# BREAKING AWAY

# MEET...

## Bob Wagner Jr

CANDIDATE FOR COUNCILMAN AT LARGE

# BREAKING AWAY THE FUTURE OF CITIES

Essays in Memory of
Robert F. Wagner, Jr.

JULIA
VITULLO-
MARTIN
*editor*

## A TWENTIETH CENTURY FUND BOOK

1996 ◆ The Twentieth Century Fund Press ◆ New York

*FTW*
*AKA 0255*

Library of Congress Cataloging-in-Publication Data

Breaking away : the future of cities : essays in memory of Robert F. Wagner. Jr. / edited by Julia Vitullo-Martin.
    p. cm.
    "A Twentieth Century Fund book."
    Includes bibliographical references and index.
    ISBN 0-87078-379-3    0-87078-386-6 (pbk)
    1. Urban policy–United States. 2. Cities and towns–United States.
3. Wagner, Robert F. (Robert Ferdinand), 1944–1993.
I. Wagner, Robert F. (Robert Ferdinand), 1944–1933. II. Vitullo-Martin, Julia, 1946–
HT123.B73    1995                          95-39950
307.76'0973–dc20                        CIP

Cover Design and Illustration: Claude Goodwin
Manufactured in the United States of America.

# FOREWORD

*I*n 1993, the Twentieth Century Fund contracted with Julia Vitullo-Martin and Robert F. Wagner, Jr., to write a book about urban affairs. At a time of widespread despair about the condition of America's cities, they promised an essentially optimistic volume. They saw their mission as scouring the country to discover the most effective and perhaps innovative solutions to the chronic problems facing big cities. They made a good case that such successes were taking place all across the nation. They were on a field trip to San Antonio, as part of the research for this book, when Mr. Wagner unexpectedly became ill and died.

Bobby Wagner's circle of friends was remarkable. All the more so because despite the prominence of his family ties and public career, his friends were overwhelmingly personal, not mere political allies or well-connected New Yorkers. They were and are people who were close to Bobby because they believed in his essential grace, sincerity, intelligence, and good intentions. They are also a remarkably thoughtful and knowledgeable group, especially when it comes to issues concerning America's large cities.

Thus, it made good sense to ask some of them to collaborate on a book that would encompass many of the issues that he and Julia Vitullo-Martin were planning to address. The group of authors who have written the essays that follow is not homogeneous; their views cut across the political spectrum. In this, however, they somewhat reflect the development over the past decade of Bobby Wagner's eclectic views about major public questions.

There are sixteen contributors to the volume, and their work ranges across the landscape of urban issues. Julia Vitullo-Martin has contributed the first chapter and a later essay on housing, as well as editing the overall work. Dick Netzer marshals facts that suggest a recasting of the conventional wisdom about the economic function and recent economic history of major cities. Joseph Fernandez and Robert Kiley use their own dramatic experiences in senior posts in New York City to illustrate the challenge and promise of reforming basic services. Paul Goldberger and Nathan Leventhal suggest ways in which the Big Apple is special and the reasons that it is likely to continue be so.

Along the way, Peter C. Goldmark, Jr., Stanley Brezenoff, Roger Cohen, and William J. Dean add material that anchors the book in the particular place that Bobby Wagner and his special causes played in the life of the city over the past three decades. And this look at our cities is rounded out by the views of Diane Ravitch, J. Phillip Thompson, Ester Fuchs, Christopher Stone, Donna Shalala, and Ellen Chesler, author of *Woman of Valor*, a Twentieth Century Fund fellow, and one of the people who shaped this volume.

None of the authors, of course, argue that what they say on a given topic is precisely what the original coauthors would have said. But they can, in all fairness, claim to have served the overall purpose of the assignment taken on by Wagner and Vitullo-Martin: opening up the conversation about urban problems to new ideas and new solutions. It is the authors' intent that this volume offer hope, chart a course for future work, and sharpen our understanding of the complexity of big city life and government.

The Fund has a long tradition of interest in urban issues. It has established numerous task forces to address the problems of cities, ranging from an evaluation of the municipal bond rating system used by private agencies to an assessment of urban preservation policies to two studies of the state of New York City. More recently, it supported Thomas Muller's book *Immigrants and the American City*, commissioned papers on public hospitals and the impact of AIDS and the issues surrounding the privatization of public hospitals, and is currently supporting projects that are examining strategies to reverse the decline of central cities and looking at various school reform proposals with a focus on New York City's schools.

This volume adds to that tradition. On behalf of the Trustees of the Twentieth Century Fund, I thank Julia Vitullo-Martin and her colleagues for their contributions and for making this memorial to Robert F. Wagner, Jr., a reality.

◆ ◆ ◆

Let me add a personal note: I first met Bobby Wagner in 1967, when he entered the graduate program at Princeton's Woodrow Wilson School. We became friends and made common cause on a number of campaigns and projects over the years. In the fall of 1968, Bobby took a course in executive leadership that I was teaching. He was the outstanding student in the class, and I gave him an "A." On everything that mattered most, in my judgment, that was the grade he maintained for the rest of his all too short life.

RICHARD C. LEONE, *President*
The Twentieth Century Fund
October 1995

# CONTENTS

# Prologue:

# The Wagner Legacy

*Peter C. Goldmark, Jr.*

*T*he name Robert F. Wagner runs like a bright thread through the tapestry of twentieth-century history in New York. From the election of Robert F. Wagner, Sr., to the state legislature in 1904 to his son's twelve years as the city's mayor to Bobby's death in 1993, the name Wagner has been identified with the defining themes of politics in New York.

Senator Wagner led the fight for the innovative New York reforms that proved to be the laboratory for the New Deal. Of the three Wagners, it was he who helped to bring about the most far-reaching changes. Mayor Wagner wielded more power than his father or his son. He presided over the expansion and modernization of city government, guided labor to the center of city politics and public policy, and took the first decisive steps to open public life in New York to black and Latino minorities.

Bobby Wagner did not hold elective office beyond New York's city council, but he often stood on the firing line as an appointed official. He worked to create humane policies in the face of the advancing tides of deterioration and division that swept the city in the last third of this century. Of the three Wagners, it was Bobby who found himself swimming against the strongest currents, and Bobby who took on the most difficult tasks and pursued them against the greatest odds.

Bobby Wagner's voice was heard often on the major issues facing New York City and, by extension, urban America. His hand was felt everywhere. His leadership was pivotal in three of the most important reform efforts in New York after the fiscal crisis—three reforms that eventually served cities across the country.

The first was the campaign to make infrastructure investment the city's major capital priority. This policy made sense in terms of quality of life, jobs, and competitiveness. It also made sense as a way to counter the trends of economic and psychological disinvestment that sap the urban experience in the late twentieth century. Bobby conceived this strategy, sold it, and pushed it into place in a succession of city budgets.

Few observers of the New York scene—where so much that is unimportant attracts attention, and so much that is critical goes unremarked—would label this strategy as one of the major successes of a city that staggered from one crisis to another in the 1970s and 1980s. Yet that is exactly what it was. In the fiscal dithering of the early 1990s, however, the city retreated from the Wagner infrastructure policy—and that retreat will cost New York immeasurably.

The second major reform in which Bobby Wagner played a principal role was the renewal of the region's mass transit system. This is a stupefying accomplishment when viewed in the context of a decline in most public services, the age and intractability of the transit system, the fiscal vise that has closed relentlessly on American cities since the 1960s, and the history of failed city-state cooperation following the fiscal crisis of the mid-1970s.

Richard Ravitch was the chief architect of this turnaround, Robert Kiley its principal implementor. Bobby was the public figure whose guidance spanned the tenure of both. His political statesmanship steadied the entire work over the course of a decade, and his conciliatory skills helped knit together the regional geographic coalition and the bipartisan political entente that made the achievement possible. The rebuilding of the crumbling subway and commuter rail system is the largest and most visible turnaround we can point to in New York City over the past two decades. It was a success for which many share credit. But Bobby Wagner was instrumental in its conception and critical to its execution.

The third great undertaking is the reform of the New York City public school system. We do not know how that drama will end, or even if it is irreversibly under way. What we do know is that Bobby sought the assignment, threw himself into it, and guided it during tumultuous years. Once it became clear that he himself could not become chancellor, Bobby accepted the position of board chair and ran a search for the best person to fill the job.

History's final verdict on Joseph Fernandez is hard to discern today; his tenure will probably be more easily forgotten than evaluated because of its short duration. Bobby's approach to school reform, however, was completely consistent with his approach to all big problems: think through and set the general direction; sign on talented people to lead the effort; reach out to all the major parties; enlist, explain, persuade, and moderate; compromise on the little issues, hold fast on the big ones; and make vividly clear to all participants their stake in the battle and its outcome.

Bobby Wagner was one of the city's few public figures who dealt on a sustained basis with both Mayor Edward I. Koch and Governor Mario Cuomo, the two elected officials who dominated New York in the 1980s. Bobby shared Cuomo's interest in conciliation and finding common ground. Unlike Cuomo, however, Bobby shared Koch's involvement in the operations of the vast bureaucracies over which all three men presided. Like Koch, he understood how essential they were to the performance of modern government.

Far more self-effacing than either Koch or Cuomo, Bobby Wagner worked in the poorly understood zone that lies between the city and the state. He understood, as few public figures do, the complex dynamic between city and state that functions as the force field for each of the large operating systems in the New York governmental structure: health care, education, welfare, transportation, and criminal justice.

In this zone, Bobby knew that the role of the state legislature is more crucial than that of either the city's or the state's chief executive. Here, too, the power of the municipal unions is most clearly felt. Following the tradition initiated by his grandfather, Bobby Wagner worked at the intersection of legislative process, union power, and public opinion; like his grandfather and father, he was always trying to move the great forces of the center forward toward the next progressive objective through challenge and compromise.

Of the battles the three Wagners fought, it is Bobby's that are the most fateful for us. For the first 175 years of America's history, its cities were magnets of opportunity and powerful engines of economic growth and individual advancement. Today, American cities play that role only for immigrants and, in highly specialized locations like central Manhattan and a handful of other cities, for young professional elites. The domestic imperative of the 1990s is to counter the trends of growing inequality, social disorganization, and institutional arteriosclerosis. In this drama, against great odds and at great personal cost, Bobby Wagner committed himself to the search for workable paths to renewal, shared values, and opportunity for the great urban populations of the country.

Bobby Wagner's support for Rudolph Giuliani for Mayor in 1993 surprised many, although for real connoisseurs of New York politics it held an interesting echo of his father's carefully staged endorsement of Republican-Independent Mayor John Lindsay the morning of election day in 1969. The Wagners were fierce and committed Democrats, but in the end they cared more about the city than they did about the party.

Bobby's decision to support Giuliani represented more a conclusion on his part about incumbent Mayor David Dinkins than a statement of unqualified faith in candidate Giuliani. Giuliani's stance toward the city school system and its leadership in the first two years of his mayoralty would have saddened Bobby deeply. I am certain that either he would have invested the time necessary to deter the Mayor from this reckless course, or he would have broken with him over it at great cost to Giuliani. It is a measure of Bobby's importance to the city and of our loss that neither happened.

There have been very few paladins of civic renewal who were kind. Bobby's astonishing moral strength lay in the continuity of his values, from his most personal interactions to his most painful public decisions. There were no false notes, no paralyzing disjunctions. That seamlessness probably contributed to the heavy personal and physical toll that public engagement exacted from him. But it also was at the heart of the three outstanding qualities by which we knew him—his integrity, his passion, his grace.

# ACKNOWLEDGMENTS

*T*his book, begun in great hopefulness by Bob Wagner and me, was made possible by the financial and editorial assistance of the Twentieth Century Fund. After Bob's death, Fund president Richard C. Leone provided the concept—a collection of essays by Bob's friends and colleagues—that allowed us to finish the book in Bob's memory and honor. Beverly Goldberg, vice president, facilitated the editing; Jason Renker, assistant vice president, saw the volume through production; and Sarah Wright typeset the volume.

I would like to thank the Citizens Housing and Planning Council for opening their extensive library; Mara Tapp of WBEZ in Chicago for making available tapes of her many excellent radio interviews with housing and political officials; and the Wagner Archives at LaGuardia Community College for providing the photographs of Bob, his family, and friends.

I am deeply grateful to four people who helped bridge the chasm between November 15, 1993, and today: Julius Edelstein, Bob's lifetime friend, whose reflections on the Wagner heritage are invaluable; Ellen Chesler, friend and fellow of the Twentieth Century Fund, who helped think through every detail of the new structure and without whom this book could not have been finished; Margaret Hunt, superb editor, who worked through the many different voices and ideas to help mold a united manuscript; and Tom Vitullo-Martin, my husband and Bob's friend, who was with us at every stage of the project, including the saddest.

# 1

# INTRODUCTION

## JULIA VITULLO-MARTIN

*I*n all areas of public policy, Bob Wagner and I had been looking for the breakaway, a term we had borrowed from the racing cyclists in Central Park. The strong cyclist looks for the opportunity—a steep climb, a treacherous descent, a building that blocks the wind—to break away from the pack. Central Park's wind, however, is so ferocious that it can be more of a hazard than competing bikers. As a result, small groups of cyclists from different teams join together to form an echelon or paceline. The first or point person challenges the wind and accepts it, allowing the rear cyclists to be pulled through by the draft, saving 15 to 20 percent of their energy. The rank revolves. The last person of the echelon cycles to the front, maintains the speed, and takes on the wind. The rotation is repeated until the wind eases or the last moment when staying with the pack makes sense. When the time is right, someone breaks away.

When we interviewed Vincent Lane, chairman of the Chicago Housing Authority (CHA), we knew we had met our first breakaway. This was astonishing to us in part because public housing had become such a disturbing, monolithic, destructive presence in so many neighborhoods. Yet, here was a man who challenged the forces arrayed against him. He took on HUD, and the welfare bureaucracy in Washington. He defied Chicago's powerful politicians and its Board of Education. He stood up against the countervailing winds and pulled away.

But just as the first breakaway seldom wins the race—almost never in the long, arduous tours for which the great bikers train—so Lane dropped out of contention, resigning from the CHA in June 1995. In the end, he had needed HUD's permission to implement his most daring plans, and HUD said no, replacing Lane with its Assistant Secretary for Public and Indian Housing, Joseph Shuldiner. Shuldiner's announced plans are Lane's plans, but HUD can implement them when Lane could not. Will HUD break away from decades of its own destructive policies? Shuldiner and HUD Secretary Henry Cisneros say they will.

The forces controlling and impeding breakaways are enormously strong. That is what this collection of essays, written in memory of Bob Wagner, is about: the battle between the structural constraints that are weakening cities, and the people and innovations striving to save them.

The contributions to the book represent three complementary dimensions of Bob Wagner's life. He was for many years an instructor at Princeton and Columbia universities and the New School for Social Research, and his sophisticated understanding of the problems facing urban America reflected his solid academic training in history, political science, and economics, as well as urban policy and politics. In recognition of Bob's great love of learning, the first three essays provide a background perspective by three prominent New York City scholars on the enduring fiscal, economic, and racial problems that confront American cities.

But beyond theory, of course, Bob Wagner had many opportunities to put good ideas to work through the prominent positions he held in public life. With the consummate skills that were his birthright, he wedded abstract policy considerations and practical politics at the New York City Planning Commission, the Metropolitan Transportation Authority, the Board of Education, and in City Hall itself. Bob always understood that the basic tension in public life is between theory and practice—that so often it is not enough to understand the complexity of a given problem to resolve it. The real challenge is to move a cumbersome political structure to take action.

For the second section of this book, then, a number of commentators were asked to take a look at some recent policy and programmatic developments in specific urban policy arenas, including criminal justice, education, urban planning, housing, and social welfare. Like Bob, these contributors bring academic training to their policy positions in and outside government. For a third and concluding outlook, several of Bob's prominent friends and colleagues in government and civic life provide hands-on lessons from the field.

## THE SCHOLARLY PERSPECTIVE

Even in the best of times, America's cities have been home to rich and poor alike. What distinguishes cities today is not the objective conditions of poverty, which are far better than in the past. What's most troubling is the subjective loss of faith among so many of the urban disadvantaged that their children will ever have a better life—that there is any way out of their existing poverty.

Political scientist Phil Thompson looks at a range of theories about the causes and consequences of deeply rooted urban poverty, particularly as it affects African-Americans. But in examining poverty and race, Thompson really examines class and race, analyzing census data for New York City to ask which is more important. While a non-white middle-class is growing, income disparities between them (especially African-Americans and whites) are widening. Because middle-class blacks may realize that their status is eroding relative to whites, they are likely to conclude that race, not class, limits their progress.

Theorists holding to a "trickle-down" explanation of black economic progress believe racial discrimination against the black middle-class is the preeminent issue facing black communities. Poor urban blacks may have an entirely different perspective, as do social scientists with a class perspective on economic development. Seeing fewer affluent whites and increased numbers of affluent blacks and Asians, poor urban blacks are likely to notice that advances for the black middle class have not trickled down to them. Thus, says Thompson, racial issues may remain critical for the black middle class—and for urban dwellers in general—but not for the black urban poor. Far more important for the black urban poor is their economic well-being, which depends to a large extent on the fiscal well-being of the cities in which they live.

During the past twenty years, many academics have been rethinking the common understandings of the fiscal base of American cities. In the 1960s, students were routinely taught that the major difference between public and private finance is that governments cannot go broke. In the 1970s, everyone learned that this was no longer true of municipal governments: cities could and did face bankruptcy.

New York City's ongoing fiscal crisis was announced to the world on April 1, 1975, when the Standard & Poor's bond rating agency withdrew its rating of New York City bonds. This effectively closed the city out of the public market: it could no longer borrow short or long. Since it had been borrowing to pay operating expenses, New York faced the very real possibility that it would no longer be able to pay for basic services. Its longstanding lenders, the huge commercial banks headquartered in Manhattan, announced they were now barred by federal and state regulation from lending any more. They were prepared to walk away from their enormously indebted sovereign.

The officers of the Wall Street rating agencies and banks were denounced by nearly every newspaper and commentator, including the then Senate Finance Committee Chairman William Proxmire, first, for having lured New York into borrowing irresponsibly large sums, and then for abandoning the city to its debts. Attacking banks is a long and honorable American tradition. Even President John Adams, the scion of a merchant family, once complained, "Banks have done more injury to the religion, morality, tranquillity, prosperity, and even the wealth of the nation than they can have done or ever will do good." Adams could have been speaking in advance for New Yorkers.

Yet, as it turned out, both the lending banks—seemingly dominant, rich, and powerful—and the borrowing cities were facing a new world. The 1990s would find banks impoverished in comparison to their earlier wealth, and cities enmeshed in fiscal difficulties.

Economist Dick Netzer, takes an optimistic view, pointing out that since the mid-1970s, nearly all large cities have benefitted from a considerable expansion in a wide range of advanced business, financial, and professional services; telecommunications; health services; and tourism (even in some fairly unlikely places such as Cleveland and Milwaukee). Moreover, most cities have done well as incubators for new service activities, but some have also proved to be successful incubators of new manufacturing enterprises.

As a result, says Netzer, the 1980s saw substantially higher labor force participation by young inner-city residents, demonstrating that if jobs are available, large numbers of people will move from welfare to employment. Netzer notes that most large cities seem to have been successful in replacing old economic specializations with new ones. Throughout this century, he maintains, these cities have renewed themselves—without government help or even much awareness that the renewal is actually taking place.

The prospects for the economies of large American cities, says Netzer, are generally good, provided governments do not undermine these private-sector developments with self-destructive policies. Damaging economic policies are made, often unintentionally, by both liberals and conservatives. Some levy onerous business taxes, which are relieved only by waivers in the most conspicuous situations. Others exhaust available fiscal resources by granting tax incentives to large firms at the expense of upgrading public amenities—thus missing an opportunity to improve the quality of urban life.

In contrast, Ester Fuchs argues that cities have entered a period she calls the permanent fiscal crisis. As is often true, she points out, New York has simply been the dramatic and aggressive initiator of events that would eventually encompass smaller cities across the country.

Fuchs notes that a serious consequence of the permanent fiscal crisis is that cities are increasingly unable to provide good basic services, even though doing so is a matter of urban survival. American cities find themselves simultaneously trapped by local fiscal crises and a relentless global competition for their productive businesses and residents.

## NEW POLICY PERSPECTIVES

For the urban poor, education may be the single most important factor in guaranteeing economic opportunity, regardless of race. Educator Diane Ravitch points out, however, that only about 40 percent of incoming ninth-graders in New York City public schools graduate four years later, while, at the same time, nearly 40 percent of the city's schools have been identified by the State Commissioner of Education as among the lowest-performing schools in the state. Ravitch argues that a new model for successful schools must be found, one that guarantees public school students a choice in determining what schools they attend. Her solutions include granting true autonomy to public schools—equivalent to the school-based management of private and parochial schools; offering meaningful flexibility for teachers as well as students; contracting out management of many schools; and providing scholarships for low-income students in educationally bankrupt schools that can be used at any school, public or private—including parochial—in the city. The hallmarks of public education in New York and elsewhere, Ravitch argues, should be equality of opportunity, quality of instruction, and diversity of providers.

Keeping young people in schools not only enhances future economic opportunity, it also helps guard against both the enticements and the dangers of crime—surely the most destructive and divisive urban problem, especially among the poor. Violent crime not only destroys lives and property, it divides neighbors and colleagues. Yet few agree on how best to wield effective punishment.

Like most urban criminal justice systems, New York's is so overburdened that the city would be unable to respond with sure, fast punishment even if it chose to do so. New York Ascendant, the 1987 report of the Commission on the Year 2000, chaired by Bob Wagner, noted that for the 600,000 felonies committed annually, only 110,000 people are arrested—about 40,000 of them for serious crimes. The State of New York has about 42,000 prison cells, which puts a ceiling on how many felons the system can permit itself to punish. In fact, only 4.2 percent of felonies committed in New York City are punished by incarceration of any kind—and only 1.9 percent by prison.

Chris Stone, director of the Vera Institute of Justice, is pessimistic about the effectiveness of most efforts to reform the criminal justice system, even though Vera has designed and implemented some of the country's most innovative criminal justice demonstration projects. He argues that the most meaningful initiatives under way in criminal justice involve trying to make failing systems more responsive to the urban communities they serve. Thus, community policing, community courts, community prosecution, neighborhood defenders, and community corrections, though not yet well-defined or fully implemented, represent, in the hands of their more talented practitioners, a sincere commitment to dealing with crime, victims, and offenders in the broader contexts of their communities.

The contradictions—and failures—of programs targeted at the urban poor can, perhaps, be most clearly seen in the federally financed public housing program, whose original, authorizing legislation was sponsored by Senator Robert F. Wagner during the Great Depression. Public housing is the ultimate liberal program, and one with auspicious beginnings. From the start, however, one of its weak elements was that it was a jobs program as well as a housing program. And it was not just any jobs program, but a union program employing high-priced plumbers, electricians, carpenters, and other crafts workers. The deliberate intention of Congress in the 1930s was, after all, to employ people. If workers were actually productive and built decent housing, so much the better, but they didn't really have to. In fact, they could and did build some very bad housing—in St. Louis, Philadelphia, Chicago, Washington, D.C., and New Orleans. In my essay on public housing, I concentrate on Chicago, an affluent city that oversees what many observers consider to have once been the most troubled major public housing program in the country, but where concerted efforts to bring about change were begun by the local authority, halted by HUD, and then restarted by HUD bureaucrats.

Biographer and historian Ellen Chesler, currently a Twentieth Century Fund Fellow, looks to the past in search of ideas to reinvigorate contemporary social welfare policy. She finds a compelling model for decentralizing delivery of services and benefits to the community level in the pioneering social settlement houses of the progressive era. The model is based on a single case-worker working in one caring and concerned institution, coordinating and addressing as many of a family's needs as possible. Chesler links recent scholarship reevaluating the imaginative and formidable role of progressive era women in the building of the social welfare state to practical innovations now under way by New York City settlements trying to reorganize and integrate government programs in order to meet the needs of poor families and communities. These institutions represent another dimension of Bob Wagner's vision for cities that work, since, along with his father, he was for many years a dedicated member of the board of United Neighborhood Houses, the umbrella organization for New York's settlement houses.

The next essays address the question, which Bob himself often asked: What, in addition to good schools, safe streets, decent housing, and strong civic institutions, are the ingredients of a viable urban environment? The answer, embraced by *New York Ascendant*, is that New York must one day become a truly civil society thriving in a beautiful setting and a more humane environment.

*New York Times* cultural correspondent Paul Goldberger discusses what physical, social, and cultural elements must combine to create a successful city today. In other words, what still attracts people to live in cities? Goldberger finds a new, safe, serene, and tidy urban paradigm in places like Charlotte, Minneapolis, Dallas, and Seattle that offer "a gentle sprinkling of those aspects of traditional urbanism that middle-class residents value in small doses" with very few of the traditional problems of city life, particularly chaos or crime. Yet, he argues that only a few great cities—New York, Los Angeles, Boston, San Francisco, perhaps Miami—remain as incubators and promoters of culture, and as such possess an ultimate form of urban authenticity.

## PERSPECTIVES FROM THE FIELD

Viable cities must also provide a healthy environment for families through a combination of preventive public health measures, including advanced sewerage treatment, stringent building codes, an ample supply of clean water, and reasonably responsible private behavior. In modern times, the field of public health has generally done well at all but the last of that list of problems. Particularly after World War II, as American doctors came to believe that antibiotics and other advanced drugs had conquered epidemics, public health increasingly confined its oversight to relatively neutral areas like clean water, and moved away from regulatory concern over sexually transmitted diseases, drug and alcohol abuse, and other individual matters.

Nonetheless, outbreaks of disease, such as the newly virulent strain of drug-resistant tuberculosis, and deadly individual behavior, such as drunk driving, periodically force a reassessment of the tools and programs of public health. The reassessment is particularly pressing today as officials reflect on recent findings of the Centers for Disease Control and Prevention that risk factors due to life style contribute about 46.8 percent of premature mortality in the United States, while health care system inadequacies account for only 10.8 percent.

At the same time, it is clear that government programs directed at large urban populations have often proved invaluable. From the turn of the century on, city governments were innovators in health because they had to be, and New York City was usually far ahead of other cities. Its public school system became the country's public health model for preventing illness among and caring for the medical needs of children. Yet in recent years, so many programs have been dismantled that the typical public school today does not even have a nurse or a health care worker on campus; most schools are visited once every six-to-eight weeks by one or two nurses who spend part of a day addressing a multitude of health problems.

Thousands of children come to school too sick to learn and often ill with communicable diseases. Nearly one of five students entering school in New York reported some health problem on his or her admission form in 1993. New York City school children are hospitalized at nearly twice the national rate for asthma. The city has the country's highest rate of infection by HIV among adolescents.

Secretary of Health and Human Services Donna E. Shalala urges a third revolution in public health—one that will restore the commitment of earlier generations to education and disease prevention. And she suggests that these efforts be harnessed to a reformed system of welfare—one based on job training, counseling, and employment.

In the best sense, Shalala's strong voice at the end of the twentieth century echoes the ideas of social reformers at its beginning. America's great progressive reformers believed they could rescue a generation of immigrants from poverty by demanding that governments provide every citizen with the fundamentals of a healthy and good life: clean, safe neighborhoods; sound housing; good schools; immunizations from disease; playgrounds and parks; job training and counseling. Secretary Shalala urges a recommitment to that idealism today.

Just as urban public health systems have deteriorated so have urban rail systems. As automobiles gained ascendancy after World War II, and suburbanization became the dominant development pattern, older cities heavily dependent on rail systems (Boston, New York, Chicago, Philadelphia) lost an existing advantage and an opportunity for the future. Options and rights-of-way for public transportation were left open in cities such as Chicago, but they were closed in others, such as New York. Chicago today is a spaghetti soup of railroads and holds far more possibilities than Eastern cities for mixing different kinds of transportation. New York, on the other hand, is restricted in what it can do. Early plans for the Long Island Expressway, for example, included a right-of-way for public transportation, but it was eliminated before the highway was built.

At the same time, New York City's once magnificent—though nearly always financially troubled and controversial—subway system set out on a long course of deterioration. As a member of the Metropolitan Transportation Authority (MTA) board, Bob Wagner searched the country for a transportation executive capable of rescuing this flagship system. He found Bob Kiley running the trains and buses in Boston. By the time Kiley assumed the MTA chairmanship in 1984, the system's operations were a mess, and its riders were angry, hostile, and declining in numbers. But Kiley had one distinct advantage. His predecessor, Richard Ravitch, had put together the largest and most innovative financing package in the history of any urban subway system. In his essay, Kiley examines the problems he faced and the management solutions he and his principle lieutenant, David Gunn, implemented.

Only a few years later, in 1990—at the urging of its then President Bob Wagner—the New York City Board of Education hired Joseph Fernandez as its new chancellor. A nationally known educator serving as superintendent of schools in Miami, Fernandez had a successful track record as a school reformer. As a Latino and a native New Yorker, he was also seen as politically savvy. But Fernandez's performance in Miami had been secured by structural supports not in place in New York, notes former deputy chancellor Stanley Litow: an elected school board of seven members who ran at-large and were directly responsible to voters; a well-funded school system with its own independent taxing authority; strong city and state backing; and forward-looking leadership on the side of management and labor, which was represented by a strong American Federation of Teachers affiliate. In New York, Fernandez started with great fanfare but left at the end of his three-year contract with the board deeply split and any number of public figures clamoring for his resignation. His essay reflects on this experience and recommends a course for the future.

On a more optimistic note, Nathan Leventhal, the President of Lincoln Center, who was Bob Wagner Jr.'s closest colleague in the Koch administration, reflects on how public investment in the arts promotes economic development in New York City while sustaining the spiritual well-being of so many of its citizens. And Bob Wagner's long-time ally in city government, Stanley Brezenoff, teams up with his former Port Authority colleague, Roger Cohen, to provide a measure of the distinguished legacy of the Wagner family by looking at how each successive generation left its mark on the work of that agency. Brezenoff and Cohen see the realization of each Wagner's vision in Port Authority efforts to restore the region's airports and improve access to them; to integrate the region's public transportation; to revitalize and improve public access to New York's spectacular waterfront; and to reestablish commuter ferry service. But beyond these specific initiatives, they credit Bob Wagner, Jr., for establishing a principled framework for cooperation among elected officials and appointed policymakers in the region, one that encourages fiscal discipline but also recognizes the need for sustained capital investment in public infrastructure and social needs.

And to close, William Dean calls forth the words of another devotee of New York City, Walt Whitman, allowing him to speak for Bob in words Bob himself often quoted. The love of New York City life that Bob so personified rings clear and true.

# PART I    THE SCHOLARLY PERSPECTIVE

# 2

# URBAN POVERTY AND RACE

## J. PHILLIP THOMPSON*

Since the 1950s, cities have steadily lost population to the suburbs: 60 percent of metropolitan-area residents lived in suburbs in 1990; only 30 percent did so in 1950.[1] The twelve largest metropolitan areas have increased their population since 1950, but only two of the twelve largest cities have done so: New York and Los Angeles, both gateways for Latin, Asian, and Caribbean immigrants.[2] Virtually all metropolitan growth in recent decades has occurred in the suburbs, facilitated in large measure by federal transportation and housing policies that built roads and subsidized suburban home-ownership, thereby encouraging white flight from central cities. These factors in turn increased fiscal strain and worsened already deteriorating services in cities, pushing out more middle-class residents.[3]

Those remaining in cities, and those arriving, are increasingly poor and minority.[4] Poverty rates in the top one hundred U.S. cities rose from 14.5 percent in 1970, to 16.7 percent in 1980, to 18.3 percent in 1990.[5] At the same time, blacks, Latinos, and Asians became a majority in six of the nation's eight largest cities. Only

---

* Lori Minnite and Jocelyn Sargent offered valuable insights and assistance in the preparation of this chapter.

Philadelphia (48.4 percent) and San Diego (42.5 percent) had less than a 50 percent minority population in 1990.[6]

Poverty has not only increased, it has become more concentrated. Poor (mostly minority) inner-city residents increasingly live in neighborhoods characterized by joblessness, welfare dependency, extraordinary levels of poverty, failing schools, and violent crime.[7] This combination of woes now popularly, if imprecisely, defines the "underclass." Half of all poor African-Americans live in such "extremely" poor neighborhoods—that is, defined as a census tract having more than a 40 percent rate of poverty.[8]

The composition of the poor population has also changed. Fewer of the poor are elderly; more are children—40 percent, according to the 1990 Census.[9] Social Security and Supplemental Security Income (SSI) have been relatively effective in reducing poverty among the elderly. Unlike Social Security, however, Aid to Families with Dependent Children (AFDC) has not been indexed to inflation and has declined in value. A study of poverty in New York City found that AFDC had virtually no effect on reducing poverty among single parents with children in 1990, while government programs for the elderly cut the poverty rate in elderly households by more than 40 percent.[10] Many studies have noted that, although children are a large component of the poor population, they receive a relatively small share of poverty-related spending. This is important because recent longitudinal studies confirm linkages between the nature of childhood development and improved outcomes in later life.

## CLASS DIFFERENTIATION WITHIN THE BLACK COMMUNITY

In the 1970s, sociologist William Julius Wilson argued that the growth of the black middle class showed that present-day racial discrimination had declined and that class factors were more important in explaining inner-city poverty among blacks.[11] Wilson's work was significant because it implied that race-specific policies such as affirmative action were less important than programs directly benefiting the poor. Subsequent studies, however, have shown large and persistent gaps between the earnings and wealth of the black and white middle classes, suggesting that racial discrimination is still an important cause of racial inequality.[12]

Both Wilson and his critics are right in important respects, as data for New York City demonstrate. Whether race or class is more important depends on one's perspective. New York City's economy did exceptionally well in the 1980s, and offered a relatively robust setting for black economic progress (see Table 2.1). Over the decade, New York City's white population dropped sharply—by 683,000, or 24 percent—and the Puerto Rican population declined negligibly. But all other groups grew: non-Puerto Rican Latinos by nearly 283,000, Asians by nearly 242,000, and blacks by just over 183,000. Total family population in the city was constant, but racially and ethnically New York became a different place.

As shown in Table 2.2 (see page 16), New York City's poverty population grew by over 69,000 in the 1980s.[13] The whites who stayed in the city included a significant poor, mainly elderly, population. The number of poor blacks and Puerto Ricans declined slightly, and poor non-Puerto Rican Latinos and Asians increased by over 179,000. As shown in Table 2.3 (see page 17), the size of New York City's middle class (and upper class), defined as those persons living in families earning more than median income, was reduced by the departure of nearly 433,000 white middle-class families. That reduction, however, was almost offset by an increase of about

## TABLE 2.1

### PERSONS IN FAMILY HOUSEHOLDS BY RACE/ETHNIC GROUP
### New York City, 1980, 1990

|  | White | Black | Puerto Rican | Other Latino | Asian/ Other | Total |
|---|---|---|---|---|---|---|
| Persons in 1980 | 2,861,960 | 1,453,780 | 789,480 | 532,080 | 234,717 | 5,872,017 |
| Persons in 1990 | 2,178,157 | 1,637,089 | 759,803 | 814,798 | 476,517 | 5,866,364 |

**Increase/(Decrease),
  1980–1990**

|  | White | Black | Puerto Rican | Other Latino | Asian/ Other | Total |
|---|---|---|---|---|---|---|
|  | (683,803) | 183,309 | (29,677) | 282,718 | 241,800 | (5,653) |

Source: Author's calculations based on the U.S. Department of Commerce, Bureau of the Census, 1980 and 1990 Public Use Microdata tapes. Such tapes reflect data collected the previous calendar year.

## TABLE 2.2

### RACE/ETHNIC GROUP BELOW 50 PERCENT FAMILY MEDIAN INCOME
### NEW YORK CITY, 1980, 1990

|  | White | Black | Puerto Rican | Other Latino | Asian/ Other | Total |
|---|---|---|---|---|---|---|
| **1980** | | | | | | |
| % in Poverty | 12.80 | 32.60 | 45.90 | 29.20 | 16.90 | **23.80** |
| No. of Persons | 367,460 | 473,880 | 362,760 | 155,180 | 38,260 | **1,397,540** |
| **1990** | | | | | | |
| % in Poverty | 13.40 | 28.60 | 44.00 | 33.60 | 13.40 | **25.00** |
| No. of Persons | 292,150 | 467,686 | 333,944 | 273,801 | 99,010 | **1,466,591** |
| **Increase/(Decrease), 1980–1990** | | | | | | |
|  | (75,310) | (6,194) | (28,816) | 118,621 | 60,750 | **69,051** |

*Source*: Author's calculations based on the U.S. Department of Commerce, Bureau of the Census, 1980 and 1990 Public Use Microdata tapes. Such tapes reflect data collected the previous calendar year.

157,000 black, 125,000 Asian, 80,000 non-Puerto Rican, and 35,000 Puerto Rican middle-class families. As a result, while whites are still proportionately overrepresented in New York's middle class, in 1990, one of every two middle-class families was black, Latino, or Asian, a change from 1980, when only 37 percent of the middle class was nonwhite. Today, it can no longer be said that New York City's middle class is white.

Does Table 2.3 imply narrowing differences between whites and nonwhites generally? No. Income inequality actually increased between middle-class whites and all others during the 1980s (see Tables 2.4 and 2.5, page 18). Income inequality also increased between poor whites and blacks, as well as between poor whites and Latinos. The differences between the black and Latino middle classes compared to the black and Latino poor is particularly striking, however. Poor black

## TABLE 2.3

### RACE/ETHNIC GROUP ABOVE FAMILY MEDIAN INCOME
### NEW YORK CITY, 1980, 1990

|  | White | Black | Puerto Rican | Other Latino | Asian/ Other | **Total** |
|---|---|---|---|---|---|---|
| **1980** | | | | | | |
| % above Median | 66.50 | 39.40 | 25.60 | 39.30 | 58.60 | |
| No. of Persons | 1,904,080 | 572,500 | 201,900 | 209,240 | 132,720 | **3,020,440** |
| **1990** | | | | | | |
| % above Median | 67.50 | 44.50 | 31.20 | 35.50 | 34.90 | |
| No. of Persons | 1,471,158 | 729,319 | 237,356 | 289,069 | 248,015 | **2,984,917** |
| **Increase/(Decrease), 1980–1990** | | | | | | |
| | (432,922) | 156,819 | 35,456 | 79,829 | 125,295 | **(35,523)** |

*Source*: Author's calculations based on the U.S. Department of Commerce, Bureau of the Census, 1980 and 1990 Public Use Microdata tapes. Such tapes reflect data collected the previous calendar year.

and Puerto Rican families experienced losses in real income of 12 and 14 percent respectively, while their middle classes experienced significant rises in real income.

Two trends can be gleaned from this census data for New York City: the minority middle class is growing and, simultaneously, income disparities between the minority (especially black) middle class and the white middle class are widening. The concurrence of these trends has produced separate socioeconomic perspectives within the minority community. Middle-class blacks may realize that their status is eroding relative to whites. From their perspective, race, not class, limits their progress. Those holding to a "trickle-down" theory of black economic progress believe racial discrimination against the black middle class is the preeminent issue facing black communities. However, poor blacks in the city may have an entirely different perspective, as do analysts

## TABLE 2.4

### MEDIAN NEW YORK CITY INCOME BY RACE/ETHNIC GROUP
FOR FAMILIES EARNING ABOVE MEDIAN FAMILY INCOME, 1980, 1990

|  | White | Black | Puerto Rican | Other Latino | Asian/ Other |
|---|---|---|---|---|---|
| 1980 Median Income | 29,010 | 25,010 | 23,010 | 24,300 | 27,890 |
| 1980 Median Income in 1990 Constant Dollars | 51,165 | 44,110 | 40,583 | 42,858 | 49,190 |
| 1990 Median Income | 63,032 | 52,208 | 49,500 | 49,800 | 57,000 |
| Increase, 1980–1990 | 11,867 | 8,098 | 8,917 | 6,942 | 7,810 |

*Source*: Author's calculations based on the U.S. Department of Commerce, Bureau of the Census, 1980 and 1990 Public Use Microdata tapes. Such tapes reflect data collected the previous calendar year.

## TABLE 2.5

### MEDIAN NEW YORK CITY INCOME BY RACE/ETHNIC GROUP
FOR FAMILIES EARNING 50 PERCENT OF MEDIAN FAMILY INCOME OR LESS, 1980, 1990

|  | White | Black | Puerto Rican | Other Latino | Asian/ Other |
|---|---|---|---|---|---|
| 1980 Median Income | 5,530 | 4,490 | 4,325 | 4,710 | 5,225 |
| 1980 Median Income in 1990 Constant Dollars | 9,753 | 7,919 | 7,628 | 8,307 | 9,215 |
| 1990 Median Income | 10,000 | 7,000 | 6,664 | 8,160 | 10,000 |
| Increase/(Decrease), 1980–1990 | 247 | (919) | (964) | (147) | 785 |

*Source*: Author's calculations based on the U.S. Department of Commerce, Bureau of the Census, 1980 and 1990 Public Use Microdata tapes. Such tapes reflect data collected the previous calendar year. All poverty statistics are for persons for whom poverty status could be determined.

maintaining a class perspective on economic development. Seeing fewer affluent whites but more affluent blacks and Asians, they may notice that advances for the black middle class have not trickled down to them. Racial discrimination and class polarization, however, are not a zero-sum equation. Both perspectives can be accurate to some degree.

Understanding the two trends is important politically. "White versus black" may remain the critical issue for the black middle class, although it might not be the primary political paradigm for many of the city's poor. Barring major social transformation, the minority middle class will soon be the dominant voice in city politics. That class's outlook toward the poor will take on increasing importance in local policy; it was already an important issue during the Dinkins administration.

These trends are not unique to New York City. A growing, politically significant but economically imperiled black middle class, and a large and stagnant poor black population, are the norm in the nation's big cities. Similar trends exist for other minority groups, but little work has been done in this area. Because so much of the literature on poverty analyzes black poverty, the remainder of this chapter will focus on the black poor.

## CAUSES OF INNER CITY POVERTY

Simply stated, explanations of persistent inner-city poverty can be grouped according to four causes: cultural deprivation; racial discrimination; structural transformation (economic class); and social breakdown in the black community.

### Cultural Deprivation Theory

There are two critical differences between culture theories and others: culture theorists emphasize "deviant" values and "immorality" of the poor, and they hold the view that poverty is the result of dependency bred by the government dole.[14] Cultural deprivation theorists are hard pressed to explain the persistence of poverty among poor families and particular ethnic groups, but basically rely on two theories, one old and the other new. The old theory argues that certain families and some ethnic/racial groups are simply less intelligent than others: differences in achievement are genetic, and deprived culture is a natural biological phenomenon. The new theory is that poor families are usually stuck in poor communities, where conditions are ripe for a negative subculture, including excessive teenage sexual promiscuity, a separate language ("street English"), and a depreciation of school and academic learning. The latter theory attributes deviancy to the spatial isolation of the poor from the presumed superior culture of upper classes, or in some cases, the isolation of poor blacks from the normative white culture.

Not all culture analyses have predictable conservative intonations, however. Christopher Jencks rightly raises the question of whether centuries of racial subordination and continued racial prejudice have alienated African-Americans from low-wage, racially subordinated labor.[15] He implies that some black joblessness can be explained by blacks' unwillingness to do certain types of work, or to work in white cultural environments. While studies indicate that blacks are no less willing to work than whites, black (and white) alienation from certain types of racialized work relations is seldom discussed in analyses of poverty.

## Racial Discrimination Theory

These theorists primarily base their arguments on evidence of continued racial discrimination in housing and employment. Sociologists Douglass Massey and Nancy Denton maintain that discrimination in housing location limits educational and employment opportunities for low-income blacks.[16] The effects of poverty are made worse because poor blacks are densely concentrated, in isolated public housing developments, for example.

Discrimination is not new, however, and so it alone cannot explain rising crime or family instability, which are recent developments. To explain new social pathologies, Massey and Denton borrow the concept of "the values and attitudes of the street" from traditional culture-of-poverty theory. They argue that race—and to some extent class—discrimination in housing works to concentrate poor blacks in segregated inner-city neighborhoods. In this model, these neighborhoods become a greenhouse for a negative subculture; investors avoid them; their residents lack the mainstream cultural norms and skills that employers demand. To Massey and Denton, low black educational achievement is less the result of faulty school administration or teaching than the inevitable result of concentrating poor blacks together: "Given the burden of 'acting white,' the pressures to speak Black English, the social stigma attached to 'brainiacs,' the allure of drug-taking, the quick money to be had from drug dealing, and the romantic sexuality of the streets, it is not surprising that black educational achievement has stagnated."[17]

## Structural Transformation Theory

Structural arguments explaining the persistence of poverty highlight unemployment and underemployment. The exodus of manufacturing businesses to the suburbs and overseas has had an especially hard impact on blacks, who were heavily concentrated in blue-collar industries.[18] The main growth in inner-city employment has been in services, where wages tend to be high or low. High wages require secondary or professional education, which most low-income blacks lack.[19] Job opportunities for the black poor therefore tend to be low-wage, or very low-wage, and dead-end.[20]

Unemployment alone, however, does not explain ghetto pathology. Like race discrimination theorists, structuralists use culture-of-poverty theory to explain the breakdown of families and institutions in the ghetto. Wilson, a groundbreaking structuralist, emphasizes that middle-class blacks have departed inner-city ghettos at the same time that blue-collar jobs (employing mostly males) have declined. Young women cannot find stable, working marriage partners. Teenagers have nothing to do and no one to look up to. Working-class men have been under-mined, the middle class has fled, and a tangle of pathology remains. Wilson believes that economic—not racial—isolation of poor "under-class" blacks ferments a negative culture. However, several empirical studies challenge the view that cultural characteristics of the black poor, rather than race discrimination, account for employers' reluctance to hire low-income blacks.[21]

## Social Breakdown Theory

The fourth explanation for the persistence of poverty focuses on social breakdown in poor communities. These theorists argue that poverty does not automatically cause crime, educational failure, and other ills associated with poor neighborhoods. They point out that there are considerable variations within and between poor neighborhoods that cannot be explained by simplistic culture-of-poverty arguments. Anthropologists have long known that poor communities contain a variety of cultures and that the poor also respond to attitudes in the broader society.[22] Community and neighborhood studies that are informed by social breakdown theory look for the factors within poor communities that indicate the level of social success. Students of social breakdown pay attention to informal networks of family and friends, to local (even building-specific) institutional practices, and to governmental practices in poor communities. Some studies suggest that poverty disrupts family networks and weakens participation in community organizations, which in turn leads to crime and neighborhood downturn.[23]

## HOW TO REDUCE POVERTY

Different analyses of urban poverty prompt different remedies. Culture theorists' proposals vary, but they emphasize the personal responsibility—or lack thereof—of those in poverty. At one extreme, some analysts call for the removal of children from incompetent poor mothers in favor of placement in government child-rearing programs. More mainstream arguments hold that the poor should be forced to work, regardless of the status of the job; unwed fathers should be forced to pay child support; and government benefits should be temporary at best.

One problem with culture arguments is their assumption that reforming the bad attitudes of the poor will somehow lead to job opportunities with sufficient pay to support poor families. Research indicates a dearth of such jobs and the need for a public jobs program to back up any forced-work program.[24] Culture theorists do not study social processes within poor communities, so they have no idea how their proposals would affect poor people. Simply forcing poor mothers to work at low-wage jobs, for example, might lead to less supervision and development of children, weaker performance in school, and more community violence. Fortunately, Congress and most states have thus far treated such proposals with caution.

Race discrimination theorists want stronger federal residential desegregation efforts to break down barriers between cities and suburbs. They also want vigorous enforcement of antidiscrimination laws. However, desegregating the United States would not only be a great moral challenge, but an unprecedented physical challenge as well. For example, to completely desegregate Chicago, New York, Cleveland, or Philadelphia, more than 80 percent of blacks would have to move.[25] Given the lack of progress in achieving racial desegregation thus far, and Congress's apparent lack of political will to pursue it, desegregation is unlikely to alleviate urban poverty anytime soon.

Structuralists emphasize labor market solutions, such as a public jobs "Marshall Plan" for the inner cities, or linkage strategies among minority workers, entrepreneurs, and regional businesses. Some also call for community enrichment programs—such as day care, job training, and drug treatment—that help the poor enter the workforce. The Clinton administration's liberal pragmatist approach to welfare reform is most closely linked to Wilson's structuralist arguments. It combines a conservative cultural emphasis on morality, the work ethic, and limitations on welfare ("two years and out") with job opportunities and social supports such as subsidized day care. Such a program would be expensive, however.

Given the federal budget deficit, and the unwillingness of Congress to tackle poverty and urban decay even in relatively prosperous times, a comprehensive, adequately funded Marshall Plan is unlikely to emerge. Also, given the general lack of knowledge about internal community social processes, it is unclear which social supports are critical for program success or even whether the same supports would work in different communities.

There has been little generalization from community and social network studies about how to "solve" poverty. Nonetheless, such studies can be placed within the framework of efforts to improve poor communities as places to live and work. Local strategies are different from any of the strategies mentioned earlier in that they do not necessarily require expanded and expensive federal action. One such approach is what economist George Galster calls the "parallel institutions" approach.[26] The basic goal is to create vibrant community-owned businesses in low-income, minority neighborhoods. This approach is embodied in federal Enterprise and Empowerment Zone programs. Many scholars, and some elected officials, discount the effectiveness of the parallel institutions approaches, often citing reasons such as inadequate government funding for such programs, the limited market for goods and services in low-income neighborhoods, the tendency of property owners (but not others) to benefit from such programs, the likely political opposition from mainstream businesses if local entrepreneurs are successful, and the danger that such targeted neighborhood approaches may allow the broader political community to avoid responsibility for urban poverty.[27]

Other local strategies include building community-based organizations to develop housing, prevent crime, provide social services, and organize neighborhoods. Although it has received little attention in academia, there has been a near-explosion in community organizing and development efforts over the last ten years. Because there have been few studies, we do not know much about what effect they are having on reducing (or preventing) poverty. The implications of increased community organization on political participation of the poor are likewise unexplored.

Community studies answer some questions that the other theories do not: Why do some families, buildings, and blocks do better than others? Although community scholars offer no solutions to extreme economic and racial inequality, they expose a range of policy options for local officials to lessen the effects of poverty on poor communities and individuals. Does public housing policy, for example, promote and develop intergenerational kinship ties or undermine them? Do police organize poor communities to participate in their own security? Do social service caseworkers have low enough caseloads to know the problems of their clients? Are they flexible enough to customize programs for their clients to prevent family breakdown? What incentives are there for experienced public school teachers to work in troubled schools? Or do their contracts allow civil servants and government professionals to move out into less challenging neighborhoods? What types of special training do police, parole officers, school teachers, social service workers, housing managers, and firefighters receive for working in complicated and difficult low-income environments? Are programs coordinated across agencies? Is there a centralized youth referral system? The answers to these questions have major implications for poor people living in cities. In most cases, they are not significant budget issues. They involve work-rules negotiated by unions and city officials, government regulations, and force of habit. They are areas where local government officials can exercise great initiative.

## BLACK POLITICS

Absent from much of the debate on these issues is discussion of the role of local political leadership. This absence is especially glaring in the case of black mayors, who run many large cities. One of the hopeful changes in urban politics was the election of black mayors in major cities, a phenomenon that began in the early 1970s. Many believed that black mayors would be able to relieve much of the racial conflict that devastated American cities in the 1960s and help lead the urban poor on the road to economic recovery.[28] Today, those hopes are long gone. Implicit and largely unspoken in much of the urban poverty literature is criticism, if not condemnation, of black political leadership.

Advocates of racial integration promote the fragmentation of black communities into larger white communities. Some critics argue that black political leaders cynically promote de facto racial segregation only to protect selfish political interests. Others argue that black politicians have performed poorly and that massive deconcentration of poor black communities is thus more important than preserving black political power. Similarly, structuralists advocate universal antipoverty programs that do not "over-identify" blacks with poverty programs.

This recommendation results from a determination that local city politics, especially black politics, matter little when it comes to poverty.

Given the substantial efforts of blacks and liberal whites to elect black mayors in major cities over the last twenty-five years, the absence of a discussion of black politics in relation to poverty is surprising. Even conservative culturalists now provide a better model for the self-determination of local poor communities than do the otherwise more liberal structuralists and racial integrationists—whose theories tend toward paternalism and whose proposals lack any significant role for community organization or local political participation of poor minorities. To the extent that such issues are addressed, it is usually to deride local "empowerment" efforts.[29]

What went wrong? Why did black political leadership fail, and liberals lose their faith? What are the prospects for a renewed black politics, and a renewed black/liberal alliance? Should this even be a goal?

Admittedly, black mayors have not been successful in reducing inner-city poverty, stemming black-on-black violence, or in maintaining black voter participation in local elections.[30] Black mayors recently lost elections in Philadelphia, Chicago, Los Angeles, and New York. The losses seem to heighten the sense that black leadership has lost its power. Why have black mayors not been more successful?

The familiar answer is that black mayors, like white ones, have little or no control over national economic trends—such as the decline of manufacturing industries in the Northeast and Midwest in the 1970s—that devastate cities. Mayors cannot stop businesses from leaving their cities, and they are loath to adopt social programs that enhance the risk that bond-rating agencies will downgrade their city's credit ratings. Programs directly affecting the poor, such as social services and public housing, are federal and state regulated—making local innovation more difficult. Mayors also must confront hostile city bureaucracies and unions that frequently oppose reforms benefiting low-income communities.[31]

Mayors have to deal with structural political-demographic problems as well. The loss of city population, relative to suburbs, has led to an increase in suburban representation not only in the U.S. House of Representatives but also in state legislatures. Bill Clinton has been called the first president elected by the suburbs (although many governors already have been). The U.S. Senate severely under-represents urban areas. New York City alone has roughly the same population as the ten least populated states, but these states control *one-fifth* of the votes in the Senate. Disproportionate political power leads to disproportionate distribution of national resources and gives rural legislators the ability to block important urban initiatives.[32]

Structural problems aside, questions remain as to why black mayors have not been more aggressive in drawing public attention to urban problems or in organizing low-income communities. Why have they not invested more resources in low-income neighborhoods? And why have black mayors not mobilized poor blacks more effectively to vote in national elections?[33] Political scientists Richard Saerzopf and Todd Swanstrom have shown that cities fell further behind suburbs in turnout for presidential elections in recent decades—the same time that Black Power came to cities.[34]

Former Atlanta mayor and civil rights leader Andrew Young attributes many of the shortcomings of black electoral politics to two factors: the lack of open criticism within the ranks of black mayors, and the middle-class bias of civil rights legislation:

> There have been missteps and misjudgments on our parts, as on the parts of many elected officials, but we have been reluctant to say so. We must in order to understand where we are and move on. For example, the civil rights movement was not aimed at ending poverty. It did not focus on economic issues; not because we didn't think economic issues were important, but because we did not think we could win on economic issues. . . . The primary battle in the 1950s and 1960s was to right the wrongs against a population that was already qualified and middle-class, but was still denied the basic right to public accommodations in America. We set out to break down the color barriers for those who were exceptionally well qualified, and we succeeded.[35]

Of Young's two explanations, the second is more important, if only because the lack of social criticism within the black community extends far beyond black mayors. If the needs of poor minorities in cities eclipsed the 1960s civil rights legislation, why have civil rights organizations not recognized that fact and pushed forward with a new agenda?

A key problem has been the disjuncture between the national legislative, legalistic, and defensive nature of the civil rights movement and the immediate, practical, complex, and often contradictory requirements of local communities. On the national level, growing conservatism has put civil rights advocates on the defensive since the late 1960s. Increasingly, they relied on the courts to protect voting rights, equal employment, affirmative action, educational desegregation, fair housing, and other gains won in the 1960s.[36] While these programs were under constant attack on the national level, newly elected black mayors were facing new problems—such as drug abuse, teenage pregnancy, black-on-black crime, homelessness, and chronic unemployment—that cannot be solved in court and cannot wait for incremental federal legislation.

Civil rights leaders, however, have been loath to question old civil rights programs or to take on new battles while civil rights programs continue to be opposed strenuously by conservatives. Black elected officials have come up with few alternatives to the old agenda. The objective problems in black communities have thus been compounded by national conservatives' continuing challenge of the (mostly black middle class) gains of the 1960s, as well as a lack of social accountability of elected and civil rights leadership to the poor. The result has been policy stagnation.

In practice, there are numerous policy contradictions and political disjunctions among civil rights advocates, black elected officials, and low-income black city residents that cry out for resolution. Below are some examples.

## HOUSING INTEGRATION VERSUS NEIGHBORHOOD DEVELOPMENT

In response to the concentration of blacks in high-rise segregated public housing projects by racially prejudiced city administrations in the 1960s and 1970s, civil rights advocates pushed the Department of Housing and Urban Development (HUD) to enact regulations mandating that public and senior citizen housing cannot be constructed in neighborhoods with more than a 40 percent concentration of government subsidized housing or more than a 60 percent minority population. The explicit aim was to desegregate communities and to deconcentrate low-income housing.

Over time, and frequently under political pressure, mayors in many cities began initiatives to redevelop low-income minority communities. High-rise family public housing was abandoned in favor of low-rise, low-density, and mixed-income subsidized housing. Residents living in overcrowded sub-quality housing, with no options for suburban living, clamored for new community housing. Banks were encouraged, and eventually required, to invest in these low-income communities.

But HUD stood fast to its regulations. Now, mayors investing millions in low-income communities cannot use federal funds there without obtaining a federal waiver. Cities spending the most in developing subsidized housing, such as New York, must obtain a waiver from federal regulations to spend federal funds to develop those same neighborhoods. What's more, current HUD regulations inadvertently penalize cities whose minority populations are rapidly increasing. New York City's Department of City Planning has demonstrated to HUD that there are no census tracts in the city that meet HUD's site and neighborhood development standards—except the most expensive real estate in the city.[37] The expensive sites are useless because their cost alone exceeds HUD's limits on total development costs. In short, HUD's site and neighborhood standards, though established to thwart segregation, now impede development, especially in cities with large minority populations striving to redevelop low-income communities.

Similarly, racial integrationists advocating that federal Section 8 rent subsidies be used to relocate blacks to the suburbs are at cross purposes with community housing developers and owners who want the same federal subsidies to finance and improve buildings in low-income black communities.

## HOUSING INTEGRATION VERSUS MAINTENANCE OF FAMILY SUPPORT NETWORKS

The New York City Housing Authority (NYCHA) is required to allocate apartments to applicants without regard to the applicant's length of residence in a particular neighborhood or family ties in the neighborhood. The policy was enacted after NYCHA was sued, under the Fair Housing Law, by civil rights advocates for using a "zip code preference" policy in allocating apartments. The zip code preference gave residents living in the same zip code as the housing development a leg up in gaining apartments. The zip code preference was no secret. It was negotiated in the 1970s by Mario Cuomo, then a lawyer seeking to allay community resistance in Forest Hills, Queens, to the development of public housing. The suit, brought in 1990, argued that since many neighborhoods are racially segregated, zip codes populated by whites give whites a preference in obtaining public housing in those neighborhoods. Such a policy therefore maintains segregation in public housing.

At the time the suit was brought, however, whites had essentially abandoned public housing. Today's whites occupy less than 5 percent of public housing apartments and account for less than 5 percent of the names on the waiting list for new apartments. The result is an admissions system that promotes inter-ethnic integration among African-Americans, Asians, Dominicans, Puerto Ricans, and other minorities on the waiting list. But young single mothers with children, senior citizens, and disabled applicants comprise the bulk of the twelve-year public housing waiting list. For them, it is doubtful that the benefits of inter-ethnic minority integration outweigh the value of sustained family and local network supports.[38] This admissions policy is the frequent target of criticism from public housing residents and tenant leaders.

## VOTING RIGHTS ACT VERSUS EXPANSION OF POLITICAL CHOICE

Voting rights remedies are based on the premise of residential segregation: minority political districts must be geographically linked. Because blacks in cities are more segregated than any other group, the Voting Rights Act (VRA) continues to be a useful tool for drawing African-American legislative districts. The same is not true of Latinos and Asians, who tend to live in more integrated neighborhoods. As a result, the VRA is not as helpful to them in gaining representation. In the most recent New York City Council redistricting, Asians were too geographically dispersed to gain a majority Asian district, although they had sufficient population to do so. Likewise, Latinos did not gain majority districts in proportion to their population, also because of residential dispersion. The inequity in district formation was a source of bitter conflict among minority groups. As the Latino and Asian populations continue to swell in New York, and in cities across the nation, black leaders will be criticized for their support of voting rights remedies that favor black voters.

A mounting criticism of voting rights remedies, and geographic representation generally, is that drawing districts by race and geography ignores associations that may be more important at a given time than race or geographic proximity. The voting problems in cities sometimes have more to do with class than race. For example, there are 700,000 public housing residents in New York City, with some clearly defined common interests. Yet they have no representation on the City Council, the state legislature, Congress, or even the Housing Authority Board. Voting systems and procedures that recognize multiple identities—that being poor may be as important as being black—are being promoted by dissident civil rights activists/scholars such as Lani Guinier.

## CRIME VERSUS THE CIVIL RIGHTS AGENDA

No issue shows the distance between the civil rights agenda and the demands of low-income blacks more than crime. The historic emphasis in civil rights has been on issues such as citizen protection against the police, opposition to the death penalty, and disparate sentencing for blacks. These are major issues in the black community. Indeed, in Baltimore, 57 percent of black men between age eighteen and thirty-five are either "in prison, on probation or parole, out on bail, or being sought on an arrest warrant." The corresponding figure in Washington, D.C., is 42 percent.[39]

Yet there are many more victims in black communities than criminals. Low-income black communities are demanding increased police protection, harsher police crackdowns, and longer sentencing. Black elected officials and administrators have been under intense pressure to respond, which increasingly pits them against traditional civil rights allies and against each other. In response to community outrage over the rate of violent crime, several black elected officials, including former Mayor Sharon Pratt Kelly of Washington, D.C., publicly called for the National Guard to patrol high-crime neighborhoods. Nightly curfews for persons under eighteen years old have been instituted in several black-led cities. The black head of the Chicago Housing Authority, against opposition from the American Civil Liberties Union (ACLU) and other civil rights groups, instituted police sweeps in public housing projects to rid them of suspected drug dealers and gang members.[40] The recently passed Omnibus Crime Bill split the Congressional Black Caucus, with two-thirds of the caucus supporting the bill, despite the expectation that its death penalty provisions would be used to punish blacks disproportionately.[41]

## EDUCATION

City schools have been in crisis for decades, and the hopes placed in racial integration of the schools have been foiled by suburbanization. The crisis is especially acute for black males. Since the mid-1970s, black males have experienced the sharpest decline in college enrollment of any group: far more go to prison than college.[42] Clearly, the condition of young inner-city black men is beyond the crisis point. Responding to community initiatives, the Milwaukee Public Schools Task Force recommended the creation of two "African-American Immersion Schools" for males. The aim of the schools was to help reorient black males by increasing positive self-image though identification with the achievements of African-Americans. Popular support in low-income black communities led to the creation of several similar schools across the country. The move spurred national controversy among civil libertarians, women's groups, and the National Association for the Advancement of Colored People (NAACP), all of whom focused on what they perceived as institutionalization of racial and sexual discrimination in the schools. In 1991, the ACLU and the National Organization for Women (NOW) Legal Defense and Education Fund sued the Detroit Board of Education to admit girls in three specialized academies. In response, the Milwaukee Board of Education voluntarily agreed to admit girls. The Detroit board agreed to admit girls to the all-male academies only after a U.S. district judge ruled the all-male schools unconstitutional.

The point is not the merit of all-male academies, but the dissonance between the directions being taken by inner-city black residents and those taken by traditional civil rights and liberal organizations. Ben Chavis, despite his problems in the position, generated intense and long-needed debate by publicly articulating these contradictions during his brief tenure as head of the NAACP.

The problems of inner-city poverty demanded an agenda from black mayors dealing with neighborhood economic development, reform of education, police, human services, public housing bureaucracies, and relations with Latinos and Asians. Such an agenda might have required alteration of traditional liberal coalitions that elect black mayors, with possible fallout from municipal and teachers unions, civil rights organizations, and fellow black politicians. Few black mayors have pursued such a politically risky and administratively arduous course.

In the absence of a positive, collective approach to these issues, more black politicians are comfortable running as "deracialized," problem-solver candidates. The danger in this is that many of them appear to have abandoned even the rhetorical concern for the poor that has been characteristic of black politics. In this environment, it is not surprising that advocates and scholars look outside local black leadership for initiatives dealing with poverty.

## What Comes Next?

Although pessimism about the ability of local government, local black elected officials, and civil rights organizations to fight poverty is understandable, it is short-sighted. In the likely event that no major structural reforms come out of Washington, the burden of coping with social chaos in poor neighborhoods will continue to fall on those who govern, work, and live in cities.

Cities can do a lot to help poor neighborhoods without massive federal programs. They can improve service delivery, fund community organizing, identify policy factors promoting and hindering success in low-income communities, and implement changes. Although community-building strategies have little chance of ending poverty, they can rapidly improve conditions and social organization within poor communities in the short-term.

Organizing and community-building in black (and other) poor communities could have a significant impact on political turnout.[43] This is important because, as political scholar Hugh Heclo has repeatedly noted, the poor are currently a political nonentity. As long as this is the case, garnering national political support for major structural reform benefiting inner-cities will be highly unlikely. The unrealized political resources of poor communities may be their most important asset.[44]

# 3

# THE ECONOMIES OF CITIES

## DICK NETZER

*I*n an earlier era, when the pace of technological, economic, and social change was seemingly much slower, a city or region was identified with a specific set of economic specializations. Pittsburgh was the center of the steel industry. Chicago was not only "hog-butcher to the world," but also the country's most important producer of industrial machinery and the hub of its land transportation system. The smaller Massachusetts cities were preeminent in textile and leather goods manufacturing, North Carolina cities were dominated by cigarettes and furniture; Memphis was the banker and shipper for the cotton growers; Fort Worth was the world's leading cow town; Seattle and San Francisco were dominated by their maritime industries; and so on. And, of course, Detroit and eastern Michigan cities (as well as a good many others in the Midwest) were auto cities, Los Angeles the movie capital, and Florida cities were resorts.

But these seemingly fixed specializations were changing— sometimes quite rapidly—by the middle of the twentieth century, and the rate of change has accelerated since then. By 1960, there was no meat-packing in Chicago, little steel-making in Pittsburgh, and almost no textile or leather goods manufacturing in Massachusetts. By 1980, high-tech manufacturing and office activities were far more important in Seattle, North Carolina, and many other places than their "traditional" economic specializations.

## THE SUCCESSION OF INDUSTRIES

In fact, since the eighteenth century, American cities have grown more by mutation than by steady development of their traditional industries. New specializations, often born to serve existing ones, supplant the old and in turn are supplanted. Nowhere is this seen more sharply than in the economic history of New York City. It is no surprise that the most cogent depictions of the dynamics of economic change in large American cities are those written by analysts of New York City's economy: Robert Murray Haig in *The Regional Plan of New York and Its Environs*, completed in 1929; Raymond Vernon in *The Changing Economic Function of the Central City, Anatomy of a Metropolis* (with Edgar M. Hoover) and *Metropolis 1985*, written between 1959 and 1961 as the basis for a second regional plan for New York; and Jane Jacobs in *The Death and Life of Great American Cities* (1961), *The Economy of Cities* (1969), and *Cities and the Wealth of Nations* (1984).[1] Most contemporary writing about urban economic dynamics accepts the reasoning in these classic works as self-evidently true. So, in this chapter, we go back to the sources of these accepted truths.

In the first half of the nineteenth century, New York became the country's largest city and economic capital because its harbor was by far the best of any city on the Atlantic coast and because, after 1825, it had access to the interior of North America via the Erie Canal. Maritime commerce spawned new industries, notably marine insurance, which was the foundation of the city's preeminence in finance (Philadelphia was the financial capital before 1840), ship building, repair and outfitting, and the processing of raw materials that arrived by water. By 1900, New York City was the most important sugar and copper refining area in the nation.

But even before 1900, finance, printing and publishing, and a variety of manufacturing industries that depended on the existence of a large labor supply and quick access to supporting services had become more important to New York than the economic activities more closely tied to its port. In the early twentieth century, New York City became the country's number one location for the manufacture of apparel, electrical and electronic goods (such as radios and parts), various types of fabricated metal products (such as builders' hardware), toys, jewelry, and motion picture films. Meanwhile, New York's dominance of finance grew with the nationalization and internationalization of financial markets, reducing the relative role of rivals like Boston, Philadelphia, St. Louis, and Chicago. The city became an increasingly attractive location for the headquarters of national businesses.

Over the past forty years, with surprising speed, New York's major industries of the 1950s have shrunk or even disappeared. For example, manufacturing employment, which was about 850,000 in the middle-1950s, fell to 280,000 by 1994. Much of the manufacturing that remains is feeding the service sector of the local economy, rather than making finished products and shipping them around the world. There also have been many well-publicized departures of corporate headquarters, at first for locations within the New York metropolitan region, more recently for other parts of the country. Offsetting the declines of such industries, finance, advanced business services, tourism, health, and education services have greatly increased in importance. As is true of most of the country's larger cities, New York's economy today bears only a passing resemblance to that of fifty years ago.

## EXPLAINING URBAN ECONOMIC TRANSFORMATION

Historically, a city captured a commanding position with respect to an economic specialization because of some natural endowment, a specific physical locational characteristics. A city would be located at the head of navigation or "fall line" of a major river (Richmond, Virginia) or junction of waterways (Chicago and Pittsburgh) or the easy crossing point of a major river (Minneapolis). Or, it was a natural seaport (Boston) or near important natural resources—fishing grounds, ore deposits, or timber. The city may have been a convenient place from which to service a relatively rich surrounding agricultural area and process its farm products. Or, going way back in history, the city simply was located on a site that was easy to defend.

In time, technological and other changes vitiated most of these locational advantages. The substitution of overland and air transportation for shipping by water makes Columbus as well situated as Cleveland and Charlotte as well situated as Richmond. Changes in the way steel is manufactured and the exploitation of new sources of iron ore have made tidewater sites around the world superior competitors to the Pittsburghs that once dominated the steel industry. Indeed, today few decisions on the location of manufacturing plants are made on the basis of the location of natural resources. Instead, the key factors are the size and nature of markets for output and the costs and quality of inputs other than natural resources—particularly labor. As the world economy and world trade expand, the number of places where an efficient, cost-minimizing scale of production can be achieved is increasing, as is evident in the spread of the auto industry from the American Midwest to other regions in this country and to Asian countries.

Such changes explain absolute and relative declines in a city's "traditional" economic specializations. They do not explain why most large cities seem to have succeeded in replacing old specializations with new ones. It takes more than the presence of site-specific advantages like climate in some places to explain the self-renewal that has gone on in this century—without government intervention or even much awareness that the renewal process is occurring. And whatever role chance—or good luck—may have played in some cases, that too is an insufficient explanation. The location of some enterprises and industries is, in a sense, accidental. The developer or inventor happened to live in that place or chose to live there after the product had been conceived for personal reasons rather than because of economic imperatives relevant to that line of economic activity. For decades, most valve spring compressors, a tool indispensable for the servicing of autos made before 1940, were made in Waterloo, Iowa—rather than a hundred other possible places—simply because a Waterloo man had developed a superior model.

Those astute observers of the renewal process in New York—Haig, Vernon and Hoover, Jacobs—first demonstrated that the replacement of economic specializations has occurred fairly regularly over time. They then provided the explanation. In Vernon's formulation, the essential economic role of the large city is to incubate new industries.

The city is equipped to be such an incubator because it can offer all sorts of services, supplies, skills, and talents that few fledgling enterprises have available. Consider work space. While thousands of business enterprises are run from homes, millions more have long outgrown the garage or home office and been moved to dedicated premises. A new enterprise seldom is sufficiently well capitalized to permit the purchase or construction of such premises. Typically, new businesses are renters. The supply of rental space for all types of commercial and industrial enterprises is likely to increase geometrically with city size.

The same is true of other business "inputs":

▼    Specialized parts and supplies (the small garment firm that has been typical of New York's apparel industry for decades was able to buy almost any kind of buttons and other trimmings from suppliers located within a few blocks and thus was unrestricted in its fashion design decisions)

▼   Professional services, notably legal and financial services

▼   Workers with unusual skills (carpenters and electricians are ubiquitous, but carpenters who can build stage sets or electricians who know how to work on stage lighting are not)

The collection of these specialized inputs and the clusters of industries they serve is what economists call "agglomeration." Agglomerations characterize big cities and cities that, if not huge in overall size, are exceptionally large in one specialized industry or collection of activities (like Las Vegas in gambling or Nashville in country music). In such places, the demand from many enterprises, small and large, for services, suppliers, and specialized labor is large and stable enough in aggregate—however unstable individual enterprises may be—that clusters of the specialized suppliers emerge and persist. Their presence makes it possible for new users of these suppliers to start up and expand. To be sure, there is always the possibility of importing specialized supplies or services from other cities or regions, or substituting for them, but at some cost in time, versatility, and flexibility, if not in money. Technological changes continually threaten existing agglomerations by making it easier and cheaper to get services from distant locations, but successful cities develop new specialized services and supplies that are, for the moment, best provided in that one city.

Agglomerations can dissipate, if the economic activities that provide the core of the demand shift on a wholesale basis from the city. For example, there was concern twenty-five years ago that the entire cluster of theater, television, and film production and supporting activities might fade in New York, because of the shift in television drama production to California and a succession of very poor seasons on Broadway. The mass of activities that remained was critical, and the cluster survived, but the concern was justified.

Moreover, agglomerations can be and have been duplicated, at least in part, in other places over time. So the special competitive advantage to the original city, for the location of those core industries, of having the agglomeration will be reduced over time. As an economic sector grows nationally and internationally, its local size generates competitive agglomerations in more and more places. But that is not necessarily a disaster for the first city. In fact, if the growth process is successful, the existing agglomeration will be attractive to new types of economic activities, ones that in time become important in their own right. That will happen as the supporting services and suppliers make themselves useful for new types of enterprises, products and services, and the city becomes the incubator for them.

## DEMAND-SIDE VERSUS SUPPLY-SIDE

This account of the economic growth process of cities differs from the story that seems to animate local government officials and business spokespersons concerned with "urban economic development." Their story is that the road to economic success for a city lies in capturing or retaining firms and industries that *export* their output from the city to other places, firms and industries that could locate in any number of places. Their strategy is to bribe firms to locate in their cities by tax concessions, waiver of land use and other regulations, gifts of land and/or buildings, below-market interest rate credit, or if the firm is the owner of a professional sports franchise, which usually exports nothing at all from the city, all of the above.

In rare cases, the public policies of a city may have been so hostile to the economic growth process that such bribery truly is essential. And there are industries and economic activities that really do not need what it is that cities have to offer. A new automobile plant, for example, hardly requires anything like an incubator, and new auto plants and other large-scale manufacturing plants have not been located in cities for decades. If the economic activity in question can be located almost anywhere, then bribery can work. But, on balance, the bribery strategy has not been a spectacular success, however persistent its advocates are in pushing it. For most cities, the key to attracting and fostering new activities to replace the old ones lies not in bribes, but in the quality of the supporting services that the city economy (*not* the city government) has to offer.

In the 1950s, when the study of urban economics was emerging, Hans Blumenfeld, a highly perceptive city planner in Toronto, vigorously criticized the apparent infatuation of economists and urban geographers with the export-led, or demand-side, theory of urban economic growth. Blumenfeld argued that the prime mover, for most large cities, was to be found on the supply side. Whether new activities are invented in the city, attracted to it, or flourish once there will depend on the supply of inputs the city has to offer, ranging from directly supporting services and suppliers to the quality of life in the city. The quality of the city's physical inputs—such as the internal transportation systems and the availability of state of the art telecommunications equipment services—matters. But ultimately the most important input is the human one: the talents, inventiveness, and entrepreneurial energies of the people who live and work in that city. The concentration of such people in a city is, of course, another form of agglomeration.

Blumenfeld's views moved from the pages of city planning journals into common currency when they were elaborated by Jane Jacobs, beginning in 1969. The supply-side perspective, however, was also imbedded in the work of Vernon, who added an important dimension to the Blumenfeld account. For many types of economic activities carried on in cities, Vernon argued, the principal attraction of agglomeration is that the concentration of related activities makes possible face-to-face communication on an everyday basis. Indeed, in Vernon's functional classification of economic activities in New York, the most important category was what he called "communications-oriented" industries. He did *not* mean industries that are heavy users of telecommunications; he meant industries that function on the basis of extensive face-to-face communication among the participants (most of which also are telecommunications- intensive).

The essence of the advantage of extensive face-to-face communication lies in its utility when multiple parties must make complicated decisions, and implement them rapidly. Vernon offered several prototypical cases for New York:

▼   The high-fashion end of the apparel business, where speedy responses from producers and buyers determine success or failure—for firms and individuals, for a season or for good

▼   National advertising, where there is a complicated interaction among the creative people, the media people, and the sponsors

▼   Major corporate and government financing deals, where huge potential gains or losses hinge on face-to-face negotiations

In each of these industries, there are many cases of less complexity, with less need for instantaneous action and so less need for face-to-face communication. In other industries, the ratio of cases where face-to-face communication is important to those where it is not may be much lower. But in any industry, there will be situations in which it is highly desirable.

## VERNON'S FORK

Vernon had no illusion that the need for face-to-face communication or any other aspects of agglomeration guaranteed the indefinite economic success of New York or any other city. He wrote that growth in the scale of individual industries, changes in their organization, and improvements in transportation and communications technology could work to encourage *either* decentralization (from the largest metropolitan regions and from the large central city to its periphery) or centralization of specific economic activities. He thought that, on balance, the activities that in 1960 were heavily communications-oriented would continue to be quite centralized, especially in New York.

The reality, as always, is mixed. Even activities for which face-to-face communication is vital have decentralized, but that decentralization has been relative, not absolute. Most of this type of economic activity has expanded nationally and globally, and New York and other older large cities have shared in the expansion, even while losing their earlier shares of the then-smaller industries.

Improved long-distance transportation, as well as the radical improvements in telecommunications of the past two decades, has supplanted or reduced the need for being within a few meters or blocks of those with whom you deal regularly. A United Airlines television commercial in the depth of the 1990–91 recession made the point well. The CEO of a company in serious economic trouble summons all the officers of the company and tells them that the company will not get by simply by dealing with its customers by phone. He then proceeds to give each a United ticket to a specific destination, where there is a key customer. The message is: When push comes to shove, face-to-face communication with customers is critical for the company, but flying with United can dissolve distance and assure that necessary element.

It also is true that there are advanced economic activities that really do not need much in the way of face-to-face communication. Securities traders can spend their whole careers with no more than telephone contact with their most active and longstanding counterparts in other firms, except possibly for personal contact at a dealers' convention at some resort every year or so. And in some of the most rapidly growing cities of the South and West—like Charlotte, Phoenix, and Salt Lake City—many economic activities that have been the sources of most of the growth really do not interact much. Instead, each of these activities finds that city a good place to be for reasons other than face-to-face communication. It might be because of the city's telecommunications and transportation infrastructure. For example, because Federal Express has its major central sorting operation at Memphis airport, a Memphis law firm has the unique advantage of being able to give Federal Express a letter or package at midnight for delivery anywhere in North America before 10 a.m. that day. Or the city may be centrally located for the firm's operations, like a regional insurance company or bank.

The effect of changes in telecommunications technology on the degree of economic decentralization is, in any event, ambiguous. Reduced cost and improved quality of long-distance transmission of voice, facsimile, and data do make it possible to conduct sophisticated operations in dispersed locations that were once too costly, including one's own home. But some telecommunications costs still increase directly with distance, like dedicated lines, making it advantageous to have operations that must be linked with dedicated lines close together. (That factor was the basis for the virtually complete concentration of the dealer market for U.S. government securities in New York by the 1950s.)

Other technological improvements—like local fiber-optics networks—have economies of scale. They are not cost-effective unless they carry very large volumes of messages, which means that such improvements are made first in the largest cities. Eventually such improvements will spread to other places but, initially, they strengthen the position of the largest cities. Mitchell Moss, a leading authority on telecommunications and the economies of cities, argues that the process of technological and organizational change in telecommunications is such that a small number of the world's largest cities always will have some advantages over smaller places, although the specific nature of the advantage will change from time to time.[2]

The limits of the extent to which technology can abolish the advantages of face-to-face communication, and thus the most important economic reason for concentrations of people in cities, were explored in a leading article about scientific research and cyberspace in the *Economist*. The article serves as a parable for the larger question of the economies of cities:

> Not everything can happen on line: geography will have its due. A technological researcher cannot, unless he works entirely in virtual worlds, do his job just anywhere. The complex mixture of social, mental and physical skills that makes laboratory science work requires equipment and expertise all in one place, however quaint that may come to

seem to free-floaters in corporate finance. And the net cannot yet provide the fantastically flexible labor markets of true science cities. A researcher in Silicon Valley has hundreds of potential jobs within reach of his house; a researcher in Plains, Georgia, may not, however deeply he is plugged in.[3]

These are some of the reasons why networking, which is often taken to mean decentralization, may yet strengthen big and mature concentrations of science and entrepreneurship, with their labor-market advantages, at the expense of smaller or newer ones. It may attract people to the places where their e-mail buddies congregate, rather than encourage hermit-like telecommuting.

## A Bright Economic Prospect for the Cities?

Since 1960 (when he wrote about the economic function of the central city), Vernon's forecasts about the future of New York and other large old central cities (in the Northeast and Midwest) have come to pass, but more rapidly and to an even greater extent than he had anticipated. Manufacturing and other goods-handling activities (like wholesale distribution) have declined drastically. Retailing has decentralized almost as drastically. And while the cities' economies have become overwhelmingly dependent on services, most types of service activities have expanded much more rapidly outside older central cities than within them. A dramatic example is that of corporate headquarters offices, increasingly located in smaller central cities or on green fields well beyond the city.

But the rates of growth in the service activities overall have been so large that most city economies have grown considerably, if inter-mittently, since what now seems to have been the low point of urban economic prospects in the 1970s. In the early 1980s, in the country's old industrial heartland, the large cities that still had substantial manufacturing activities suffered greatly as their industries contracted sharply. A little later, some cities in Texas and elsewhere had major setbacks associated with the worldwide oil glut. Then, at the end of the 1980s, California and the Northeast suffered severely from huge retrenchment in defense spending, major contraction in some parts of the financial services sector, and a collapse in local real estate markets.

Through all these difficulties, however, important parts of the local services sector were growing in nearly all cities, and in all of them overall economic growth resumed within a relatively short time. Over the twenty years from the mid-1970s, nearly all large cities have experienced considerable expansion in a wide range of advanced business and professional services, financial services, health services, and tourism (even in some fairly unlikely cities). Moreover, while most cities have done well as incubators for new service activities, some have even proven successful at incubating new manufacturing enterprises.

Today, Los Angeles is perhaps the world's best incubator for new enterprises of all types, including manufacturing. In part, that success is related to immigration, which provides both entrepreneurs and workers for the new enterprises. That is also important in New York and some other cities.

The supply-side conditions of most large American cities—in physical and human resources—have substantially improved over the past twenty years, notwithstanding the "rotting infrastructure" myth of print media. The amenity levels of most central business districts are far higher, with pedestrian streets, "skywalks," and refurbished theaters, as well as the ubiquitous espresso bars and other sophisticated retail establishments. Operating and capital subsidies to public transportation have restored or created attractive, well-functioning, central-business-district-oriented transportation services that increase the competitiveness of those districts (although few transportation economists believe that the huge subsidies, especially to new rail transit systems, are cost-effective from the standpoint of national transportation policy).

Also, in many cities, a good deal of housing within or on the edges of central business districts has been created, including cities where such housing never existed. For example, in Chicago in 1960, there were fewer than a hundred housing units within one mile of State and Madison Streets (the zero point in Chicago's street grid), and all of them were probably substandard. Today, there are many blocks converted from low-grade business to high-grade residential use, as well as extensive new housing development east of Michigan Avenue. In the largest metropolitan areas, the real possibility of living within walking distance of work makes the city a far more attractive business location for many of the people who must be present if the city really is to function as an incubator.

## THE DOWNSIDE

Most readers will be skeptical of the upbeat tone of the preceding section of this chapter. After all, the economic conditions of large American cities do include the continued exodus of businesses and traditional industries, higher than national unemployment rates, spectacularly high youth unemployment rates, low rates of participation in the labor force, high poverty rates, and all sorts of social ills, including crime.

All of those conditions are real enough, but they are symptoms. Some more basic factors do not bode well for the economic prospects of the cities. One continuing disability of the central city—and the larger the city, the more pronounced this disability is—is what Vernon's collaborator, Benjamin Chinitz, called "the changing nature of centrality" more than thirty years ago. For most of cities' histories, the location that was optimal with regard to transportation access, was the actual geographic center of the central city. As cities grew in the nineteenth and early twentieth centuries, the geographic center of a city moved (for example, northward in New York). But wherever that center was, it was the best point for almost any form of economic activity (with the exception of those activities that had to be located at the water's edge and of huge space-consuming heavy industrial plants).

But after 1950, that was no longer the case. The most accessible location, that is, the location with the lowest transportation costs in money and time, became different for different types of economic activity. The most "central" location in that sense for wholesale distribution of goods is now invariably outside the central business district. Usually, in larger cities, the most central location is not one but several locations, a result of the patterns of motor vehicle traffic and highway facilities. The most "central" location for department stores is in the suburbs, even for New York, because of the dispersion of the consuming population. And for most low-density cities whose growth has come mostly after 1950—Phoenix may be the prototype—there are virtually no functions, public administration aside, for which the center of the city is truly the most central location.

For a medium-sized city whose boundaries have expanded to include newly settled sections on the outskirts—Tucson, Tulsa, Nashville, Jacksonville—the changing nature of centrality does not impose serious economic problems. Jobs are accessible from any residential location in the city, and the economic activity falls within the central city's tax base. But in the largest cities, jobs do become relatively difficult for some residents to get to, and the central city's ability to tax the economic activity of the urban area is circumscribed. The central city as a provider of jobs and taxes becomes increasingly dependent on those specializations for which the agglomeration effects continue to make the central locations truly central. The difficulty, for the largest cities, is that these specializations are to some extent boutique industries, which are not only difficult to tax (for example, they may use little physical space and thus contribute little in property taxes, the most important source of city revenues) but also provide limited numbers of jobs only for especially well prepared candidates.

Another negative factor is the greatly increased difficulty in reusing land within the central city for other purposes. In large American cities in the nineteenth and early twentieth centuries, new land uses were not found only on the outskirts of cities. Both residential and non-residential structures were replaced readily by new ones, often repeatedly. New York is, as always, the extreme case. In a city of 250 square miles and nearly one million buildings that was founded in 1625, we find a single building dating from before 1700, three from the eighteenth century, and fewer than a hundred from the first quarter of the nineteenth century. In the late 1960s, it was commonplace to tear down and replace office buildings that were between fifteen and thirty years old.

Any replacement is much more difficult today, because of concern about neighborhood effects and environmental problems, and vastly increased rigidity in land use controls and other regulatory systems. This tends to be least true of central business districts (outside New York), where replacement of old structures and parking lots with new buildings is seldom all that difficult, given the enormous profits usually expected and the history at frequent land use changes within central business districts. But beyond the central business district, it usually is hard to convert residential land uses to nonresidential ones, increase the density of residential uses (both were major aspects of the earlier growth process in the largest cities), or make major changes in the character of the nonresidential ones—even when the previous nonresidential uses, long since abandoned, were con-spicuously noxious. A good many of the "incubator industries" cannot be economically housed in new central business district office buildings, nor will their employees and inventors be able to afford or even want to live in high-priced condos in and near the central business district.

If the regulatory systems make the costs and hassle of finding suitable space high enough in the erstwhile incubator city, entre-preneurs are likely to forego the advantages of agglomeration and face-to-face communication and locate in exurbs or far away places and countries. This problem cannot be solved through the con-ventional bribery process—offering huge tax and other incentives to identifiable firms, usually large ones, and to well-connected real estate developers—because the city won't know which firms to bribe. The firms in the incubator industries tend to be invisible until they are successful. Even the most aggressive city economic development officer cannot bribe an entrepreneur who cannot be identified.

Another reason for concern about the future of cities lies in the economic circumstances of large portions of the African-Americans and Latinos of the big cities. Thirty years ago, the common diagnosis and prognosis in this regard was that it was not surprising that income levels and labor force participation rates were very low and unemployment rates very high among urban minority populations, who had suffered from decades of racial discrimination in employment. Moreover, many of the minority people of working age in that era were recent arrivals from places that offered appallingly bad education, and most migrants had few skills that were needed in urban labor markets. But with general prosperity, the dismantling of racial discrimination in employment, better educational opportunities for young people, and supporting social and job-training services—all of which *were* occurring in the 1960s in American cities—we could, the theory was, expect the minority newcomers to the cities to move up the ladder of economic and social mobility, much as earlier generations of newcomers did.

In fact, this happened during the 1960s. Poverty rates among urban minorities declined substantially and the gap in earnings levels and unemployment rates between whites and minorities narrowed considerably. True, youth unemployment rates remained high, but they were almost as high among young whites as among minority young people. However, in the 1970s, with slow growth in income levels and higher levels of unemployment across the board, the relative economic position of minorities stopped improving and, in some places and respects (notably, in youth unemployment rates and the incidence of poverty) got worse.

After 1982, the country prospered, but there was considerable geographic unevenness. Most cities on the coasts, and in the Southeast and Northern Plains regions boomed, but growth was much less marked in most of the old industrial Midwest. In the cities that did well, prosperity did have positive effects on the economic circumstances of minorities, but these positive effects were much less dramatic than had been the case in the 1960s. For example, in the country as a whole, the incidence of poverty increased somewhat during the 1980s and the real income of the poorest one-fifth of the households declined. The opposite occurred in the cities that had the most pronounced booms: the poverty percentage declined a bit and the real income of the poorest fifth also rose. In some of these cities, minority labor force participation rates, which had declined sharply in the 1970s, increased significantly. Minority workers, including young people entering the labor force, found jobs in large numbers in the expanding services sector, often low-paying jobs in restaurants and similar places, but often in the "high-end" services, like finance, as well.

However, because the rate of absorption of the inner-city unemployed was modest, there were, and are, huge numbers of minority people in cities who are outside the formal labor force. The recession at the beginning of the 1990s, most marked in those cities like Boston, New York, and Los Angeles that had done best during the 1980s, exacerbated these conditions. Nonetheless, the experience of the 1980s does show that a city economy that is prosperous will be one in which there are reductions in minority poverty and youth unemployment, albeit smaller improvements than occurred in the 1960s.

## ON BALANCE

The prospects for the economies of large American cities are generally good, provided city governments (and other levels of government) do not undermine things with self-destructive policies. These policies— some of which are existing practice in too many cases—include especially damaging taxation and regulation relieved only by waivers in the most conspicuous situations (for the incubator-dependent General Electrics and IBMs) or exhausting available fiscal resources by giving large firms tax incentives at the expense of amenity-improving public expenditure.

But success as an incubator will not necessarily assure the creation of large numbers of new jobs. For most activities that are likely to find the central city the appropriate location, the very real disadvantages—concern about high taxes and space costs, crime, municipal regulation, and the quality of life in general—of that location will require economizing on the use of labor. Over the next generation, we can and probably will have successful cities housing a by-passed underclass that is far from small. Growth and prosperity will help, as in the 1980s. It is too much to expect improving economic conditions to solve all the social problems of the city, however. Wasted areas and wasted people, and the money and other costs of coping with them, will remain and will continue to be drags on the city economy and challenges to public policy.

# 4

# THE PERMANENT URBAN FISCAL CRISIS

## ESTER R. FUCHS*

O nce the domain of public accountants, finance experts, and political insiders, municipal budgets are now front page news in every major city across the country. And the news is not good. Cities are routinely confronting budget shortfalls, laying off municipal employees, and cutting services to bring spending in line with available revenue. Philadelphia, Bridgeport, and East St. Louis are all casualties of the 1990s. They actually experienced New York City-style fiscal crises, requiring state rescue and oversight. Philadelphia was on the edge of fiscal collapse in August 1990, when former Mayor Wilson Goode reported a $73 million budget deficit for the 1990 fiscal year. Moody's rating agency promptly dropped the city's bond rating to *Ba*, dropped it again in September to *B*, and effectively closed Philadelphia out of the credit market.

Urban fiscal crises are not new. During the Great Depression, 1,434 incorporated municipalities defaulted on their loans.[1] The current condition of constant urban fiscal crisis, however, dates only to 1975, when New York City—carrying a $12.3 billion debt and projecting an operating budget deficit of $1.68 billion—was closed out of the bond market.[2] New York's fiscal crisis was a wake-up call for the nation's mayors.

\* I would like to thank Rachel Stevens for her expert research assistance.

Before 1975, cities could rely on anticipated cycles of economic growth to fund their expanding budgets and pay back their mounting debt. The bond market was willing to support the municipal debt habit, so long as the profits were risk-free. But as central cities faced growing competition from an increasingly suburban and, ironically, global economy, recessions hit the cities hardest, and periods of economic growth tended to be weak and less frequent. Now, savvy businesses are willing to exploit a city's vulnerability by threatening to leave if they are not given significant tax abatements, and middle-class homeowners are organized to defeat any mayor who proposes raising property taxes.

The fiscal consequences of these trends have been devastating. It is now generally more expensive for most cities to borrow money from a more cautious bond market, even as their own revenue base has either shrunk or become less predictable—or both. Cities are more efficiently managed today than in 1975, but mayors have fewer sources of revenue available to fund more costly services.

It doesn't matter whether a city is governed by a Democratic or Republican mayor or whether it is an older Rustbelt city like Chicago or a newer Sunbelt city like Houston, balancing the budget is the issue that dominates mayoral campaigns and preoccupies a mayor's time. Campaign rhetoric about improving the quality of services has become fashionable. Once in office, however, mayors face a hard political reality: they simply cannot provide effective basic services to all their citizens and consistently balance their budgets.

City budgets have always been political documents, but in this environment of scarce resources, fiscal policy has become the center of urban politics. Understanding the implications of this dramatic change requires answering three questions:

1.  How did fiscal issues come to dominate the urban policy agenda?

2.  How do persistent budget problems affect the capacity of mayors to run city governments?

3.  What impact does the permanent fiscal crisis have on ordinary citizens living in America's cities?

## FISCAL POLICY DOMINATION

Sound fiscal policy simply means a balanced budget at the end of the fiscal year, with enough money available to pay back what has been borrowed. The mayor formulates the budget, but its final version must be approved by the city council. The council, representing a broad array of interests, is generally responsible for holding the brief (and usually irrelevant) public hearings on the budget mandated by most city charters.

Cities adopt both expense budgets (the projected costs of day-to-day operations) and capital budgets (the projected costs of long-term capital projects, such as roads, bridges, and sewers). Expense budgets are financed by local taxes and fees, state and federal assistance, and short-term debt (payable within a year). The capital budget is really a set of borrowing authorizations for specific projects financed primarily by long-term debt (payable over a designated period of time beyond one year). The city's public officials make such basic fiscal policy decisions as how much to spend, how much to tax, and how much to borrow. Sounds simple enough. Spending decisions determine the level to which services are funded, which services are cut, and which new services, if any, are added to the budget. Taxing and borrowing are alternatives for raising revenue. Taxing decisions (that is, property taxes, sales taxes, city income tax, user fees) and levels of inter-governmental aid determine the mix of revenue for funding city services; borrowing decisions determine the level and type of debt a city incurs.

Since budgets are really estimates of expenditures in anticipation of future revenues, the probability of a city coming up short at the end of the fiscal year is quite high. Cities may be legally required to balance their budgets, but political factors lead mayors to project that revenues will grow and expenditures will decline. And in the face of revenue shortfalls, mayors prefer any form of borrowing to proposing tax increases or spending cuts. The golden rule of urban fiscal policy has been: never pay for anything today that can be dumped on another mayor tomorrow.

Budget deficits are not simply a consequence of irresponsible fiscal management or an inefficient workforce. There is a political and economic context to fiscal policymaking that constrains the choices that mayors make, and it is not the same in all cities.

The economic piece of the fiscal policy puzzle has been well understood for decades. Since the mid-1950s, the older cities of the Northeast have been losing both their middle-class tax base and the manufacturing jobs that were once the backbone of their local economies. This trend, coupled with the growing number of poor people concentrated in the central cities, has weakened the urban tax base and contributed to persistent cycles of fiscal problems: despite the loss of revenue, the demand for services in declining cities remains high, and the cost often increases when cities have to provide for the special needs of the poor.

The economic dimension of fiscal policy is important, but it is the political dimension that must be addressed if cities are to get any long-term relief from their current fiscal problems. Intergovernmental relations have an extraordinary impact on a city's budget and, ultimately, its fiscal condition. While most of us think of mayors as powerful public officials, in the realm of fiscal policy they are weak players. In 1819, the U.S. Supreme Court ruled in the *Dartmouth* case that cities were simply creatures of the state.[3] The Iowa State Supreme Court clarified the state supremacy doctrine in *Clinton v. Cedar Rapids* and the Missouri Railroad Company in 1868. Judge John F. Dillon stated that municipalities "owe their origins to, and derive their powers and rights wholly from, the legislature."[4] This formulation, now known as "Dillon's Rule," means that cities are completely dependent on their state governments for the authority to make laws. Many cities have been given "home rule," but it is limited, especially in fiscal policy. Moreover, the state can always supersede local decisions with state laws. State governments retain significant control over a city's fiscal policy choices, limiting the city's authority and discretion over its own revenue and expenditures policy and determining jurisdictional responsibility for service delivery.

The state mandates that impose the greatest fiscal burden on local governments are those that stipulate programs without allocating state funds to pay for their implementation—particularly in health, education, social services, environmental protection, and transportation. States can also mandate personnel policy by setting salaries, fringe and retirement benefits, and working conditions for municipal employees. Special interest groups can go to the state legislature and make their appeals for spending, even after city officials have refused their demands. This tactic has been especially successful for municipal employee unions.

On the revenue side, the city is severely limited by state regulation of its taxing and borrowing authority. States can remove certain properties from the local property tax rolls, restrict the level of local sales or income taxes, and restrict the type of taxes cities can levy. States can also limit the amount and type of debt that cities can incur.

States also assign functional responsibility. The state determines which level of government will be responsible for providing and funding a particular service and the extent of intergovernmental cooperation for service delivery. Cities benefit fiscally when they can (1) shift responsibility for particularly costly services to their county or state governments; or (2) share the cost with other, wealthier political jurisdictions by creating special districts or authorities. These non-city entities usually have separate borrowing and taxing authority, relieving the municipal government of the direct debt and revenue raising burdens associated with those services. Regional transportation authorities in cities like Chicago and San Francisco, metropolitan government in Minneapolis, and regional government in Miami-Dade County are examples of sharing fiscal burdens.

Since municipal corporations are not the only legal entity providing city services, any comparison of city budgets that does not recognize these differences is extremely misleading. New York City's comprehensive government is certainly not the norm. For example, Chicago, Philadelphia, Los Angeles, Houston, and most other cities have independent boards of education with separate budgets and taxing authority. New York City and Boston have dependent school districts. Fulton County provides Atlanta's library services, so they do not appear in the city budget. In Chicago, mass transit is provided by a regional authority; the state provides public welfare; low-income housing is provided by a public authority; and public hospitals, courts, and corrections are administered and funded by Cook County.

A comparison of New York and Chicago at the time of New York's 1975 fiscal crisis shows the dramatic effect on urban fiscal stability caused by differences in functional responsibility. New York spent 72 percent of its budget on nontraditional services, such as mass transit, public welfare, health and hospitals, housing, and higher education, while Chicago spent only 16 percent. New York had more functional responsibilities than any other city in the country and, as a consequence, spent more on services per capita.[5]

A comparison of expenditure patterns for the five largest cities in fiscal 1991 shows that not much has changed since 1975.[6] New York is still spending more per capita on service delivery than any other city in the country. In fact, New York's per capita budget is almost three times greater than Philadelphia's and five times greater than Houston's (see Table 4.1, next page). Housekeeping services also remain most expensive in New York City.

The extraordinary variation in jurisdictional responsibilities, however, accounts for the most significant differences in spending among the five largest cities. New York City still spends 72 percent of its budget on noncommon services and 16 percent on traditional services. In contrast, Chicago spends 49 percent and Houston 53 percent of their respective budgets on housekeeping services. Education and social services devour 47 percent of New York's budget, but they barely appear in the corporate budgets of Los Angeles, Chicago, or Houston because these are either county or special district functions (see Table 4.2). Noncommon services are generally assumed to be redistributive—that is, support services for low-income people. Interestingly, aid to mass transit (included in utility expenditures)

## TABLE 4.1

### Per Capita Expenditures, Five Largest Cities, 1991

| | New York | Los Angeles | Chicago | Houston | Philadelphia |
|---|---|---|---|---|---|
| **COMMON SERVICES** | | | | | |
| Police | 244 | 187 | 205 | 154 | 206 |
| Fire | 96 | 73 | 79 | 89 | 76 |
| Environmental Protection | 216 | 111 | 81 | 157 | 149 |
| Highways | 121 | 53 | 128 | 56 | 41 |
| Libraries | 33 | 13 | 42 | 15 | 22 |
| Governmental Administration | 130 | 86 | 44 | 34 | 110 |
| **Subtotal** | **841** | **523** | **579** | **505** | **604** |
| **NONCOMMON SERVICES** | | | | | |
| Education | 1,047 | 4 | 11 | 0 | 10 |
| Social Services | 1,396 | 3 | 65 | 33 | 304 |
| Criminal Justice | 208 | 14 | 7 | 21 | 186 |
| Transportation | 68 | 109 | 158 | 59 | 72 |
| Parks & Recreation | 61 | 78 | 13 | 37 | 44 |
| Housing & Community Development | 346 | 66 | 43 | 16 | 53 |
| Utilities & Liquor Store | 618 | 664 | 66 | 132 | 378 |
| **Subtotal** | **3,743** | **938** | **363** | **298** | **1,047** |
| *Interest on* | | | | | |
| ***General Debt*** | 208 | 62 | 92 | 113 | 91 |
| **Total** | **4,584** | **1,461** | **942** | **803** | **1,651** |

*Source:* U.S. Department of Commerce, Bureau of the Census, *City Government Finances, 1990-91* (Washington, D.C.: Government Printing Office, 1991).

## TABLE 4.2

### COMMON AND NONCOMMON SERVICE EXPENDITURES AS A PERCENTAGE OF TOTAL EXPENDITURES, 1991

| | New York | Los Angeles | Chicago | Houston | Philadelphia |
|---|---|---|---|---|---|
| **COMMON SERVICES** | | | | | |
| Police | 244 | 187 | 205 | 154 | 206 |
| Police | 5 | 11 | 17 | 16 | 10 |
| Fire | 2 | 4 | 7 | 9 | 4 |
| Environmental | | | | | |
| Protection | 4 | 7 | 7 | 16 | 8 |
| Highways | 2 | 3 | 11 | 6 | 2 |
| Libraries | 1 | 1 | 4 | 2 | 1 |
| Governmental | | | | | |
| Administration | 3 | 5 | 4 | 4 | 6 |
| **Total** | **16** | **32** | **49** | **53** | **31** |
| **NONCOMMON SERVICES** | | | | | |
| Education | 20 | 0 | 1 | 0 | 1 |
| Social Services | 27 | 0 | 6 | 3 | 15 |
| Criminal Justice | 4 | 1 | 1 | 2 | 9 |
| Transportation | 1 | 7 | 13 | 6 | 4 |
| Parks & Recreation | 1 | 5 | 1 | 4 | 2 |
| Housing & Community | | | | | |
| Development | 7 | 4 | 4 | 2 | 3 |
| Utilities & Liquor | | | | | |
| Store | 12 | 41 | 6 | 14 | 19 |
| **Total** | **72** | **58** | **31** | **31** | **53** |
| *Interest on* | | | | | |
| *General Debt* | 4 | 4 | 8 | 12 | 5 |
| *Total Expenditures* | **100** | **100** | **100** | **100** | **100** |
| *Total Expenditures* | | | | | |
| *($ thousands)* | 38,112,900 | 5,686,172, | 3,262,714 | 1,557,741 | 31,122,862 |

Note: Percentages may not total 100, due to rounding.

Source: U.S. Department of Commerce, Bureau of the Census, *City Government Finances, 1990–91* (Washington, D.C.: Government Printing Office, 1991).

accounts for virtually all of Los Angeles's and Houston's noncommon service spending. Cities that are investing in their mass transit systems certainly view public transportation as an essential service and a necessary part of any sound economic development strategy. Nevertheless, mass transit systems are costly to build and generally operate with a deficit and, as a consequence, produce a fiscal burden for cities that fund them directly through their own budgets. The cost of mass transit is highest in Los Angeles and lowest in Chicago, because Chicago effectively shares the cost of its mass transit system with a regional authority.

Cities show remarkable similarity in spending priorities—if we examine only their common function budgets (see Table 4.3). In all five cities, police spending accounts for the lion's share of the common function budget, with environmental protection (sanitation and sewerage) coming in a close second.

## TABLE 4.3

### COMMON SERVICE EXPENDITURES AS A PERCENTAGE OF TOTAL COMMON SERVICE EXPENDITURES, 1991

|  | New York | Los Angeles | Chicago | Houston | Philadelphia |
|---|---|---|---|---|---|
| Police | 29 | 36 | 35 | 30 | 34 |
| Fire | 11 | 14 | 14 | 18 | 13 |
| Environmental Protection | 26 | 21 | 14 | 31 | 25 |
| Highways | 14 | 10 | 22 | 11 | 7 |
| Libraries | 4 | 2 | 7 | 3 | 4 |
| Governmental Administration | 16 | 17 | 8 | 7 | 18 |
| **Total** | **100** | **100** | **100** | **100** | **100** |
| $ Per Capita | 840.98 | 522.90 | 579.46 | 504.91 | 604.05 |

Note: Percentages may not total 100, due to rounding.

*Source*: U.S. Department of Commerce, Bureau of the Census, *City Government Finances, 1990–91* (Washington, D.C.: Government Printing Office, 1991).

Chicago and Houston have kept the proportion of their budgets spent on government administration, as well as the actual cost, lowest by combining contracted-out services, low pension benefits for city workers, and weak or nonexistent municipal employee unions. This fits the commonly held view of Houston as a weak labor city, but Chicago's status may surprise many. Despite Chicago's reputation as a union town, its municipal employees were among the last to gain collective bargaining agreements. Harold Washington, Chicago's first black mayor, supported changes in state law to extend collective bargaining rights to white-collar workers in July 1984, and allowed them to be represented by the American Federation of State, County, and Municipal Employees (AFSCME) in negotiations. Before June 1985, when Washington fully implemented the Shakman Decree, most city workers were exempt from civil service and could be fired without a hearing. The Shakman Decree was the outcome of a 1969 lawsuit (*Shakman v. Democratic Organization of Cook County*, 1970) brought by a disgruntled reformer defeated by a machine candidate in his bid to become a delegate to the Illinois State Constitutional Convention. Despite signing a consent judgement in 1972 that would have ended the patronage system, Mayor Richard J. Daley and subsequent mayors had never really implemented the Shakman Decree. Richard M. Daley, who succeeded Washington, became one of the first mayors in the country to contract out janitorial services, reducing both city costs and union power.[7]

Since the 1980s, federal mandates have also been having an increasingly negative impact on a city's ability to balance its budgets. Early mandates, such as those found in the Water Quality Act of 1965 and the Air Quality Act of 1967, were directed at state governments, which now often share the cost of compliance with their local governments. A U.S. Conference of Mayors survey of 314 cities in 1993 found that compliance with ten unfunded federal mandates accounts for an average of 11.7 percent of local revenue.[8]

Between 1984 and 1994, according to Mayor Steve Bartlett, Dallas spent $90 million on water treatment plant improvements and another $200 million on sewage treatment facilities to comply with the federal Clean Water Act. In Dallas, $20 million is equivalent to the cost of 800 additional police officers for one year. Dallas expects to spend another $3 billion to bring its sanitary sewer lines into compliance.[9]

The Americans with Disabilities Act mandates that curb cuts and ramps be installed in city intersections by 1995. In Philadelphia, compliance will cost $140 million, more than three times the amount

While the trend line is not constant, state governments do tend to reduce the level of their assistance to city governments during economic recessions—just at the time when cities need it the most.

State aid is becoming even more significant as the federal government has been reducing its assistance to local governments since 1978. Federal aid as a percentage of local government revenues peaked at 9 percent in 1978 (see Figure 4.3).

The early optimism that states would step up to replace lost federal aid faded when few did. Most states that increased aid during the flush 1980s did so in the areas of transportation and education and did not pick up the tab for the majority of federally funded programs. In a recent survey conducted by the National Conference of State Legislatures,

## FIGURE 4.3
### Federal Aid to Local Governments as a
### Percentage of Total Local Revenue, 1927–91

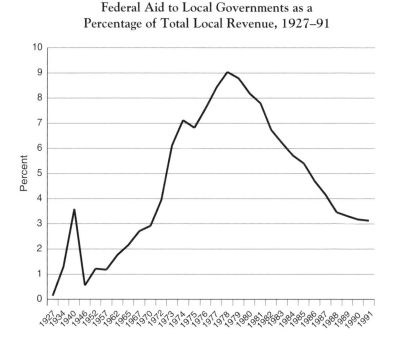

Sources: U.S. Advisory Commission on Intergovernmental Relations, *Significant Features in Fiscal Federalism*, Vol. II, Table 18, 1993: Washington, D.C.

twenty-six states—as different as California, Montana, and New Hampshire—reported revenue shortfalls in their fiscal year 1992 budgets. As a consequence, even states like Massachusetts, New York, and California, which increased spending in the 1980s, cut back their local assistance, worrying about balancing their own budgets in the 1990s.[13]

By 1994, the recession had ended and most states found themselves with surpluses. The political climate led governors and state legislatures to enact tax cuts rather than significantly increase aid to local governments.

Direct federal assistance to city governments is relatively recent, dating from only the 1930s. The failure of state governments to alleviate urban unemployment and social welfare problems during the Great Depression changed federal policy. It was Franklin Delano Roosevelt's New Deal that established the direct fiscal link between city governments and Washington. Recognizing that cities could no longer be viewed as economically self-sufficient, Roosevelt's federal government accepted responsibility for ensuring the survival of city governments and the welfare of their residents, beginning what some have called the great liberal experiment.

This liberalism took on a peculiarly urban form, encouraging city governments to get involved in programs that actively redistributed income and to increase their workforces to help offset widespread unemployment in the private sector. In 1927, direct federal aid to local governments in constant dollars was $17.3 million. By 1940, it reached $661.9 million—an increase of 3,724 percent.[14] In short, federal aid became a substantial and dependable slice of the cities' revenue pie. Federal urban policy really began with such New Deal programs as the Federal Emergency Relief Administration (FERA); the Works Progress Administration (WPA), with half its money spent in the fifty largest cities;[15] the Public Works Administration (PWA), with more than half the money it spent between 1933 and 1939 going to urban areas; and the U.S. Housing Authority (USHA).[16] Whether it was Harry S Truman's Highway Act, Lyndon Johnson's Great Society, Richard Nixon's General Revenue Sharing, or Jimmy Carter's Urban Development Action Grants, every president after Roosevelt and until Ronald Reagan had at least one signature piece of legislation that helped cities meet their growing service delivery and consequent revenue needs.

Johnson's Great Society, of course, was pro-urban by design. It provided the greatest infusion of federal funds to cities since the New Deal. Much of this assistance went directly to city governments, circumventing the states completely. Between 1957 and 1967, federal aid to local governments grew by 331 percent.[17]

The seminal Great Society programs included Model Cities, Community Action, Head Start, the Economic Opportunity Act, Mass Transit Aid, Educational Aid for the Disadvantaged (Title I), and the Manpower Development Training Act. Johnson also created the cabinet-level Department of Housing and Urban Development (HUD). This period might be viewed as the second phase of the liberal experiment.

Direct federal assistance peaked in 1978, during Carter's presidency. But not until the Reagan years did the federal government make a concerted effort to end the urban liberal experiment. Reagan's New Federalism was designed to change fundamentally the fiscal relations among federal, state, and city governments. In some sense, this was a frontal assault on the New Deal and Great Society's liberal agenda. The major piece of urban legislation passed during the Reagan presidency was a 1988 amendment to the federal municipal bankruptcy code, allowing cities to declare bankruptcy without jeopardizing their tax-exempt municipal bonds. Ironically, cities understood that their fiscal vulnerability had increased during Reagan's tenure, so this change was welcome.

It is not simply the failure to pass pro-city legislation during the 1980s, but the all-out attack on existing urban programs that continues to hurt urban fiscal capacity. Between 1978 and 1988, federal aid to localities dropped 51 percent.[18] The reduction in the federal government's revenue-raising potential as a consequence of the 1981 Tax Act, combined with the 1985 Gramm-Rudman-Hollings Act requirement to reduce the federal deficit, has made discretionary spending a prime target for budget cuts. In retrospect, it is not surprising that a Republican president who, according to the New York Times/CBS polls, twice won elections with support from only 35 and 36 percent of the voters in large central cities would consider this constituency a vulnerable target.[19]

The Omnibus Budget Act of 1981 cut domestic spending by $35 billion, eliminated fifty-nine grant programs, and consolidated nearly eighty categorical grant programs into nine broad-based block grants. Most important, many of the eliminated grants were direct aid to local governments, while the new block grants were all to state governments.[20] Not only did this legislation erode the federal-city policy link while enhancing the state role, it reduced the overall level of federal intergovernmental aid.

The elimination of General Revenue Sharing for states in 1980 and local governments in 1986 was the final fiscal assault on local governments. According to the General Accounting Office, revenue-sharing funds constituted as much as 23 percent of total revenue in some fiscally distressed cities.[21] And because of its "no-strings-attached" approach, revenue sharing was an especially important tool for balancing city budgets.

Bush continued Reagan's policy of urban disengagement—reducing federal aid, proposing no new programs, and finally succeeding in eliminating Urban Development Action Grants. During the Reagan-Bush years (1981–1991), federal funding of urban programs dropped 68 percent, the first real dollar decline since World War II.[22]

All five cities were hurt by the decline in federal aid (see Figure 4.4). Ironically, in 1980, cities with limited functional responsibilities, like Houston and Los Angeles, relied on the federal government for a larger share of their revenues than New York or Philadelphia. By 1990, New York was receiving less than 3 percent of its revenue from Washington—very close to the percentages in Houston and Los

## FIGURE 4.4
### Intergovernmental Federal Aid as a
### Percentage of Total Revenue, 1960–91

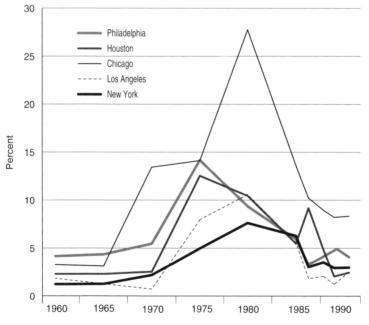

Sources: U.S. Bureau of the Census, *City Government Finances: 1960, 1964–65, 1969–70, 1974–75, 1984–85, 1987–88, 1988–89, 1989–90, 1990–91*, Table 5.

Angeles. Even Chicago, which has always been politically effective in Washington, found its federal assistance was down from a high of 27.8 percent (in 1980) to a low of 8.3 percent (in 1990). In 1991, all the cities except Philadelphia saw a slight recovery. Senator Daniel P. Moynihan points out the irony of these numbers for states like New York, Pennsylvania, and Illinois, which had significant balance of payment deficits with the federal government between 1983 and 1993[23] These states were joined in recent years by California. Rather than being a drag on the nation's economy, the states holding the largest cities have paid the federal government far more in taxes than they've received in outlays.

The Reagan-Bush urban agenda was not simply a temporary cutback in federal aid attributable to an economic downturn. It was an intentional, fundamental reordering of relationships in the federal system that had been established by Roosevelt and reinforced by Johnson. What better way to end the liberal experiment than to eliminate the funds that supported its programs?

The enormous national debt, a legacy of the Reagan years, has made it difficult to introduce any new domestic policy initiatives without cutting others. President Bill Clinton's one major piece of urban legislation, The Empowerment Zones, Enterprise Communities and Rural Investment Centers Program, enacted as part of the 1993 Omnibus Budget Reconciliation Act, was significant, but the level of funding indicates that he will not change the downward slope of federal aid to urban areas. Only six neighborhoods will be eligible for $100 million each in federal funds over the next years. His proposals for welfare and health reform and the crime bill may help cities as part of a broadbased, universalistic approach to domestic policy. Since the 1994 mid-term Congressional election victory for the Republican party, cities are once again the targets of proposed cuts in federal spending. In 1994, the federal government granted $218 billion in aid to state and local governments. The Republicans in the House have proposed cutting aid by $390 billion between 1996 and 2002, representing a 5 percent decline in aid in 1996 and 17 percent in 1998.[24] It is unlikely that Clinton or the Democrats in Congress will do much to oppose this trend. Philip Dearborn of the Advisory Commission on Intergovernmental Relations predicts that there will be no real financial help in discretionary aid to cities from the federal government for the remainder of the century.[25]

Reagan's New Federalism supported the position that states and localities could better determine their needs without the "interference" of the federal government. In reality, New Federalism meant that states and localities would have to pay for most domestic programs without federal funds. In fact, the 1980s saw a resurgence of local economic growth in cities such as Boston, Philadelphia, New York, Baltimore, and other older cities that had suffered most during the previous decade. The subsequent boon to local revenues helped all these cities balance their budgets while increasing spending. Once growth ended, however, the impact of lost federal revenues began to take its toll. In effect, the end of the urban liberal experiment may have been postponed until the 1990s.

How did cities get into this mess? New York's fiscal crisis was perfectly timed to assist the Republicans in their ideological assault on local redistributive programs and their more far-reaching efforts to divest the federal government of responsibility for urban problems. New York City was judged "guilty" of creating its own fiscal problems, and most important, its "generous" redistributive programs were seen as the cause. Without much effort on the part of conservative ideologues, the enterprise of providing redistributive services at the local level was completely delegitimized. Moreover, cities such as New York that relied on federal funds were labeled "dependent." The label implies that federal money was a gift from a generous relative rather than a sharing of mutual burdens by a political partner.

New York City's near-default in 1975 instilled the fear of fiscal crisis in virtually every city across the country. Mayors became obsessed with fiscal management issues. If they did not show that they could balance their budgets and keep their credit ratings high, their political opponents would surely make fiscal irresponsibility an issue in the next election. Mayors had no choice but to accept responsibility for the fiscal health of their cities, but they failed to realize that in doing so they lost the battle over federal assistance and helped marginalize cities in the political conscience of most Americans, who now live in suburbs. Once their budgets were balanced, mayors had trouble arguing that their cities "needed" federal funds.

During the 1980s, mayors of both parties tacitly accepted the terms of the political debate defined by the Reagan republicans and unintentionally allowed the threat of fiscal crisis and instability to obscure the basic economic reality discovered during the Great Depression: cities are not economically self-sufficient government units and need both federal and state assistance to provide adequate services for their residents, businesses, workforce, and visitors.

## HOW DO PERSISTENT DEFICITS AFFECT MAYORS' ABILITY TO GOVERN?

With limited legal authority over fiscal policy decisions in their own cities, American mayors are weak executives preoccupied with gaining control over policymaking and with assuring their reelection. Mayors tend to be targets both of the public's expression of discontent and its demands for improved services. Yet cities have access to fewer resources than state or federal governments. Increasingly, mayors are telling their constituents that the only responsible course of action is a combination of cutting spending by reducing the municipal workforce and encouraging business development through tax incentives.

The structure of the American federal system forces cities to compete with one another for all tax revenue, leaving virtually every local government with insufficient resources to finance needed services. The threat of budget shortfalls has been the only reliable way for mayors to control the otherwise persistent interest-group demands for increased spending. The political survival of mayors depends on their ability to reduce the public's expectations for effective services and to minimize citizen involvement in determining needs. When facing a constant battle to reduce spending, mayors have trouble focusing on the substantive policy issues—improving public education, reducing crime, keeping streets clean. The reality is that cities can balance their budgets, but it is most often at the expense of basic services.

The following examples illustrate the pervasiveness of urban fiscal problems and the limited policy options that mayors have to remedy their situations.

## Philadelphia

In September 1990, Philadelphia experienced a real fiscal crisis.[26] After being locked out of the bond market and cutting $65 million from social service programs, Philadelphia still faced a $193 million shortfall in its $2.16 billion fiscal 1991 budget. Unable to get approval of any of his revenue measures from the city council, Mayor Wilson Goode had a serious cash flow problem. After much delay, the state assembly passed legislation in April 1991 enacting a 1 percent city sales tax. In June, the assembly created the Pennsylvania Intergovernmental Cooperation Authority (PICA), a financial oversight board with legal authority to float bonds for the city and to secure city tax revenue for repayment of debt. This was insufficient to resolve the crisis, however, and when Mayor Ed Rendell took office in January 1992, Philadelphia was on the brink of fiscal collapse, with a $230 million deficit on a $2.3 billion budget. Like New York City in 1975, Philadelphia had experienced a serious decline in its economic base. In 1960, the city had 300,000 manufacturing jobs; in 1993, only 72,000.

According to the 1990 U.S. Census, 20.3 percent of Philadelphia's 1,585,557 residents lived in poverty, while only 10.1 percent of the metropolitan region's residents were poor. Federal aid had dropped to

$54 million in 1990 from $250 million in 1981. Philadelphia's spiraling budget costs had been caused in part by increased spending on drug and alcohol treatment, AIDS, and the homeless—and a political structure that assigned Philadelphia (also a county) the costs of criminal justice services. Moreover, much of Center City redevelopment was accomplished in the 1980s through property tax abatements, forcing the city to become increasingly reliant on wage and business taxes.

Mayor Ed Rendell understood that Philadelphia's fiscal problems were not simply a matter of balancing the budget for one year and reentering the bond market. He ran on a platform of reforming government, cutting spending, and promoting economic development. He also refused to raise city taxes. At the same time, Mayor Rendell used the city's fiscal crisis to demand concessions from the municipal labor force—personnel accounted for 60 percent of the city's budget. In October 1992, he signed a union contract that provided for a three-year wage freeze, a reduction in the number of paid holidays, surrender of control over union health plans, and revised work practices that allowed for greater flexibility in dividing jobs between union and nonunion workers. In March 1993, Rendell negotiated a four-year contract with the police union, which included a two-year wage freeze, 2 percent and 3 percent raises in 1995 and 1996 respectively, and a cut in city contributions to police medical plans for each worker by $90 per month. He reduced the number of firefighters, civilianized many jobs in the police department, and cut library hours. In 1993, Ed Rendell balanced the city's budget for the first time in seven years and effectively resolved the city's fiscal crisis.

Nevertheless, Philadelphia still confronts a structural imbalance in its budget and a stagnant revenue base. Between 1989 and 1994, Philadelphia lost some 20,000 jobs annually. Mayor Rendell proposes to reduce Philadelphia's business, wage, and real estate transfer taxes to make the city more economically competitive with its suburbs.

## Washington, D.C.

The most recent fiscal crisis occurred in our nation's capital city. In 1993, Washington D.C.'s mayor Sharon Pratt Kelly faced a $52 million budget gap in a $3.4 billion budget. By 1994, she had eliminated 6,000 positions in city government.[27] Criticized for Washington's growing fiscal problems, she was defeated in her party's primary by Marion Barry, a convicted felon and former mayor. When Barry took office in January 1995, the city's fiscal problems escalated. Washington, D.C.'s deficit was estimated to be $722 million in a $3.2 billion budget. In February 1995, the mayor asked federal authorities to take over the city's welfare, medical, court, and corrections systems. On February 15, when Moody's Investor Service lowered the District's bond rating from Baa to Ba—junk bond status—the district joined the growing group of cities that, in the post-Great Depression era, had experienced certifiable fiscal crises. Washington's situation is somewhat different than other American cities because of its direct fiscal and administrative links to the federal government. Congressional auditors declared the district insolvent on February 21. Despite Mayor Barry's efforts to cobble together a bailout plan, the city's track record at cutting spending was so poor that some form of financial control board takeover was inevitable. In April, Washington's city council actually voted to lower property taxes, increasing the deficit by about $40 million. In May 1995, President Clinton and the Congress stripped power from the city council and the mayor and appointed a five-member control board to manage the city's finances with a mandate to balance the district's budget in four years.[28]

While Washington has clearly been mismanaged for decades, the Greater Washington Research Center has documented a decline in the district's economy that includes a loss of middle-class households and jobs to surrounding suburbs, which will only worsen its fiscal situation.

## Los Angeles

Other cities have not reached a crisis, but are enduring chronic fiscal problems. Facing its worst fiscal problems since the Great Depression, Los Angeles confronted a $198 million deficit in its $4.3 billion budget for fiscal year 1995 before deciding to transfer revenue from semi-autonomous, proprietary departments such as water, power, airports, and the harbor to the general fund.[29]

## San Francisco

San Francisco has been facing chronic budget deficits since former Mayor Art Agnos took office in 1988. California's water shortage has left San Francisco with yearly revenue shortfalls of $20–$40 million due to lost sales of hydroelectric power.

## Detroit

Detroit mayor Dennis Archer faced a $63.3 million budget deficit in the spring of 1994, just as the city council approved a $2.2 billion budget for fiscal year 1995, his first since taking office. The shortfall was caused mostly by a cut in revenue sharing by the state of Michigan. Archer restructured the city debt to eliminate the shortfall and narrowly averted a downgrading of city bonds. Moody's had already dropped Detroit's rating to Ba1 in July 1992. Any further drop would have jeopardized Detroit's ability to borrow in the bond market.[30]

## New York

New York mayor David Dinkins, who ran on a platform of improving services for all New Yorkers, began his first term in 1990 by calling for an austere budget to fend off an impending deficit. Dinkins's fiscal problems continued to escalate as he faced a $73 million shortfall in fiscal year 1991's budget and a possible takeover of city finances by the state Financial Control Board. The city's $28.5 billion fiscal year 1992 budget included a $400 million increase in property taxes and a $335 million increase in income taxes, along with $1.5 billion in service cuts, including drastic cuts in social services, parks, and libraries, as well as 10,000 municipal employee layoffs.

Elected in 1993 as the city's first Republican mayor in more than twenty years, Rudolph Giuliani ran on a platform of fiscal austerity and "reinventing government" and took office challenged by an estimated $3.2 billion budget gap. Giuliani adopted a $31.6 billion budget for fiscal year 1995, which included cutting 15,000 people from the workforce, $358 million from education, and $129 million in social services while keeping the police and fire departments untouched. While many advocacy groups called these cuts draconian, three agencies that monitor city finances estimated $1 billion in "budget risks."

In 1995, Mayor Giuliani again faced a budget crisis. He closed a $3.1 billion gap in his proposed fiscal year 1996 budget, with a $400 million cut in welfare and Medicaid spending, a $750 million reduction in the Board of Education's general budget, and significant cuts in foster care, corrections, youth programs, and the arts. Despite this effort to balance New York City's $31 billion budget for fiscal year 1996, Standard & Poor's, a major municipal credit rating agency, lowered the city's General Obligation Bonds from A- to BBB+. They sighted fiscal gimmicks, too many "one shot" revenue sources, and a chronic history of cash flow problems as factors contributing to their decision.

Though committed to fiscal responsibility, Giuliani may not be able to overcome structural imbalance. He did not create the city's chronic revenue shortfalls, and only a strong economic recovery can relieve the problem—temporarily.

## Atlanta

In January 1994, Atlanta's mayor Bill Campbell took office, confronting a $30 million budget deficit. Campbell had pledged during the campaign not to raise property taxes. He called the situation a crisis that could be resolved by "enormous cuts or wonderful innovations to find additional revenue." Campbell also ran on a public safety platform and a populist "no frills" approach to governing. Since three-fourths of Atlanta's budget goes to employee wages and benefits, Campbell's major strategy for reducing spending targeted the municipal workforce. In August 1994, the city council approved the second early retirement program for city workers in two years.[31]

## Boston

Mayor Thomas Menino of Boston had to close a budget gap of $21 million in his fiscal year 1994 budget. He was able to do this with a small increase in state aid after three years of cutbacks and an increase in the property tax. With three-fourths of its revenue coming from property taxes and state aid, Boston constantly worries about hitting the property tax limit set by Proposition 2 1/2, as well as the political disposition of the state government. Former Mayor Raymond Flynn already put into place efficiency-management measures, reducing the workforce by 1,750 and hiring no new police or firefighters between 1991 and 1993.[32]

## IMPACT OF THE PERMANENT FISCAL CRISIS ON URBAN RESIDENTS

Clearly, the issues on the urban political agenda and the language of political discourse have changed as a consequence of the permanent fiscal crisis. Questions of redistribution and participation that were part of the liberal experiment and American politics in the 1960s have been replaced by issues of efficiency and financial management. During the 1980s, the language of government responsibility was replaced by "downsizing," "privatization," and "treating citizens like customers and forcing governments to think like private businesses." This shift from redistribution to management has had an important impact in the urban political arena. Defining the fiscal crisis as a management problem implies that solutions to the problems of city governments are technical in nature, not questions of political value open to public debate. It has promoted acceptance of reduced services from government without sufficient public debate about what to fund and what to cut.

In the 1993–94 election cycle, mayors across the country ran on platforms of making government more responsive to citizens. Promising to improve the quality of life for all city residents became the new populist creed. The promises of urban liberals—equity, redistribution, employment—disappeared from mayoral campaigns. Mayor Richard M. Daley of Chicago describes his mission as low taxes and high-quality services. Keeping business and middle-class taxpayers happy are the limited objectives of most mayors who confront shrinking revenue bases.

The prospects for urban America in the 1990s are in many ways worse than they were during the Great Depression. During the 1930s, cities were supported in their relief efforts by a massive infusion of federal aid, which also went into public works projects. As they enter the 1990s, many cities are crumbling under an old, rapidly deteriorating infrastructure—and have no money to make the necessary repairs. Most cities have already abandoned redistributive programs. Their budget concerns for the 1990s are how to raise money for roads, bridges, and public buildings, and provide the basic services of police, fire, sanitation, and education adequately. Interest costs will consume an increasing proportion of budgets because the rates for municipal borrowing have tripled since the end of World War II as cities compete with the federal government's insatiable appetite for debt. Cities are not simply limited in their ability to provide redistributive services, as Paul Peterson argued in City Limits.[33] They no longer have the revenue base to keep their infrastructure intact or to provide basic housekeeping services effectively. The Great Depression put an end to the economically self-sufficient city. Yet, as a nation, we continue to make policy that ignores this important change.

## What Is to Be Done?

The fiscal problems that American cities face are structural. For most cities, fiscal instability has been a chronic condition that was generally ignored before 1975. After New York City's crisis, many cities cut spending, increased taxes, and improved worker productivity to ensure balanced budgets. Just as cities were reaching the limits of retrenchment strategies, the economy of the 1980s tricked many policymakers into thinking that improved management had cured the urban fiscal crisis. Fiscal problems during the 1980s in many Sunbelt cities should have provided a clue that management was not the central problem. Yet that myth has persisted into the 1990s as fiscal problems plague cities all across the nation.

The structural problems of urban fiscal policy must be tackled now. At the very least, we need a new definition of fiscal responsibility that is not tied to yearly balanced budgets. To balance their budgets, cities have been forced to pursue short-term strategies that often cause great human suffering and are inefficient, detrimental to the tax base, and fiscally irresponsible in the long term.

We need a new model of urban fiscal policy that gives mayors the power and resources to provide decent public services without eroding the fiscal stability of their cities. There are several structural changes that would accomplish this goal.

First, the tax base that pays for urban service delivery must be expanded. The cities that have generally managed best—Chicago, Minneapolis, San Antonio, Dallas, Nashville, Pittsburgh, and Portland, Oregon—have created some form of metropolitan government, or at the very least have relied on the tax base of county or state governments to provide expensive redistributive services and deficit-producing services like mass transit.

Second, the state and federal governments should not be permitted to mandate programs without providing revenue for implementation. California offers a model. Their legislature assesses the fiscal impact of mandates before they are passed, provides funding when increased services or new programs are mandated, and establishes a commission to hear local government's claims for reimbursable state-mandated costs.

The federal government has made a first step in addressing this problem with the passage of the Unfunded Mandates Reform Act of 1995, sponsored by Senator Dirk Kempthorne (R-Idaho). The law requires that the Congressional Budget Office evaluate the cost of federal legislation to state and local governments: if mandates in any legislation are found to exceed $50 million per year in costs state and local governments, the law requires the Congress to identify a funding source for these mandates; and if it doesn't, Congress must specifically waive regulations that there be no unfunded mandates, with a majority vote. In reality, this bill does not force the federal government to pay for unfunded mandates, it only changes the process, requiring a clear statement of the costs it is imposing. Significantly, the act does not apply retroactively, leaving state and local governments a continuing obligation to pay for the Clean Water Act and the Safe Drinking Water Act. Also, laws protecting Constitutional rights, antidiscrimination laws, civil rights mandates such as the Americans with Disibilities Act, and mandates associated with seven major entitlement programs, including Medicaid, are not covered by this law. The legislation also commissioned a comprehensive review of all existing mandates to determine if any can be eliminated or streamlined.[34] The findings of this review should be used to expand the scope of the existing law. Without further legislative action, unfunded mandates will remain a serious fiscal problem for state and local government.

Third, the fiscal responsibility for social welfare services should be assumed completely by the state and federal governments. In 1991, states as diverse as Michigan, Maryland, Tennessee, and California reduced their Aid to Families with Dependent Children benefits, indicating that it is time for a federal takeover. Poverty, homelessness, and drug addiction may be concentrated in central cities, but they were not caused by city taxpayers. In many cases, city boundaries are historical artifacts that have simply served to isolate the poor from wealthier suburbs and limit their access to high-quality education, housing, and health care.

Fourth, cities must be given control over their labor force and work rules to improve the efficiency of their bureaucracies. Contracting out and privatizing should be used for services where they have been proven to be cost-effective and where quality can be maintained. Sometimes the threat of privatization can improve worker efficiency and force more reasonable contracts from municipal employee unions. Mayors must be willing to use either strategy.

Fifth, we need to create a system of responsible and competitive urban political parties, so mayors can run for office on a platform that clearly articulates a city vision. At a time when loyalty to political parties is at an all-time low and elections have been trivialized, mayors have become captives of the most organized interest groups. These groups then trade their electoral support for influence over fiscal policy. The point is not to resurrect the repressive machines of the turn of the century, but to use the party to create consensus politics. Only if the party can provide the mayor with a mandate to govern that transcends parochial and partisan interests can the mayor make interest group demands subservient to broader city interests.

Finally, national leaders of both parties must make the case for America's cities both to Congress and to the American people. This should be the time for creating a broad-based political alliance. Cities need federal revenue to balance their budgets, and the only way to change the prevailing anti-urban agenda is to change public opinion. Urban problems must be understood as national problems. Crime, drug abuse, inferior public education, pollution, and poverty have been spreading into once tranquil suburbs. Declining urban economies strain state budgets and cause a decline in the national economy, as well. By encouraging the American people to realize the common interest between cities and suburbs, we can encourage a more rational public policy to emerge.

PART II    NEW POLICY PERSPECTIVES

# 5

# THE PROBLEM OF THE SCHOOLS: A PROPOSAL FOR RENEWAL

## DIANE RAVITCH

*I*f New York City is to thrive in the future, it needs an education system that educates all of its children for productive and satisfying lives. We do not now have such a system. If high school completion can be considered a valid performance measure, then the school system educates only about half of its students. Some youngsters achieve great success; many do as well as they would in any other school system; and a very large proportion of children leave the system before they have an adequate education. Of those children who enter ninth grade, only about 40 percent graduate four years later; about 50 percent graduate five years after beginning high school.

Among the 40 percent who graduate within four years are some of the most brilliant and well-educated students in the nation, prepared not only in elite examination schools like Bronx High School of Science, Brooklyn Technical High School, and Stuyvesant High School, but in mixed-ability high schools such as Midwood, John Dewey, Edward R. Murrow, Townsend Harris, and Benjamin Cardozo. Students in the city's schools continue to win a disproportionate number of Westinghouse science awards.

But many of the system's graduates who go on to higher education are not well-prepared for college. City University of New York accepts about 40 percent of the graduates from the New York City school system. After admission, they take tests of reading, writing, and mathematics. The tests of reading and mathematics are geared to a tenth-grade level; the writing test is graded by faculty and is not keyed to a specific grade level. About two-thirds of the city's graduates pass the reading test; about one-half pass the mathematics test. Only one-quarter pass all three tests. Their poor academic preparation requires remediation, adding a costly burden to public higher education.

Although there was a time when the New York City school system was considered one of the best in the nation, that time is long past. In 1985, the State Commissioner of Education published a list of the state's schools that had the poorest performance. Of 504 schools on the list, 393 were in New York City. The schools on this list were among the 10 percent in the state with the highest percentage of students scoring below a specified reference point on state tests; they were among the 10 percent of schools with the highest failure rate on Regent's Competency Tests (basic skills), as a percentage of their enrollment; and they had an annual dropout rate greater than 10 percent. Nearly 40 percent of the city's schools were identified by the State Commissioner as among the lowest-performing schools in the state!

It may be that students in the New York City schools never performed any better than they do today; the data necessary to make a precise comparison between the present and the past do not exist. But such a comparison is irrelevant, because today we demand of schools what we never demanded in the past: to educate all—or nearly all—students. It does not really matter whether the high school graduation rate is higher or lower today than it was thirty or fifty years ago. What matters is that it is far too low to meet the requirements of today's society. Regardless of past performance, it is simply un-acceptable that only half of the students who begin ninth grade are able to earn a diploma within five years.

Where does the blame lie? It is easy enough to blame social conditions: poverty, the breakdown of the family, violence in the streets, and the ready availability of drugs and guns. But after describing the burdens and handicaps of young people, the fact remains that they must be educated in order to have a chance at a decent, productive life. So the question remains not what gets in the way of education but how can young people today get the education they need?

It is certainly not fair to place all the blame for poor performance on the high schools. Many of their students were ill-prepared in earlier grades and enter high school hostile and indifferent to their own schooling; some of their students who arrive from other nations are barely literate in any language, or have never attended school at all.

But it must be said that most of the traditional high schools are ill-equipped for students with multiple problems. Among the more than 100 high schools in New York City, not including dozens of small, specialized schools, are about 70 high schools that each enroll more than 2,000 students; some of them have more than 4,000 students. Educators used to believe that such large schools were efficient, but that view has long since changed. Many children arrive in school with enormous personal and social problems; large, impersonal, factory-style schools are often unable to give each of them the individualized attention and support they need. Such youngsters need to be in an environment where the adults know them well, rather than in an institution where they are anonymous and easily overlooked.

Student performance is clearly the most important measure of the city school system. If performance in general were high, and if students of every race and ethnic group were well represented among high-performing students, then there would probably be little attention paid to the other problems of the system. But most students are not performing well, and the system must be reorganized to help bring about high performance among all students, regardless of race or social background.

In many respects, the school system has become dysfunctional. When it was first centralized at the turn of the twentieth century, educators believed that it was possible to create an efficient and uniform system that would hire and promote on the basis of merit and that would meet the needs of all children. For a variety of reasons, the merit system was discarded, and today supervisors are as likely to be chosen on the basis of politics, race, or gender as for their talents as educators. Over the years, the centralized system has been changed again and again, most recently in 1969, when decentralized local school districts were created. Now the system is neither centralized nor decentralized; it may be said to have the worst aspects of both, and the benefits of neither. It has all the stifling controls of a centralized system, with none of its efficiencies; and it has all the vagaries of decentralization, with none of its promise of wedding responsibility and authority.

The school system is premised on the idea that no one can make a decision without getting the approval of someone else. The system is girdled about with rules, regulations, obstacle courses, and checkpoints to assure that no one does the wrong thing. Anyone who acts without all the appropriate clearances may be assumed to have done the wrong thing. Each school is a link in a hierarchical, bureaucratic chain, and every action must be referred to or authorized by someone else higher up on the chain, either in the district office, the high school superintendent's office, or ultimately, 110 Livingston Street. This is the way the system was designed to work one hundred years ago. Today, despite efforts to encourage "school-based management," the term has little meaning in a system where no school controls its own budget or personnel.

Think about it. In every private and parochial school, those in charge make many decisions about staff, students, schedules, repairs, and purchases of goods and services without the oversight of a phalanx of supervisors. Is there something special about people in public schools that requires them to be subordinate to layers of people who hold the power to grant or deny permission?

Even in minor matters, the schools have little authority because decisions over the expenditure of funds are made by central authorities. The top-down, hierarchical, bureaucratic system that was established at the turn of the century embodied the assumption that experts at central headquarters (who had passed the requisite tests) were always more knowledgeable and trustworthy than principals, and it was they (the experts) who should control all decisions about expenditures. If a window is broken, the principal cannot hire a local glass company to fix it; if a school needs a dedicated electric line for computer equipment, the principal cannot call an electrician to come tomorrow. All repairs must be done by designated Board of Education workers. Not surprisingly, the Board's division of maintenance has a backlog of 40,000 requests for repairs.

Consider the purchasing of supplies, such as paper and pencils, and equipment, such as computers and file cabinets. All purchasing is done centrally by a bureau. Given the enormous scale of purchases, there should be large economies, but this is not the case. In fact, the materials purchased by the bureau of supplies frequently cost *more* than retail. If the schools were free to do comparison shopping, they might be able to save money by buying either from the Board's purchasing bureau or a discount store, wherever they could get the best price. And the competition would produce savings that could be used for teachers and supplies. Instead, someone downtown decides which company will get the rich contract for file cabinets, and every school must take what is available, regardless of its real cost. One principal complained to me that the paper sent to his school is yellowed from sitting in a warehouse for years, and that the television set supplied by the Board cost 50 percent more than the same set in a neighborhood store.

The school system was designed on the assumption that only the central bureaucracy can be trusted to make purchases and to order repairs. If such decisions were in the hands of individual principals, it is assumed, the principals might give contracts to friends or relatives. The fact that investigations have occasionally exposed corruption among employees in the central bureaus has done nothing to shake the belief that only the bureaucratic system, with its many layers of approvals, will assure honesty.

Consider leasing. The central board has a bureau in charge of leasing space for schools, and this bureau decides which space is appropriate and negotiates leases. Since the city is trying to restrain new capital spending and since school enrollment is expected to increase every year during the next decade, leasing is an increasingly important activity for the Board of Education. Why, one might ask, is leasing performed by salaried bureaucrats who are paid regardless of whether they are able to conclude a lease successfully, instead of commercial leasing agents who are paid only for their successful performance?

Is there a better way? In the early 1990s, cries for reform rose with regularity, and most proposals for reform consisted of shifting around powers and functions among the central board, borough boards, and local community school district boards. In 1993, the borough presidents of Manhattan and Queens proposed that the schools be run by five borough boards and a city commissioner of education. Although borough boards were tried and discarded at the beginning of the century, many people see them as a reasonable alternative to the distant and heavy hand of the central board. However, the danger of the borough board proposal is that one large bureaucracy will be replaced by five middle-size bureaucracies; or worse, that a compromise proposal will leave intact a slightly diminished central bureaucracy while creating five middle-size bureaucracies, which coexist with thirty-two local school boards.

The more serious drawback of borough boards is that it is a bureaucratic reorganization that offers no promise of addressing the fundamental flaws of urban education. Boards don't educate children: teachers do. The issue that cannot be avoided is that each school must be managed by a group of adults who have direct, personal, and professional responsibility—and accountability—for the success of their students.

Where might we go from here? It is necessary to search for a new paradigm; it is necessary to look beyond the usual choices between centralization and decentralization, central and borough boards, and borough boards and community school districts. As a starting point, I argue that as much responsibility and accountability as possible should be located in the school. I note that school systems are the only large-scale social organizations in our society that have thus far remained untouched by the restructuring that has become commonplace in many other sectors; by restructuring, I mean the flattening of management and the decentralization of authority to those who are in positions of responsibility. No organization restructures because it wants to; it restructures because it has to in order to survive. The fact that school systems receive public funding regardless of their performance (and that schools receive extra funding from the federal government based on their numbers of low-achieving students, with no bonuses for reducing these numbers) has been a disincentive to any meaningful restructuring. The New York City Board of Education has "restructured" a number of failing schools by breaking them up into four, five, or six smaller schools. This is good as far as it goes, but the system itself has not been restructured, and the performance standards for the new schools are virtually non-existent. It is clear that radical restructuring is needed so that the system serves the needs of children rather than the needs of the adults who work for the system.

No organizational change by itself will make the system work better for children. Giving more or less power to borough boards or district boards is probably an exercise in futility, because it leaves intact the division between responsibility and authority, as well as the dependence of schools on outside authority for every decision, large and small, consequential and trivial.

Throughout their history, the New York City public schools have been centralized or decentralized or—as in the present case—both. But these are not the only options for managing the city's educational system. It seems to me that reformers must think about what is now called "reinventing government," in which the role of government is to steer, not to row. It may be that the best direction for reforming the schools is to seek a diversity of providers that are publicly monitored, rather than a bureaucratic system controlled by the mandates of a single governmental agency. What would a system look like in which government did the steering and let many others do the rowing?

Reinventing the school system would include three basic principles: autonomy, choice, and quality.

*Autonomy.* New York City needs a system in which bureaucracy is reduced to a minimum, in which schools exercise a high degree of professional and budgetary autonomy. Schools should control their own budgets; they should be told what funds they have to spend, and then be allowed to make choices and allocations— always cognizant of the fact that they will be rigorously audited by public officials. The money made available should be based on enrollments, with supplements from state and federal aid for schools with poor or handicapped children. Each school should decide how much to spend on staff, supplies, maintenance, food, and other needs. Similarly, schools should be responsible for their personnel, for assembling the team that will perform the mission of the school. The adults who are responsible for each school know its needs better than administrators in a distant office, and they should be responsible for making decisions about budget and personnel.

*Choice.* The city needs a system in which teachers can decide where they want to work and parents can choose the school to which they send their children. Forced assignment of teachers and children is counterproductive and undermines motivation. A school community works best when parents, students, and teachers have chosen to be there.

*Quality.* The city needs a system in which the major role of the city and/or borough authorities is to monitor fiscal and educational quality in every school. In this system, the central authorities will be responsible for setting citywide educational standards, ad- ministering regular citywide assessments, and reporting to parents and the public on the educational progress of the schools and the city's students. In addition, central authorities would oversee large capital improvements, negotiate union contracts (assuring that the contracts do not negate the other features of the system, like the power of the schools to select their own staff), and approve the creation of new schools. At the borough level, the role of authorities will be to audit each school's fiscal management, not second-guessing legitimate decisions about how to spend money but assuring that expenditures are legal and proper.

This strategy for reform is based on the principles of autonomy, choice, and quality. It reflects the belief that there is no "one best system," and that what works for one school or community may not work for another. Children and families in New York City should be able to choose among a wide diversity of schools: Family-style schools, single-sex schools, back-to-basics schools, progressive schools, work-based schools, schools organized around themes like the arts or technology. In schooling, one size does not fit all, even though the goals of schooling will be similar for all schools (that is, to enable students to become literate and numerate, and to develop the skills and knowledge that are important for work, citizenship, and further education).

The first part of the change strategy is to permit successful schools to become self-governing. Such schools would control their own budgets and make their own decisions about personnel and purchasing. Many schools that already have a culture of success will probably wish to become self-governing, if given the opportunity. Those schools that wish to manage their own affairs should be allowed to conduct an election among parents and staff, and if a majority of both groups vote favorably, the school would become a public charter school (PCS). A PCS would be free of most current rules and regulations, other than those that are necessary to protect students' health and safety and to prevent racial discrimination. Each PCS would receive an allotment of money, based on enrollment. It would also receive additional state and federal funding for students who are disabled or disadvantaged. Consequently, schools with many poor students would have much more money to spend on staff and supplies than schools with few poor students. All such schools would be audited by public officials and would be required to meet citywide educational standards, as gauged by regular citywide assessments. Any PCS that ran afoul of specific fiscal and educational commitments would be at risk of losing its status and reverting to control by the city commissioner or borough board.

A second part of the change strategy is to encourage contracting of the management of many schools. Contractors might be institutions of higher education, museums, hospitals, businesses, unions, community groups, principals of existing schools, groups of teachers, or any other kind of organization that demonstrates the capacity to run a school. The decision to invite potential contractors to manage schools could be made in either of two ways:

1. If state or city officials identify a school as educationally "bankrupt," the school would be eligible for contracting. This would be preferable to the present situation, where the state commissioner places failing schools on a list without providing any meaningful strategy to change them.

2.   Or, the decision to invite contractors to apply might be taken on the initiative of parents. If the parents are dissatisfied with the quality of their children's school, they should be permitted to vote on whether to solicit contractors to run their school.

In either case, prospective contractors should be invited to make presentations to the school community. They should present their performance goals and explain their methods to parents and the community. Prospective contractors should apply for certification by public officials, based on their experience and their financial stability. Once they win a contract to manage a school, they would be regularly evaluated relative to their performance goals. Like a PCS, schools managed by contractors would receive a guaranteed amount of money, based on enrollment. In the event that a contractor fails to meet performance goals, the contract would be cancelled or not renewed at the end of its contract period. It might reasonably be objected that the introduction of five-year contracts might also introduce instability into the lives of poor schools, but occasional turnover would be preferable to leaving the school undisturbed, without hope for significant change.

Another way to encourage new performance-based schools would be for school officials at central or borough headquarters to issue a "request for proposals" for contractors to establish new schools in neighborhoods where existing schools are performing poorly or where there is a need for a new special-purpose school, or where a large number of parents wish to establish a new school. New schools might be established to meet specific needs, for example, to work with youngsters who have dropped out or to provide an enriched early childhood program for working parents.

Using these alternatives for contracting, contracts could be arranged both to improve the management of existing schools and to open new schools with specific programs. However initiated, the contractor would be subject to public audit and review and would be expected to meet performance goals or lose the contract.

A third part of the change strategy is to provide means-tested scholarships to poor students, with high priority placed on students in schools that have been identified by public authorities as "educationally bankrupt." The state commissioner of education calls such schools "schools under registration review" or SURR schools. These children (as much as 5 percent of the total enrollment) should be eligible for means-tested scholarships that may be used in any accredited school—public, private, or religious. Schools that accept these scholarship students must be willing to meet the city's educational standards and to abide by civil rights laws. In this way, educational opportunity will be promptly extended to poor students who would otherwise be trapped in a school with a history of low performance.

Since the federal program of student aid for higher education works in the same way, there is reason to think that such an approach would be found constitutional. Public scholarships would be allocated to the students to use in the school of their choice; no public funds would flow directly to the institutions. Federal Pell grants are awarded on the basis of need and may be used at any college or university that is accredited, whether public, private, or religious. The state and city already place handicapped students in private and religious institutions when their needs cannot be met in the public schools. Publicly funded Headstart centers are run by public, private, and religious agencies. A similar approach in the city would offer an alternative for needy students.

This entire strategy, with its three complementary parts, would encourage bad schools to close or to be transformed by new leadership. It would allow the neediest students to escape bad schools and to go to the schools of their choice. It would encourage the creation of new schools geared to meet the needs of different groups of students. It would give the central or borough authorities plenty to do while withdrawing from them the power to control what happens in every school.

One of the most important features of this strategy is that it offers a means of increasing the funds available to the schools that serve the neediest students. At present, senior teachers move to what are perceived to be the "best" schools, while schools in poor neighborhoods are staffed by a preponderance of young and inexperienced teachers; since most educational expenditures go to teacher salaries, schools in "good" neighborhoods usually have a real budget that is much larger than that of schools in "poor" neighborhoods. Under the proposed plan, in which every PCS or contract school receives an allotment based on enrollment, schools serving poor children would benefit immediately. No school could afford to have only senior teachers; all would have the funds to balance senior and junior teachers. Schools in poor neighborhoods, which receive additional federal and state aid, would have more money to spend than schools in non-poor neighborhoods that have the same number of students.

What is more, everyone who works in the public schools would know that they are responsible; that the buck stops with them; that they, like their counterparts in independent and religious schools, have the ability to manage their own affairs without second-guessing from "downtown."

## CONCLUSION

The hallmarks of education in New York City should be: equality of opportunity, quality of education, and diversity of providers. Since the city itself is so remarkably diverse, with a large public sector and a vibrant private sector, as well as a broad assortment of nonprofit organizations, such a plan is well-adapted to the nature of the city. This rich pool of resources and talent should be utilized to build a vigorous and diverse array of educating institutions.

Organizations that evolve and improve thrive; those that become ossified and incapable of change do not. During the course of the twentieth century, the city has changed. As the city's economy changes, the school system must change. The unskilled jobs once so available in the city have been shrinking rapidly; high school dropouts can no longer find decent jobs and are now bound for the welfare rolls. As the city's economy shifts decisively toward technical and service industries, where strong literacy skills are required, even high school graduates who are poorly prepared are at a decisive disadvantage. In order to remain vital, the educational system must be dynamic and prepared to meet new challenges. It cannot cling to an organizational form that worked well for the first half of the century but has become increasingly unsuited to the problems and needs of new populations.

The new American economy needs well-educated people, people who are literate, numerate, able to solve problems, and capable of working well with others. To realize the principle of equality of opportunity, we must strive to prepare all children for a productive life. The dimensions of this challenge will require bold and innovative thinking. If we hope to succeed, we must imagine and invent a school system that works well for all children.

# 6

# CRIME AND THE CITY

## CHRISTOPHER STONE

C rime and cities go together, both in our imaginations and in real life. In New York City, every day an average of 3 new homicides, 100 serious assaults, 150 robberies, and 200 burglaries are recorded by the police, despite four years of declines in reported crime.[1] Yet staggering as these numbers are, New York's rate of violent crime places the city thirtieth among U.S. cities.[2] "Crime" is a popular term for a multitude of sins. Petty offenses far outnumber serious ones, and even statistics that include minor offenses miss the majority of the crime because most crime is never reported in any city. All crimes cause harm, one way or another, but not all crime threatens the city itself. Violence does pose such a threat, as does the waning commitment to justice in the enforcement of the criminal law.

## IS VIOLENCE RISING IN CITIES?

The problems of crime and violence seem all too obvious to the urban resident, to the television viewer, or to the reader of the popular press, but official reports on crime often seem to contradict one another. Some reports say violent crime is rising, others claim it is falling.

Criminologists measure the extent of crime in two basic ways: by counting crimes reported to police and by conducting victimization surveys of the population. Victimization surveys are generally regarded as more accurate measures because they do not rely on people to report crimes to the police, but they are rarely conducted on a local level.

The National Crime Victimization Survey, conducted annually since 1973 by the U.S. Department of Justice, shows that the rate of violent crime has remained relatively steady over recent years, just below the high points of the late 1970s and early 1980s. In America's central cities, experiences of violent crime are about one-and-a-half times more frequent than in suburban areas, but still below levels from 1980 through 1982 (see Figure 6.1).

The other widely used source of national crime rates is the FBI, which collects information on crimes reported to local police departments. In May 1995, the FBI reported that its preliminary analysis of crimes reported in 1994 showed violent crime down 4 percent from the year

## FIGURE 6.1

### Victimization Rates for Crimes of Violence
### (for persons 12 and over, per 1,000 people)

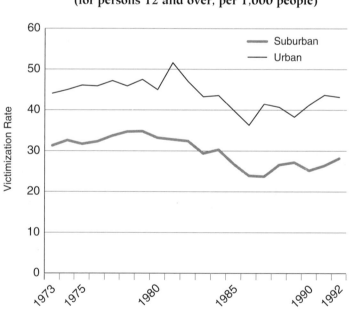

Sources: U.S. Department of Justice, Office of Justice Programs, Bureau of Justice Statistics, *Criminal Victimization in the United States, 1992*, table 18; *Criminal Victimization in the United States: 1973–80 Trends*, table 5.

before. In cities of more than one million people, violent crime reported to the police was down 7 percent, while in suburban counties there was no change from 1993.[3]

Some politicians have drawn the wrong lesson from these numbers. They have concluded that the fear of violent crime is disconnected from reality. This is an enticing conclusion, for it suggests that officials can focus on reducing *fear* rather than reducing crime itself. One might, for example, increase the visibility of uniformed police officers and marked police vehicles on busy streets, even if that pulled those officers and cars away from less travelled blocks where crime is higher. Reducing fear may, indeed, be good urban policy and might, in some circumstances, help communities prevent some crime; but it is a mistake to think that fear of crime in cities today is disconnected from rising levels of crime itself. The rising levels do not appear in the national data on victimization or reported crime because these statistics aggregate too much.

The national data obscure the fact that the rate of serious crime varies considerably from one city to another. Using data provided by individual police departments, the FBI produces comparisons of the rates of reported crime for individual cities, focusing on what it defines as index crime (murder and nonnegligent manslaughter, forcible rape, robbery, burglary, arson, aggravated assault, larceny, and theft of a motor vehicle). Generally, over the past twenty years, larger cities report higher rates of index crimes than smaller cities; but among the country's largest cities, there is significant variation unexplained by size. The number of reported index crimes per hundred thousand people in 1993 in Baltimore, Detroit, and Seattle was more than twice as high than in San Jose (see Figure 6.2, page 92).

Not only is the crime rate very different for different places, but it is changing in ways that are very different from one city to the next. While the rate of violent crime nationally is falling slightly, the rate is actually rising in some cities, holding steady in others, and falling by very different amounts in still others. From 1993 to 1994, Bridgeport, Connecticut, and Chattanooga, Tennessee, saw violent crime drop by just over 25 percent; Rochester, New York, and Oklahoma City saw virtually no change, while Las Vegas experienced a 23 percent increase. Even among the biggest cities, where the drop in reported crime has been most consistent, some had increases in violent crime in 1994 (see Figure 6.3, page 93).

What is true among cities is true *within* cities as well. By aggregating data from places where crime is rising with data from places where crime is falling, citywide statistics obscure rising rates of violent crime within individual urban neighborhoods.

FIGURE 6.2

**Rate of Reported Crime, 1993**

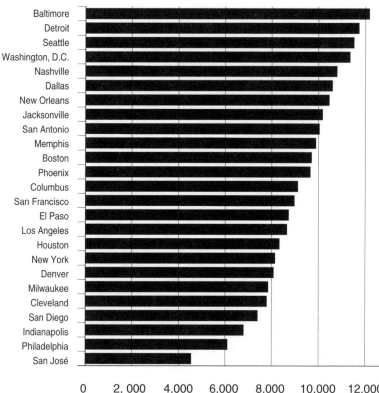

Index Crimes per l00,000 people

*Source*: Federal Bureau of Investigation, *Crime in the United States* (Washington, D.C.: Government Printing Office, 1994).

In New York City, for example, the FBI reported a 12 percent decline in violent crime for the city as a whole from 1990 to 1993. The problem is that no one lives in the city as a whole. People live and work in neighborhoods. The data at a neighborhood level show that the gradual decline in violent crime citywide over those years was the product of an increase in violent crime in traditionally safe neighborhoods combined with a decline in high-crime neighborhoods.

In the Brooklyn neighborhoods of Flatlands and Mill Basin, for example, the police recorded a 36 percent increase in violent index crimes

## FIGURE 6.3
### Change in Reported Violent Crime, 1993 to 1994

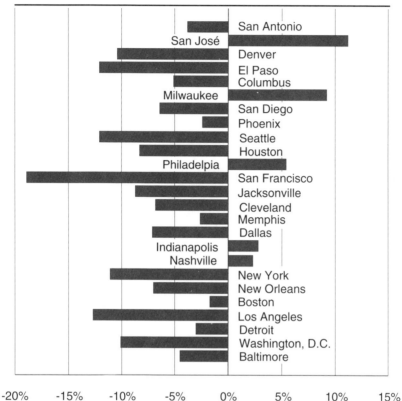

-20%    -15%    -10%    -5%    0%    5%    10%    15%

Source: Federal Bureau of Investigation, *Uniform Crime Reports: 1994 Preliminary Annual Release* (Washington, D.C.: U.S. Dept. of Justice, 1995).

from 1989 through 1993, and violent crime reports were up in all three precincts on Staten Island. In 1994, more than one-third of New York City residents lived in police precincts that had recorded an increase in violent crime over the preceding four years, even while the numbers had been falling for the city as a whole. In these neighborhoods, the perception that violent crime had been rising quickly was firmly grounded in reality (see Figure 6.4, page 94).

The belief that violent crime is rising may be similarly grounded even in the high-crime neighborhoods where reports of violent crime appear to be declining. This is because the categories used in these statistics aggregate very different crimes, such as robbery and armed robbery. When the FBI data on violent crime are examined for changes

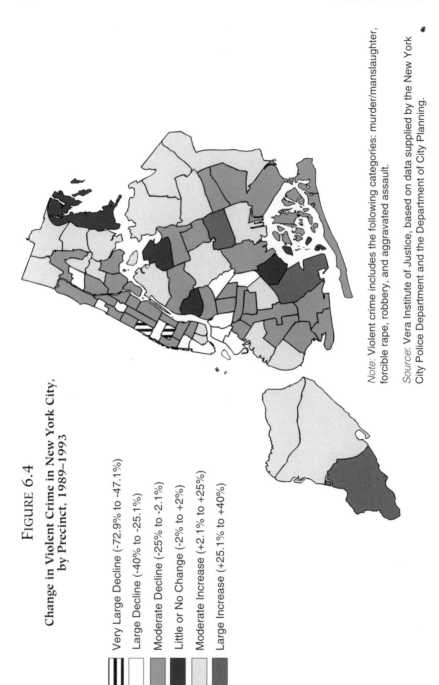

FIGURE 6.4

Change in Violent Crime in New York City,
by Precinct, 1989–1993

▌▌▌ Very Large Decline (-72.9% to -47.1%)

☐ Large Decline (-40% to -25.1%)

▨ Moderate Decline (-25% to -2.1%)

■ Little or No Change (-2% to +2%)

▧ Moderate Increase (+2.1% to +25%)

▨ Large Increase (+25.1% to +40%)

*Note:* Violent crime includes the following categories: murder/manslaughter, forcible rape, robbery, and aggravated assault.

*Source:* Vera Institute of Justice, based on data supplied by the New York City Police Department and the Department of City Planning.

in crimes with firearms, the apparent drop in crime disappears. From 1979 to 1992, while the overall rate of reported violent index crime declined, the proportion of offenses committed with pistols and revolvers increased—from 9.2 percent to 12.7 percent. In the five years from 1987 to 1992, the number of all violent crimes with firearms reported by local police to the FBI rose 55 percent.[4] From 1992 to 1993, the chances that a violent crime was committed with a gun rose by another 11 percent.[5]

These real increases in violent crime, and gun crimes in particular, have created areas within cities where fear of crime is particularly strong. In 1991, the American Housing Survey conducted by the U.S. Department of Housing and Urban Development found that 15 percent of central city households identified crime as a problem in their neighborhoods, compared with 5 percent of suburban households, and only 2 percent of rural households. Among white central city households, the percentage mentioning crime as a neighborhood problem grew from 8 percent in 1985 to 13 percent in 1991; among black central-city households, the percentage nearly doubled—from 12 percent in 1985 to 23 percent in 1991.[6]

Even for those whose neighborhoods are not particularly violent, fear of violent crime is fed by the changed atmosphere in the city, as the gulf between rich and poor has grown wider in central cities. For example, the lowest fifth of households—measured in household income—in New York City saw its average income grow by less than 1 percent from 1979 to 1989, while the average income of the highest fifth rose more than 40 percent. This gap grew fastest in Manhattan, where the highest fifth had an average income 21 times larger than the lowest fifth in 1979, but 34 times larger in 1989.[7] Ask a family in a public housing development in East New York about their daily experiences of violence and they are likely to describe the gunfire from which they must routinely protect themselves and their children. Ask a family with income in six figures in one of Manhattan's wealthy neighborhoods about their daily experience of violence, and they will probably talk about aggressive and threatening panhandling. The threat of violence in both neighborhoods is real, but fear of aggressive panhandling may be fed more by the real growth of poverty than by the experience of crime.

## CAN VIOLENCE PREVENTION WORK?

Common sense tells us that cities are much too violent, and the crime statistics support that view. Most efforts to reduce the violence, however, fly in the face of both common sense and social science.

As a society, we spend virtually every crime control dollar on prisons and the police and prosecutors needed to put people there. Twenty years ago, there were about 400,000 people in jail and prison in the United States; in 1995, there are about 1,500,000. The United States incarcerates a greater proportion of its population than virtually any other nation in the world.[8]

Since 1975, more than 20 million people have passed through America's jail and prison cells. Over that same period, the average prison time served per violent crime approximately tripled, reflecting both an increase in the likelihood that arrest leads to imprisonment and an increase in the average time served by a person when incarcerated.[9]

There is little evidence that this huge addition to the United States prison population did much to reduce violent crime. Some crime that would have been committed by those in prison was prevented, but a panel appointed by the National Research Council recently concluded that this effect has been "fairly small—preventing on the order of 10 to 15 percent of the crimes that potentially would have been committed otherwise."[10] Balanced against this is the likelihood that the experience of prison increased the number of crimes committed by inmates after their release. The net result is that while the nation's investment in prison soared in the late 1970s and 1980s, violent crime remained level nationally.

Despite this experience, most states and the federal government continue to expand their prison systems, especially for the incarceration of people convicted of violent crimes. The passage by the U.S. Congress of the Crime Bill in September 1994 represented the largest investment ever of federal dollars in state prison construction. Nevertheless, alongside their political investments in prisons, public officials are putting their hopes in a series of programs and activities assembled under the banner of violence prevention. These prevention programs vary widely, so it may be useful to distinguish three broad categories: those aimed at *people,* particularly young people; those aimed at *places,* such as schools; and those aimed at *things,* such as guns.

## People

The most ambitious prevention strategies look to the future, focusing on today's urban youth. One set of these programs tries to keep young people out of harm's way by keeping some schools open late as community recreation and service centers. Another set uses a variety of techniques to teach conflict resolution, so that young people who find themselves in harm's way will know how to get out. A third set of programs provides guidance and role models to young people through individual mentors or, in the less expensive versions, mentor-rich environments, so that more young people will choose to stay out of harm's way. One way or another, these programs all aim to affect the course of development of the adolescents they reach. They require intense, individual work, and they are therefore expensive. But their effects are meant to last beyond the period of the program, reducing violence into the future.

## Places

The prevention strategies in the second category are less ambitious but promise to produce results more quickly. This group of programs includes one set that relies on police and technology to try to keep weapons and unruly youth out of schools, another that aims to reduce the vulnerability of people at work in certain occupations, for example, by providing phones to taxi drivers or assigning more clerks to late-night shifts at certain stores; and still others that try to break patterns of violence in the home through programs such as those mandating police to make arrests when called to scenes of domestic violence. The promise of immediate impact in these and similar programs makes them more attractive to politicians than programs aimed at affecting adolescent development, but they do not generally claim to produce effects that outlast the programs themselves.

## Things

Perhaps the most controversial of all are the programs aimed at guns. These include efforts to restrict gun purchases, establish licensing of gun owners, require safekeeping of guns by dealers and private owners, and interdict illegal trade in guns. These aim principally to reduce the *severity* of violent incidents by making guns less common-place when violence flares; they do not generally aim to reduce the absolute *number* of violent incidents.

The appeal of all these prevention programs—as of prison—is grounded more in emotion than on empirical evidence of success. There is little good research on the power of individual prevention programs to reduce violence, and what does exist shows mixed results at best.[11]

The absence of compelling evidence keeps public investment concentrated in short-term rather than long-term strategies. Public officials may sense that the short-term benefits of incarceration or high school metal detectors will not reduce violence over the long term. They may even sense that the heavy reliance on prisons is increasing violence in the long term, but the damage done by prison, like the long-term benefit of practical prevention programs that try to shape adolescent development, is too uncertain to guide the investment of political resources. Prevention programs for youth may continue to receive modest funding from public funds leftover after huge investments are made in shorter-term strategies; but they will not be able to compete for funding with prisons or location-focused prevention until their impact on violence is more solidly established.

The political weakness of prevention programs was evident in the summer of 1995 when New York's Mayor Rudolph Giuliani announced a dramatic reduction in murder and other violent crime in the first six months of that year. Despite the fact that expansion of the police force over the previous four years had been accompanied by aggressive development of violence prevention programs in every category, the prevention initiatives received virtually no mention or attention in public discussion. At a time when all explanation was speculative, violence prevention programs were not part of the explanation because the programs themselves were too diffuse and lacked institutional advocates.[12]

Real evidence of program success is hard to muster, even in cities that are less complex than New York. The difficulties of conducting good research on even the simplest prevention initiative are illustrated by the story of the evaluation of the "two-clerk" ordinance adopted by the city of Gainesville, Florida, in 1987. This local law required convenience stores to employ two clerks during nighttime hours to reduce the attractiveness of the stores as robbery targets. Shortly after the law took effect, the local police department evaluated its impact using a standard technique and declared that the law had reduced convenience store robberies by more than 50 percent. The technique used by the department was to compare the number of convenience store robberies in the six months after the law took effect with the number during the same period the year before. As interest in the ordinance grew, however, the National Association of Convenience Stores commissioned a more thorough evaluation, which revealed that the earlier period had contained a rash of convenience store robberies, and that this spike in the numbers had ended with the arrest—four months before the two-clerk law was implemented—of three men suspected of many of the robberies. The rate of convenience store robberies in the four months immediately before and after the implementation of the rule had been the same, and the pattern of such robberies in the surrounding county had been consistent with that in Gainesville, despite the fact that the rule did not apply outside the city.[13]

The first lesson in this story for those who seek to build credible evidence of the value of any violence prevention program is that programs implemented in the wake of an unusual rash of incidents are almost bound to look good when the incidents subside, whether or not the programs contributed to the recovery. This is not just an issue in small cities. Even in New York, a single arson that caused multiple deaths in 1991 caused a spike in the murder rate which fell the next year.

Second, it is difficult for any program to have a significant effect on the frequency of a relatively rare event. This factor was evident in Gainesville, where there were only two convenience store robberies per month in the period when the two-clerk rule was implemented. In big cities, the same factor blunts the ability of conflict resolution programs, for example, to show results when they are implemented in the wake of a single stabbing or a shooting inside a school without baseline information about the number of less serious violent incidents that the program is expected to reduce. A single stabbing a year later will make the program look like a failure.

Third, few organizations want to fund research that is likely to show that a violence prevention program does not work. The Gainesville story presents an exception to that rule because the widespread adoption of laws requiring two clerks in convenience stores at night would have cost the stores large sums of money. This may have prompted the National Association of Convenience Stores to finance the second look at the claims being made by the police department in Gainesville.

These three lessons all point to the danger of attempting to conduct rigorous research on prevention programs that begin in a burst of political enthusiasm. The plausible impact of these efforts seldom can match the rhetoric surrounding the political decision to establish them, and even the good ones rarely have the luxury of baseline data or independent research that can credibly demonstrate their value.

This dynamic can be seen at work in the recent enthusiasm for "drug courts," in which judges make greater use of drug treatment programs than usual and monitor the progress of offenders in treatment. These courts are built on the common sense beliefs, first, that drug addiction causes people to commit crime and, second, that the courts can therefore prevent future crimes by compelling addicts to participate in treatment. Such a drug court in Miami attracted national attention in 1992, claiming success on the basis of rearrest rates for those sentenced in the special court. Other states began to replicate the court, even as researchers began to argue among themselves about the validity of the comparisons used as evidence of success in Miami. In late 1994, the Justice Department created a special office to provide new funding to states, counties, and individual cities to operate such courts. Unfortunately, the first evaluation using an experimental design to study the impact of these courts is finding no effect on future drug use or recidivism. This experimental research has found that people sentenced to treatment, and monitored in that treatment by the drug court in Phoenix, Arizona, have a rearrest rate after six months of just under 20 percent, not statistically different from the rate for those sentenced to ordinary probation.[14]

Twenty years ago, results like these were used by critics of prevention strategies to argue that nothing works, thereby helping to justify huge investments in prisons as an effective short-term response to crime. If advocates of long-term prevention strategies are to avoid losing that argument again, they must credibly evaluate and then strengthen the current generation of prevention programs. If programs that make common sense but are unevaluated are expanded, the political cost of failure by poor programs will be great, while good programs will never command the respect required to compete for funds with harsher strategies that promise immediate results.

A good place to evaluate and strengthen long-term violence prevention programs would be in urban elementary and junior high schools. In New York City, for example, the schools are spending several million dollars on metal detectors for high schools while eliminating the remaining guidance counselors and increasing class size in the lower grades—a good illustration of short-term strategies displacing long-term investments. Not only is there no research showing that metal detectors effectively reduce the level of violence in schools, but the research that does exist suggests that increasing class size is likely to exacerbate the level of violence. Twenty years ago, a national study of school violence concluded that the safest schools, even in dangerous neighborhoods, were characterized not by state-of-the-art security systems but by high teacher-to-student ratios, orderly classrooms, and good principals.[15] More recent research showing the stability of aggressive behavior after middle childhood, suggests that support for teachers and principals in elementary and junior high schools might be more effective than efforts in high schools.

Filling the gaps in this research and using that knowledge in practical programs could help us realize real reductions in violence over the long term by strengthening the ability of teachers and principals in elementary and junior high schools to keep their classrooms and schools organized, nurturing, and responsive to children.

Testing such a program through an experimental design and following the students into the first years of high school is but one example of how the case for long-term violence prevention could be made.

## JUSTICE

We can and must do much to make our cities safer and less violent, but we will never eliminate crime. We may, in the attempt, end up eliminating justice. A renewed commitment to justice—to fairness in the process by which a government protects and punishes its people— has seldom been more needed than in cities today. Public officials at every level of government are competing with one another to lengthen prison sentences, weaken laws that protect people accused of crimes, and expand the powers and numbers of police. In this frenzy, many seem to have lost sight of principles of decency, individual rights, and the value of living in a just society. Serious talk of justice has receded from public discourse to the point where the word sounds almost antiquarian.

Most urban courts are overcrowded, dirty, noisy, rude, and inefficient. Sitting in the galleries of many urban courts, listening to the initial hearings of defendants arrested the night before, you will wait in vain to hear anyone apparently interested in the question of the guilt or innocence of any defendant. Instead, judges hear cases as quickly as they can while lawyers try to keep the piles of files in some semblance of order. People accused of crimes from disorderly conduct to aggravated assault are urged to plead guilty immediately to avoid another trip to court. The courts are broken.

The same is true for the other parts of the justice system. Poor defendants expect police officers to bend the rules to get convictions. Prosecutors expect prisons to be violent places when they recommend sentences of incarceration. Judges expect lawyers to be unprepared— if they are even present on time in court. This is not a system whose rules and judgments command respect.

Still, there are glimmers of hope. Over the last several years, in a series of tentative, loosely defined experiments, a small number of urban police chiefs, judges, prosecutors, public defenders, and corrections officials have been trying, each in their own sphere, to rebuild the system of justice in urban America. To motivate change in these seemingly intractable bureaucracies, the reformers have used a variety of tactics. They have raised the threat of privatization, pointing out to police departments that private security firms are growing faster than conventional police forces and may soon become the dominant form of protection, and reminding correctional officers that private companies can replace them if they do not adopt more flexible work rules. The reformers have appealed to popular images of the past: the beat cop is back, the local magistrates court is reopened, and military discipline is back at prisons—called "boot camps." They have embraced modern computer and communications technology. Electronic ankle bracelets are monitoring the movements of offenders confined to their homes. Appointments with probation officers are being replaced by visits to computerized kiosks that recognize a probationer's hand print. Police commanders use computers to analyze current crime patterns on electronic maps and rapidly deploy their officers in response.

Individually, some of these may appear as gimmicks. The research on some boot camps, for example, shows little impact on recidivism and, occasionally, instances of physical abuse. In many cases, however, these new efforts are the visible tips of much larger organizational changes designed to make failing systems of justice more responsive, more accountable, and more inspiring to the urban communities they serve. Community policing, community courts, community prosecution, neighborhood defenders, and community corrections are not yet well-defined strategies or institutions. Some are better known to the public than others; none is well understood. Still, they all represent, in the hands of their more talented practitioners, a sincere commitment to dealing with victims of crime and offenders in the broader contexts of their communities.

The principal aim of community policing, for example, is not to deter crime with cops on foot, but to engage cops in problem-solving— working with community residents to identify and eliminate neighborhood conditions that cause crime. The point of a community court, like that in midtown Manhattan, is to help judges deal with individual cases with sensitivity to the local conditions from which the cases arise—conditions that might be improved by the appropriate disposition of the case. The point of community corrections is to impose punishment in a way that recognizes that the offender sooner or later needs to live peacefully and productively in a free community.

By placing a high priority on the community context of crime and the response to crime, these innovations reengage both citizens and officials with the fairness as well as the effectiveness of our systems of justice. These efforts face daunting obstacles, however. In most cities, differences in ethnicity, income, residential neighborhood, education, culture, and opportunity divide those who administer justice from those on the receiving end. Community justice initiatives at least acknowledge these chasms, but, even at their best, they are only beginning to build bridges across them.

The efforts in each of these parts of the justice system to build partnerships with urban residents should be accompanied by efforts to build partnerships between them. In cities where police, prosecutors, public defenders, and judges have little confidence in each other—and none of them has confidence in prisons, probation, or parole—one can hardly expect the public to have confidence in any of them. These individuals and agencies have different jobs, and they will resist being used by one another to achieve any particular ambition. Yet they might still be united with their communities in a commitment to justice. Joint training on the elements of justice would be a modest but important beginning.

Civil life in cities depends on justice. The same congregation of people that makes cities so vital makes some amount of conflict and crime inevitable. Cities will never be free of tragedy, but their vitality can be preserved. Life in cities can be good so long as urban residents maintain a commitment to meet conflict and crime with ingenuity and justice.

# 7

# HOUSING AND NEIGHBORHOODS

## JULIA VITULLO-MARTIN

The government really has only two ways of helping to house those who cannot afford decent market-rate housing. It can build directly, as it did with traditional public housing, sheltering only the poor in stand-alone projects. This is the conventional Democratic and liberal program. Or it can give low-income households some kind of voucher and let them find what they can, as best they can, in the private market, as it has done with Section 8 certificates. This is the conventional Republican and market-oriented solution.

Both programs have their advantages and disadvantages, but they share one similarity: the most egregious problems with these programs tend to arise, first, as the Department of Housing and Urban Development (HUD) creates regulations for them and, second, as Congress itself modifies them as time goes by. A program can start out fairly simple and straightforward and quickly become a mess.

Although public housing, as authorized under the Wagner-Steagall Act of 1937, is much older than the provisions of Section 8, authorized under the Housing and Community Development Act of 1974, both programs are now roughly the same size. Public housing has some 1.4 million units; Section 8 covers 1.3 million units. But public housing is highly visible, while Section 8, when working well, is nearly invisible; public housing concentrates its tenants, while Section 8 disperses them. Public housing is the program of the past; Section 8 the program of the future. Robert Armstrong, president of the Omaha Housing Authority, says, "Public housing is not the American dream. We don't want low-income people to lose sight of the fact that the American dream is still available to them." Section 8 and voluntary dispersal out of distressed neighborhoods is one route to the dream.[1]

Almost no one today is arguing for substantial new public housing construction. For one thing, it is too expensive. Partly because of federally mandated prevailing wage rules and partly because of complicated regulations, new public housing construction can be as expensive per unit as private construction. What's more, supply is not the problem—and hasn't been for years. The country has an excessive supply of housing units overall: 102 million housing units matched by only 93 million households, according to the 1990 census. The problem is the inability of very low-income households to pay fair market rents. The Republicans were right—they diagnosed the problem and came up with housing vouchers. The Democrats are now equally right in trying to make vouchers work as a channel of upward mobility.

Nonetheless, one cannot simply give up on public housing—far too many households representing far too high a proportion of the country's urban population are involved. Often, public housing projects are not only massive in themselves, but also immense in relation to the host city at large. The New Orleans Housing Authority, for example, houses 55,000 people, or one-tenth of the city's population. Boston's Housing Authority houses more than 10 percent of the city's population either in public or leased housing. The better-managed housing authorities often represent lower proportions of the local population. The New York City Housing Authority (NYCHA), for example (which accounts for some 13 percent of the nation's total public housing), houses 6.2 percent of the city's population and 9.3 percent of the city's rental population.[2]

## WHAT WENT WRONG

In the 1930s, public housing was a program that financed the construction of low-rise, small-scale, attractive projects for low-income working families. By the 1950s, public housing was building huge high-rise projects in racially and economically isolated neighborhoods to house society's poorest and most troubled members.

High-rises were thought to be cheap and efficient, but turned out to be neither. Largely because of the 20 percent of tall buildings that had to be devoted to elevators, stairs, and public corridors, high-rises were nearly always at least one-fifth more expensive than row houses. Their mass and height, considered attractive by the Modernists and efficiency experts of the 1950s, lured central bureaucrats into believing that they could and should be able to manage even the most minuscule details of life in the projects. In Chicago, for example, tenants were not able to adjust the temperature in their individual units—that had to be done by a maintenance worker called in from central headquarters.[3] High-rises were also initially advocated for their beauty—stunning though that idea may seem today. In the 1920s, Germany's Bauhaus architects had put forward a new vision for workers' housing: clean, high, pure, well-constructed buildings that rejected the false trappings of the bourgeoisie—curtains, clutter, space, individual entrances. Intent on avoiding the picturesque, the Bauhaus Modernists advocated severe horizontally in composition and perfect simplicity in design. This worked well enough when the finest materials were exquisitely crafted into housing for the wealthy, but worked deplorably when shoddy materials were carelessly employed in huge repetitive buildings.

Many projects quickly became miserable places to live. A much-quoted description of the Robert Taylor homes (the largest public housing project in the world) came from a resident: "We live stacked on top of one another with no elbow room. Danger is all around. There's little privacy or peace and no quiet. And the world looks on all of us as project rats, living on a reservation like untouchables."[4]

This pattern continued into the 1970s. Often a jurisdiction's decision to house families in high-rises was the path to disaster. Gordon Cavanaugh, former head of the Philadelphia Housing Authority, says, "Nobody in Philadelphia except the very rich and the very poor lived in high rises. The family high-rise was an affront to the neighborhood and nothing good came of it."[5] The same could be said of Baltimore, New Orleans, or San Antonio. But at the time, high-rises looked like an efficient way to clear slum land and rebuild quickly, providing many jobs and contracts to the locality.

In a famous article in *Architectural Forum* in 1957, Catherine Bauer wrote:

> The public housing project therefore continues to be laid out as a "community unit," as large as possible and entirely divorced from its neighborhood surroundings, even though this only dramatizes the segregation of charity-case families. Standardization is emphasized rather than alleviated in project design, as a glorification of efficient production

methods and an expression of the goal of "decent, safe and sanitary" housing for all. But the bleak symbols of productive efficiency and "minimum standards" are hardly an adequate or satisfactory expression of the values associated with American home life.[6]

Housing officials in many cities—Seattle, Los Angeles, Minneapolis, Milwaukee, Cleveland, Pittsburgh—saw what Bauer saw, and said no to family high-rises, thereby forestalling the worst disasters. Chicago officials incorrectly projected that ever-increasing population would result in ever-increasing housing demand. Chicago Housing Authority chairman Charles Swibel explained to the *Chicago Daily News*: "Virtually all new construction in the city is high-rise. Families who either must or want to live in an urban area will have to learn to live with the high-rise building for all large centers of population must plan for accommodating an ever increasing number of people within a prescribed land area."[7]

Historian Devereux Bowly wrote that Swibel showed

almost complete ignorance of conditions in Chicago. The fact is that most of the new residential construction in metropolitan Chicago at that time was in the form of single-family houses and walk-up apartments in suburban areas, not in high-rise buildings. Vast undeveloped areas remained available to CHA in the city, and are increasing due to large-scale abandonment and demolition of old housing in various neighborhoods.[8]

And, of course, as in most major cities, population in Chicago declined.

The one federal program that—everyone agreed—worked was housing for the elderly. Even jurisdictions that sensibly rejected family high-rises for the poor usually said yes to high-rises for the elderly. The programs functioned reasonably well until 1992, when Congress insisted that young disabled people, including recovering alcoholics and recovering drug abusers, be housed in buildings for the elderly. Now, many high-rises for the elderly are as troubled as family high-rises. Stephen O'Rourke, who heads the Providence, Rhode Island, housing authority speaks for many when he says,

Washington took the most successful housing program it ever had—housing for the elderly—and systematically destroyed it. When it was just elderly, they ran their own buildings. They had their own social programs, they cleaned and maintained their public spaces, they watched out for one another. Our management concerns were minimal. We had a roving manager for all sites. We're certainly not equipped to deal with what we have now. These buildings look like the old psychiatric institutions. Where once we had almost no turnover for reasons other than death, now we have 25 percent turnover among the elderly.[9]

Or as Billy McGonagle, director of operations for the Boston Housing Authority, says, "We messed it up. It was fixed and we broke it. Or Congress broke it and we let them."[10]

The trend is disturbingly clear: through a combination of congressional mandates and HUD regulations, public housing has become the housing of last resort. The breakdown of public housing was apparent in the early 1970s, when the Republicans, many of them hostile to public housing, proposed the new approach of vouchers. Rather than attempt to repair a clearly flawed system, they proposed providing those in need of housing with vouchers, then called certificates. With Section 8 certificates in hand, eligible low-income tenants were able to find their own housing in privately owned buildings.

For many poor people, Section 8 came just in time. By 1974, great numbers of public housing projects were being pushed over the edge by a congressional reform. This reform, the so-called Brooke Amendments of the late 1960s had, with incredible speed, transformed public housing from a low-rent but self-sustaining program into a low-income—and eventually deeply subsidized—program. The Brooke Amendments created this problem by mandating that no tenant pay more than 25 percent of household income in rent. They were passed because some tenants, often those living in the worst-run projects, were paying huge proportions of their incomes in rent (65 percent, for example, in the notorious Pruitt-Igoe project of St. Louis). Many tenants simply stopped paying rent. But the rigid congressional response—capping all rents for all apartments regardless of size or location at 25 percent of income—has probably been the single most destructive "reform" of public housing. Since tenants are allocated apartments based on the size of the household, families with several children received large apartments but continued to pay the flat 25 percent of income.

The intention was good; the results were terrible. Rents took a nose dive all over the country, eliminating the possibility of sound financial management. For its first thirty years, public housing had been self-supporting—financed with long-term bonds issued by local authorities with the federal government paying 100 percent of the principal and interest. Rents had been established according to the authority's operating expenses, much as they are in private housing. The Brooke Amendments meant authorities could no longer support themselves and had to look to Washington for deep subsidies, which came erratically over the years, further undermining the ability of local authorities to manage themselves well.

The Brooke Amendments also quickly drove out the group that had been the most stabilizing force in projects: working-class families, many of whom were overpaying for public housing once they began paying the mandated 25 percent of income (later 30 percent). They could and did find cheaper private housing. Furthermore, a number of suits by the American Civil Liberties Union (ACLU) and advocacy groups severely handicapped authorities' ability to screen residents and evict troublesome tenants. Increasingly, public housing became a holding tank for a city's unwanted population. By 1991, extremely poor households (those with incomes below 10 percent of local median income) constituted 20 percent of the total public housing population— up from 2.5 percent in 1981.[11]

Both regulations effectively increased the economic isolation of the projects and drove out working families. In 1981, HUD restricted local authorities further by requiring that 95 percent of residents be "very low income," that is, with incomes below 50 percent of the area median income. HUD simultaneously raised the rent to 30 percent of adjusted gross income.

In 1987, Congress established federal selection preferences mandating that authorities give priority to applicants who were eligible for assistance under other programs and who also were involuntarily displaced, living in substandard housing, or paying more than 50 percent of income in rent. In 1992, Congress added to this list the disabled, defined to include recovering drug abusers and alcoholics. The original concept of housing the working poor had been abandoned.

Even the NYCHA, which had resisted the most extreme federal policies, succumbed to the pressure. In 1994, NYCHA reported that, for the first time in its history, average adjusted gross family income fell—from $12,501 in January 1993 to $12,368 in January 1994— and therefore rental income fell. This was probably inevitable, given that the number of working families had decreased from 49 percent of all NYCHA families in 1984 to 31 percent in 1994.

Disasters did not go unnoticed. In 1992, the National Commission on Severely Distressed Public Housing reported that 86,000—6 percent of all units—were in nearly uninhabitable condition. The situation had "begun to cause almost unimaginable distress" to the people living in the housing. The commission cited many causes of the crisis, but one in particular came up repeatedly: isolation.[12]

Huge, geographically isolated projects invariably mean isolation from jobs. William Julius Wilson pointed out years ago that poor neighborhoods were no longer organized around work, and that, "ghetto residents represent almost exclusively the most disadvantaged segments of the urban black community—including those families that have experienced long-term spells of poverty and/or welfare dependency, individuals who lack training and skills and have either experienced periods of persistent unemployment or have dropped out of the labor force altogether."[13] The Clinton administration's Secretary of Labor, Robert Reich, has written about—and deplored—the "secession of the successful," the distancing of the wealthy and fortunate from the fates and communities of the less wealthy.[14] In public housing, the federal government mandates, and has long mandated, the secession of the successful. Indeed, an early attempt at encouraging public housing tenants to work was tried in the late 1960s by historian Richard C. Wade, then a member of the CHA board of commissioners, who recalls,

> We got U.S. Steel to agree to hire some strong young men from the projects. The men did very well. But they were working, so their incomes went up. The regional office ordered us to evict them.[15]

If an authority wants low-income working households in public housing—and, despite congressional pressures, most big-city housing administrators do—the housing must be sited with accessibility to jobs in mind. Some of the worst projects in New York City—which is generally said to be the least troubled of the large authorities—are those that present workers with a truly difficult commute. Working families moved out of projects in distant Coney Island and the Far Rockaways, for example, and were replaced with families for whom the isolation was not an economic consideration.

The Chicago family projects are not only isolated physically, economically, and racially—they are isolated by gender and age. Over 91 percent of the residents are black; three-fourths of the adults aged 25 to 54 are female. Very few residents of CHA housing are employed; most households are on welfare. Similarly, a survey in the 1980s by the Citizens Housing and Planning Council in Boston found that 70 percent of public housing households were headed by women and fewer than 36 percent of household heads were employed.

Such isolation is usually accomplished by crime, which eventually destroys everything around it, including any hope that upwardly mobile poor families may have for living normally. When Northwestern University Professor of Social Policy James Rosenbaum studied families that had moved to the suburbs from Chicago's notorious Robert Taylor Homes, he found that many newly working mothers said they had not worked while living in public housing because they feared for the physical safety of their children in their absence.[16]

## FIXING SECTION 8

While public housing was experiencing its dramatic decline, Section 8 was chugging along pretty effectively, allowing low-income families to disperse throughout urban neighborhoods. Robert C. Embry, HUD assistant secretary during the Carter administration, saw the concentration of poor people in inner cities as the major issue facing large distressed cities. He had argued that because HUD didn't have enough subsidy to help everyone, it should help those who wanted to move out of very poor neighborhoods.

> We didn't want to upset the fragile balance of middle-class neighborhoods immediately adjacent to poor areas. . . . Rather, we distributed low-income households throughout the metropolitan area. We had forty cities initiate the regional project, and nobody complained. Several hundred inner-city residents in Baltimore, for example, moved out, and no one objected.[17]

But Embry also thinks HUD made a mistake in putting Section 8 under the jurisdiction of local housing authorities, who had no interest in anybody outside their jurisdiction. Section 8 became a program of people moving within low-income neighborhoods, often congregating in changing neighborhoods and exacerbating problems. In the mid-1980s, at the urging of the Reagan administration and HUD, Congress added "portability" to the Section 8 voucher, which could now be used across jurisdictional lines. This became administratively difficult, however, as tenants, carrying a voucher from one jurisdiction moved into another jurisdiction while still reporting back to the first.

During the Bush administration, the Moving to Opportunity (MTO) program was designed by HUD secretary Jack Kemp to help motivated low-income families move into nonpoor areas. MTO was based in part on a case involving the Gautreaux family in Chicago, in which the courts had ruled that years of government action that deliberately concentrated low-income black households in black neighborhoods had to be corrected by an affirmative program enabling low-income black households to move.

With counseling from the nonprofit Leadership Council for Metropolitan Communities, the Gautreaux administrators have helped some 5,600 families move into nonimpoverished areas, for the most part successfully. Alexander Polikoff, the original Gautreaux attorney, says

> the evidence indicates that parents do better in terms of employment and/or going back to school, as compared to those who stay in the city, and a heck of a lot better than those who stay in the projects. The kids do much better in school after an initial catch-up period. It doesn't work for everybody. Moving is very hard, and the benefits come at a price, particularly for the mothers. There is also no question but that the families are eager to pay the price.[18]

Much of the Gautreaux data comes from James Rosenbaum, who found that the most significant gains came to the children, many of whom did satisfactory work in suburban schools and went on to four-year colleges, showing that "early deprivations can be reversed."[19]

What is hopeful here is that after decades of destructive programs, housing officials are again thinking about how people get out of poverty—and how federal programs can help rather than hinder them. HUD secretary Henry Cisneros has authorized local housing directors to give preference to working families under Section 8 after years of what one local official calls "federal persecution of the working family."

What is less hopeful is Congress's continuing intransigence which, in effect, forces HUD to interfere, often against its better judgment. By law, any private owner who wants to evict a Section 8 tenant for any reason other than serious lease violations must give ninety days written notice to HUD. This puts HUD directly into the act of reviewing whether an owner is being reasonable, "and really doesn't make any sense at all," notes Madeline Turner, HUD's official in charge of Section 8, who recognizes that HUD intervention has a chilling effect on the willingness of private owners to participate. "But unless we have that changed in the law, we won't be able to halt the practice."[20]

## RETURNING TO PUBLIC HOUSING'S HERITAGE

There were always those who said that public housing should be austere, even harsh, that amenities should be few or none because public housing residents should have every incentive to move as soon as possible. In many cities, such as San Antonio, Texas, this idea took hold early, and the internal quality of units moved from being simple to being grim. The Alazan-Apache Courts, for example, built in 1941 as San Antonio's first public housing, provided bathrooms that had a tub and a toilet but no sink; the kitchens had no cabinets or counters.

But in the early days, there were many policymakers and architects who were determined to produce attractive, even beautiful, public housing no matter what the constraints—New York City's First Houses; Boston's McCormack Houses; Richard Neutra's Los Angeles Channel Heights Houses. Public housing's origins had been utopian, and the first great public develpments are reminiscent of early private model developments, such as the Phipps Garden Apartments in New York or the Marshall Field Garden Apartments in Chicago. Idealistic architects believed their buildings could make a profound difference in the lives of poor families. The most compelling is the still lovely Harlem River Houses in New York, completed in 1937—several buildings arranged on nine acres, in three groups, around a central plaza and landscaped courts. The entrance has a sculpture by Paul Manship (sculptor of the Prometheus at Rockefeller Center and many others). Harlem River Houses is still managed by the New York City Housing Authority today. A parallel low-scale project, Williamsburg Houses in Brooklyn, is less spectacular, but successfully introduced a concept that was then all but abandoned: small commercial enterprises on the street. When commerce was banned in projects, street liveliness was destroyed. It was as if the designers of public housing had suddenly forgotten what makes an urban environment: intense land use, a variety of shops and restaurants, mixed uses, diverse churches and institutions, street activity.

But here's the irony: neither Harlem River Houses nor Williamsburg nor any of the historic projects could be built under today's HUD minimum design standards. The best is now outlawed. What HUD calls its "minimum design standards" are actually maximum design standards that forbid such "amenities" (HUD's term) as basements, doors on closets, ceiling fans, individual entrances. The results can be seen in the disastrous, massive public housing projects of Chicago, New Orleans, Philadelphia, St. Louis—indeed, in most big cities— where thousands of low-income households are jammed into utterly desolate neighborhoods dominated by the projects—all built scrupulously to HUD's minimum design standards. HUD does permit some good design to seep in via waivers, special programs, and local subsidies. Richmond, Virginia, for example, built traditional southern townhouses adjacent to an historic neighborhood. Said executive director Richard Gentry, "We got extra money from the city to make these look like other houses in the Fan area. HUD let us accept the city money to raise standards. A few years before, HUD had forbidden us to use city money on a new development that then ended up devastating a neighborhood."[21]

Secretary Cisneros's personal concern for poor people notwithstanding, his agency's standards are severe. Authorities that are successfully returning to the historic idea behind public housing are doing one or a combination of three things: (1) defying HUD; (2) using local money; or (3) obtaining exemptions (when politically powerful). Seattle, for example, ignores HUD on standards because it does not require HUD financing: its citizens passed a bond issue supporting locally financed—and superb—low-income housing. Wealthy, liberal cities like Seattle can succeed on their own; poor cities must depend on HUD.

## LETTING LOCAL STRENGTHS WORK

Although HUD is a federal department, the nation is made up of localities, and even a federally funded and tightly regulated program like public housing shows tremendous variation from one city to the next. For one thing, no matter what the controls from Washington, the program must operate within the context of the local housing market. Poor people respond to market forces just as surely as anyone else. They look at their options and they choose the best, rewarding well-run authorities with high demand and responding to badly run authorities with low demand.

For its entire history, NYCHA, for example, has had a long waiting list. Operating in the context of a high-rent, low-supply private market, NYCHA's apartments often offer low-income households their best option. Across the Hudson River the authority in Newark, New Jersey, faces the opposite problem: In 1991, Newark had 7,900 households living in 10,700 units, not including those scheduled for demolition. It also had—simultaneously—a waiting list of 6,500 families, and one of the highest vacancy rates in the country. In other words, Newark's 6,500 poor families were not willing to move into its ravaged, crime-ridden high-rises.[22]

Omaha Housing Authority president Robert Armstrong approves of the balance between public housing and private market alternatives practiced in Omaha where, he says, public housing is far from being the best housing has done. It's good—no graffiti, boarded up windows, litter, or broken down cars—but not so good that it locks tenants into place, as NYCHA housing once did. Armstrong argues that public housing should be transitional. No one—however good a tenant—should be able to view public housing as permanent. "We concentrate our efforts on helping people get out. We have very few multigeneration public housing families—fewer than 50 people who are second- or third-generation." The Omaha authority runs a successful business—a window and door manufacturing operation that sells to other authorities—that trains and employs residents, thereby helping them to leave public housing.

Armstrong started the window business in 1986 when an authority worker suggested that "we could do better ourselves." A professional window contractor had just supplied them with deplorably bad windows. Says Armstrong,

> We gave him and another worker space in the basement of an elderly-housing tower and let them experiment. They started building windows and doors from aluminum and they became pretty good. We took space in another building, and soon we were making the best doors and windows in the country for public housing. Then Allen Lozier, a local businessman, gave us a building, and we got some federal economic development money. Meanwhile, Peter Kiewit, a major contractor, had set up a foundation that, on his death, gave us money to purchase the right industrial equipment. We opened our doors to outside business in 1992 and have been going full blast ever since. We now employ forty-six people, have contracts to sell doors and windows to thirty-eight different authorities. Our employees must be our residents when they start, but after their apprenticeship they get an increase in pay every six months. After three years they make a pretty good living, and then they buy their own homes.[23]

It's hard to let go of the assumption that public housing should be temporary, that it should be there to get a family through a difficult period but not offer permanent shelter. This idea was basic to public housing in the 1930s, when there was no real concept of a permanent underclass. Those who argue that public housing must be transitional in all circumstances and in all jurisdictions point out that every unit taken by an upwardly mobile family is a unit denied to a desperately poor household.

Others argue that upwardly mobile tenants should be allowed, even encouraged, to stay in public housing even when their income exceeds upper limits. They believe that mixed-income projects are necessary to the formation of thriving communities. In part, the desire to keep upwardly mobile tenants increases in relation to the authority's desperation. Vincent Lane, who oversaw the country's second largest but probably most distressed housing authority, argues that these communities need every break they can get. HUD secretary Kemp and then Cisneros have offered Chicago temporary exemptions, but Lane says that's not good enough—upwardly mobile families need to be committed to their public housing communities in order for them to remain viable in the long run. As Jane Jacobs wrote, "To unslum, public housing must be capable of holding people by choice when they develop choice."[24]

Lane lost the battle with HUD in June 1995. He and his entire CHA board resigned after HUD rejected their long-planned, much-revised proposal to convert the notorious Cabrini-Green projects into a mixed-income, low-rise "village." HUD assistant secretary Joseph Shuldiner objected both to the gentrification of the project and to the complicated financing plan which would have leveraged the $40 million in HUD funds to float $96.5 million in bonds. In rejecting the proposal, Shuldiner said, "Notwithstanding our willingness to work with CHA in refining the development model presented, we do not clearly perceive its benefits over simpler models involving considerably lower complexity, costs, and fees."[25] After the resignations, HUD took over CHA, making Shuldiner acting executive director in Lane's place.

Alexander Polikoff, who represents some tenants in a suit against the CHA, commented,

> Now you have fifty percent of the bureaucratic maze you had before. Whereas before HUD was reviewing CHA proposals and in typical bureaucratic fashion finding reasons why they were wrong and why they couldn't do what they wanted to do, now that bureaucracy is actually in charge of performance. Now HUD has to find out how to do what should be done. And HUD is going to have to do what Lane was proposing: Getting a mix so that working families will be living alongside non-working families.[26]

The validity of Lane's argument is partly confirmed by the practice of the NYCHA, which has traditionally held onto its best families. NYCHA tenants have lived in public housing for an average of 16.1 years, and former NYCHA chair Sally Hernandez-Pinero argues that long-term tenants are essential to public housing's survival. The point is that there is no one answer for all jurisdictions. In complex jurisdictions like New York, and in complex troubled jurisdictions like Chicago, economic integration holds out a hope of betterment for all; in orderly jurisdictions, like Omaha, economic integration isn't necessary.

Stephen O'Rourke, who heads the mid-sized authority in Providence (2,633 units), concentrates on public housing's relationship with the rest of the city. His authority oversees families experiencing severe poverty—80 percent of its households are headed by women on welfare—but does not have to contend with geographic isolation, a problem that has plagued programs in Chicago. He says,

> We have a political program. We have to compete with other priorities. I'm a stickler for how we look publicly because we have to look good. I'm a stickler, for example, for making sure the main road into the projects looks good—people see it. They judge us.

Providence has undergone an enormous modernization program, completely reconfiguring the units inside and redesigning the outside to look like a regular apartment building, not a project.

Excellent public housing directors disagree with one another in large part because their local circumstances are different. What every complex urban jurisdiction needs is the flexibility to use the appropriate elements of the appropriate program. Cities don't all have the same needs, and they should not be required to run cookie-cutter programs just because those programs look like good ideas in Washington. Given some choice, each city would probably choose a different but effective combination of Section 8, public housing, and various financing schemes. Under the current system, most cities now push for whatever programs they can get, even when they know them to be inappropriate, because to wait for what they need to become available may mean foregoing federal funds.

## PRIVATE MARKETS

Government-supported low-income housing, though important, runs a far second to private market housing, which continues to be the main supplier for all classes. One reason poor people frequently need subsidies to find decent housing is because government actions have driven up costs. Zoning, for example, in most cities has eliminated the traditional multifamily small apartment house in many neighborhoods. New York City's outer boroughs had the three-family house, now called the illegal three; Boston had the three-decker; Milwaukee had the Polish flat. Generally, the owner lived in one part of the house, and rented out other parts to cover the mortgage.

The advantages of these buildings are clear. First, the costs of construction and maintenance were divided among two or more households. Second, an owner who cares about the building and the neighborhood is on the premises constantly. Third, and perhaps most important, low-income and working-class households became property owners. It was this factor that Saul Alinsky, among others, recognized as fundamental to saving neighborhoods. In *Upon This Rock*, Samuel G. Freedman writes that Alinsky and his Industrial Areas Foundation (IAF) set out to "restore the democratic way of life" by creating an active citizenry assembled into People's Organizations—groups that were formed and had their anger focused against a common enemy and toward practical goals through finding "specific, immediate, and realizable issues." The word *anger* derives from the Norse *angr,* meaning grief: "Grief," says IAF, "for all the opportunities lost and to be lost, for all the careers stunted and shortened, for all the hopes and dreams denied."[27]

The resurgence of Alinsky-style organizations in Los Angeles, San Antonio, Baltimore, Philadelphia, and New York is partly due to the IAF emphasis on homeownership as an organizing tool. The best known may be the Nehemiah Houses, built by a coalition of East Brooklyn Churches (EBC). EBC had pressured New York City in the early 1980s into turning over to it vacant land, modifying land-use regulations, and providing tax breaks so that EBC could build small, plain, single-family homes to be sold to moderate-income EBC members. About half of the buyers—some 1,200 families—came from public housing, which caused some critics to charge that Nehemiah was emptying out public housing, an idea IAF organizer Mike Gecan calls "really vile." Gecan argues that

> the real problem was that there's a cork at the top of public housing that keeps all families bottled up. Without Nehemiah homes, there is no dynamic movement or circulation of families upward. Instead you have to keep building stuff at the bottom because this cork isn't popped. Let people move out from the top and you won't have to keep building at the bottom.[28]

He's right, of course. If government subsidized housing is working correctly within the context of a well-functioning private market, hard-working families should be able to save a downpayment to buy a house while in public housing—in six to ten years, according to Armstrong. Within the overall housing market, Nehemiah and NYCHA function as productive, even though hostile, partners.

One fundamental difference between the federal government's and IAF's approach to housing is that IAF seeks to find and build on the indigenous community in the neighborhood. Sister Pearl Caesar, an IAF organizer in San Antonio, attacks what she calls the "mythical community participation set up by government to eliminate real community participation. Real community participation is going to lead to very different results, one of which is the American drive to own a home."

Home ownership doesn't solve every problem, but it solves many, and it usually eases the crucial problem of maintenance, which is the acute problem for low-income housing. The government's impulse is to buy, rehabilitate, or build low-income housing, and then leave its maintenance to others. This idea was fundamental to federal public housing. The federal government would finance construction, but localities were to pay for maintenance. The difficulty is that maintenance of family housing—especially housing for families with many children—is very expensive.

The overall solution is the recognition that there is no one best solution for low-income housing in troubled neighborhoods. Rather, what works is some combination of public and private systems, subsidized and at market rates, big and small developments, and with and without tax abatements—a unique combination designed for the specific needs of every neighborhood in every city.

# 8

# "BACK TO THE FUTURE": REVIVING THE SETTLEMENT HOUSE AS NEIGHBORHOOD SOCIAL SERVICE CENTER

## ELLEN CHESLER

*P*icture three children perched on folding chairs in front of a single computer. Two ogle the screen intently. A third, brow furrowed, is twisted around to face a determined, spectacled adolescent just a few years older, who is leaning down, as if to offer guidance. A ruggedly handsome middle-aged man stands in the background, studying the group's resolve.

This might be a scene out of one of Manhattan's elite private schools, where abundant investment in modern information technology has accentuated the gap in resources and in opportunities that divide the city's privileged children from those who are not. But the described photograph actually represents a very different kind of institution. It appears in a recent report of the Fund for the City of New York about its work with local organizations that serve youth. And its distinguishing feature is that all of the young people in this image—including the preppie young instructor in wire-rims—are children of color. They are participants in a technology project now under way at the Jacob A.

Riis Neighborhood Settlement House, founded on Manhattan's Lower East Side in 1888 by the legendary journalist and social reformer whose name it bears, and relocated in 1950 to Queensbridge Houses in Long Island City, the country's largest public housing project.

The Riis Settlement is again flourishing under the direction of its executive director, Bill Newlin, who arrived there five years ago, when nearly half of Queensbridge's twelve thousand residents were living below the poverty level, and the neighborhood had one of the highest homicide rates and worst drug problems in the city. Yet there were few programs in place to address these issues, and despite its proud history, the facility was closed much of the time and struggling to survive.

Today, Newlin and a staff that now numbers sixty-two have breathed new life into the idea of attacking poverty by building local community-based institutions of the sort that flourished at the turn of the century. They have transformed Riis into an agency that now serves more than thirty-five hundred clients, mostly African-American and Latino, through a variety of social, educational, and cultural services, including outreach and family counseling, a senior center, a community garden, and a wide array of after-school enrichment and recreation programs for young people, including the computer center. Just as progressive reformers once provided language proficiency and other necessary tools of assimilation to the children of the immigrant poor, so Newlin and his associates are launching today's disadvantaged youth into the orbit of cyberspace so that they may one day compete in an advanced information-driven world.[1]

Institutions such as this, however, now largely depend on public funds (indeed, approximately 80 percent of New York settlement house budgets come directly from government),[2] and recent cuts in the city's budget are all but crippling their efforts. Multiple rounds of painful reductions have severely compromised after-school programs that provide computer instruction, along with homework assistance, college readiness, and other education supplements. Some fifty-five separate settlement house initiatives have already been affected, and still further reductions may be necessary as funding from other governmental and private sources, which are frequently awarded as matching grants, are also lost. Small after-school programs like these may seem expendable to City Hall number crunchers, but, in fact, they often provide exactly the leverage that an overextended working parent, and especially a single mother, needs to keep her family intact. And despite the reigning perception that private charity can pay for them, the simple truth is that without the assurance of at least some sustained public contribution, their long-term outlook is bleak.[3]

How much is the city really saving by these actions? And have immediate savings been weighed against what are likely to be longer-term costs? City contracts for services provided by some three thousand local nonprofit organizations in the fields of health, education, and social service now add up to as much as $3 billion annually. These expenditures result from the purchasing of services ranging from ambulatory health clinics and homeless shelters, to small, but increasingly valuable, after-school programs like those in settlements that nurture the children of the working poor. The Department of Youth Services alone dispersed some $68 million annually to more than five hundred community-based organizations until this past year's round of severe budget cutting reduced that figure by nearly one-third. Still, what this means is that nearly a tenth of New York City's overall $32 billion operating budget continues to be spent each year through a collaboration of the public sector and the private. And this figure constitutes an even more significant proportion of what's actually left for discretionary spending after the city's essentially fixed costs for health, welfare, pensions, and interest are covered. Contrary to what most people believe, local social service programs are most often paid for by government, but then contracted out and administered elsewhere, usually by a nonprofit organization.[4]

The sheer dimension of this alliance underscores two major fallacies in recent conservative attacks on government social welfare assistance. First, it hardly makes sense to argue that private secular or religious charities would do a better job of performing most of these service functions than unwieldy public bureaucracies when in substantial measure they are already doing so, albeit mainly with public funds. Second, it is unreasonable to assume that private charity can ever hope to make up for reductions in government subsidies that finance programs of such extraordinary magnitude. As a group of national foundation executives recently observed, even if they were to divest their institutions completely and distribute all their assets, there still wouldn't be enough money to go around.

Speaker of the House Newt Gingrich's now infamous remark about bringing back orphanages as an alternative to sustaining troubled families on welfare payments has been exposed for what it really was—an entirely cynical political ploy which ignores the sober reality that residential facilities (today commonly known as "group homes," not orphanages) already care for thousands of children who have been removed from dysfunctional situations and placed in the country's overburdened foster care system. While many of these programs are run by private philanthropies, such as Catholic Charities or the Protestant and Jewish welfare federations, their costs, which typically run to about $30,000 annually per child, are substantially reimbursed by government. And this public expenditure is, of course, a significant multiple of the stingy subsidies typically available for children on welfare who remain in their own homes. On economic grounds, if moral ones alone are not sufficient, the idea of removing more and more children from their own homes simply makes no sense.

What does make sense is to think about how public-private partnerships in social welfare can work better to sustain and support the poor and prevent continued cycles of dependency. Instead of contemplating how to do away with these programs altogether, responsible critics of current policies should be working to devise and implement strategies that make them work better to bolster families and prevent the long-term costs and problems associated with their breakdown.

This essay on the history of social settlements and their potential for widespread replicability today is intended to present one such strategy. It proceeds from the assumption that New York City and other jurisdictions ought to further decentralize social services to the neighborhood level, where personalized, case-management of benefits and programs can be provided conveniently to families at risk. A model for this kind of program integration already exists in the city's thirty-seven still thriving settlement houses, many of which, like Jacob Riis, began at the turn of the century as progressive era innovations in social reform. The value of the historic role played by settlement houses as providers of services targeted to meet specific needs of individuals, within the framework of a broad, innovative calendar of recreational, cultural and social offerings that anchor the lives of their families and of communities as a whole, is being rediscovered.

At least one useful path into the future of urban America, then, may be found by peering back into its past. And policymakers may, indeed, find information and inspiration in history, despite the recent dishonor heaped on the enterprise by its most vocal popular devotee of late, the lamentably misguided Speaker of the House. As a recent report of United Neighborhood Houses (UNH), the dynamic umbrella organization for New York's settlements, suggests, we may succeed best at reinvigorating progressive social policy, by moving "back to the future."[5]

## THE ROOTS OF THE ENTERPRISE

University Settlement, America's first neighborhood house, was founded 108 years ago by Stanton Coit on New York's Lower East Side. Known best for addressing the needs of European immigrants in the early years of this century, the settlement house model for providing integrated social welfare services under one roof commonly evokes nostalgia for what many want to believe was a simpler, gentler era in American life. Conventional portraits of settlements summon to mind a time long ago when the idealistic sons and daughters of the nation's affluent took up residence in the ghetto and taught hordes of newcomers some valuable lessons about economic enterprise, social comportment, and good citizenship.

This version of the story is at least grudgingly respectful of settlements as benevolent, but ultimately naive, undertakings that did a bit of good for their clients while also providing meaningful civic involvement for their benefactors—many of whom were either unmarried women, like Chicago's Jane Addams or New York's Lillian Wald, who needed to create alternatives to the biological families they never had themselves, or married, well-heeled volunteers, like the young Eleanor Roosevelt, who were seeking a way out of otherwise frivolous and unfulfilling lives. As the tale is oft told, these unorthodox arrangements inevitably gave way to specialized social service organizations and government welfare bureaucracies that grew up in their wake and established more reliable sources of funding and more exacting professional standards for dealing with the poor, and that was a good thing. The best to be said for the settlement house legacy from this perspective is that it helped create the popular demand for government activism that, in turn, spawned the modern, regulatory, social welfare state.[6]

Today this view is changing, on practical as well as theoretical grounds, and settlements are experiencing a renaissance, fueled by disenchantment with the public welfare bureaucracy that was meant to render them obsolete. A recent national survey suggests moreover that early reports of the settlement movement's demise were definitely premature, and not just in New York City. Three-hundred comprehensive social service facilities in 80 cities continue to identify themselves as neighborhood associations or settlements today, as compared to 413 such institutions in 32 states listed in a national directory published in 1913, when their reputation and influence was preeminent. Few of these facilities have residential staff, although a small but increasing number are expanding to round-the-clock operation, complete with resident staff, in response to the growing need to shelter the homeless and people with AIDS. Many are direct descendants of the progressive era, while a handful, like the Harvard Community Services Center in Cleveland, Ohio, have origins in the community-based political and social activism of the 1960s. Harvard was opened in 1968, following the repeated outbreaks of urban unrest that plagued America's cities in

those years, when a group of local residents were able to obtain foundation and grant funding and take title to an abandoned group of buildings
that had formerly housed a convent. Today, the facility is so central to the
neighborhood that a police substation was located within it.[7]

How does one account for this capacity to endure through an era
in which the idea, if not always the reality of settlements, certainly
went out of fashion? Settlement houses, after all, assume the
possibility of building and sustaining institutions that achieve a
harmony of class, ethnic, racial, and gender interests, a premise that
has been mercilessly attacked on conceptual, as well as practical,
grounds in recent years for being hopelessly quaint and dangerously
paternalistic. Most well-intentioned liberal thinkers since the 1960s
have advanced a broad, rights-based agenda of reform that positions
individuals and groups in opposition to one another, provoking
conservative attacks that they have neglected the larger, collective
interests as a community.

As the historians David Rothman and Alan Brinkley, among others,
have so ably documented, it was America's turn-of-the-century progressive reformers who first repudiated laissez-faire traditions of
government in this country and organized services and programs to
serve those needs of citizens that an unregulated marketplace was
not addressing. Motivated in large part by a desire to present
alternatives to socialist demands for wholesale economic and political
reconstruction, these progressives rationalized a limited social welfare
activism on the premise that civil society constitutes a sort of family,
which obliges its most advantaged members to take care of the needs
of those less fortunate, all under the watchful eye of a parent-like state.

What they failed to consider, however, was the coercive potential
of this arrangement, which essentially ceded unchallenged authority to
self-proclaimed social do-gooders in private charities and in
government. And so by the 1960s, the progressive formula came
under relentless attack for allowing the expansion of acceptable
boundaries for political intervention on behalf of the needy without
sufficient concern for their right to protect themselves against
unwarranted or unwanted exercises of power, ostensibly, but not
necessarily always, in their own best interest. As a result, in Rothman's
words, "progressive intervention in the name of equality gave way to
a commitment to restrict intervention by the state in the name of
liberty." In the decade that followed, an immense amount of litigation
occurred that placed unprecedented limits on the discretion of public
and private social service agencies and their professional staffs —
from welfare caseworkers to mental health attendants. As far as I

know, there are no specific examples of litigation with settlements in this civil rights legacy, but it is not hard to see how larger suspicions and tensions damaged the hybrid culture of social service professionalism and cross-class voluntarism that the settlement movement had long accepted as its operating premise.[8]

"It is not that benevolence is itself mischievous or cynically to be regarded with mistrust. It is not benevolence we should abandon, but rather the naive faith that benevolence can mitigate the mischievousness of power so feared by those who wrote our Bill of Rights," wrote Ira Glasser, then president of the American Civil Liberties Union, in 1978. "We have traditionally been seduced into supposing that because they represented charity, service professionals could speak for the best interests of their clients. But now we should know better. Power is the natural antagonist of liberty, even if those who exercise power are filled with good intentions."[9]

Glasser made clear that he was not arguing for neglect of social obligations when he demanded that social programs designed to help the dependent ought to be evaluated, not on the basis of the good they might do, but rather on the basis of their potential for harm. But the undermining of good intentions by the political left, as well as by the political right, has, perhaps inevitably, fueled a mounting frustration across ideological and partisan lines, not just with government's ability to do good, but with its ability to do much of anything at all.

As a result, in recent years the pendulum has begun to swing again, and the delicate balance that liberal activists sought to achieve between meeting social needs and protecting individual rights is again shifting. Once-entrenched, liberal traditions of rights-based social activism are now blamed by conservatives for pitting individuals and interest groups against one another with no satisfactory definition of the commonweal. And, perhaps in turn, once-discarded, progressive notions about the importance of building consensus and cooperation among different groups within communities are enjoying a resurgence across ideological and political lines. Voluntary institutions like settlement houses are again being identified as examples of the possibility not only of social change, but also of social healing, because of the human dimension they contribute to social policy and because of the class, ethnic, and (more recently) racial divisions they seek to bridge. The question now most frequently asked by concerned policymakers is not how to protect clients from social services, but how to make those services friendlier and more accessible.

What has been called the "professionalization of compassion" simply did not work, says political philosopher, Jean Bethke Elshtain.

Modern efforts to create formal distance between the state and its clients in order to protect their rights lost the idea of providing "assistance aimed at self-reliance, competence, and, above all, citizenship," the goal of settlement house activists like Jane Addams. Without compromising client rights, we must recognize the value of personalized direction from competent and caring professionals. Without denying the state's ultimate responsibility for social welfare, we must dismantle the distant public bureaucracy we have in place today, which in Elshtain's words "undermines civic capacities . . . and perpetuates the very thing it aimed to cure; hopelessness, dependency, even despair."[10]

## REINTERPRETATIONS OF THE PAST

Elshtain's insights are part of a larger reevaluation of the progressive enterprise begun by scholars who are rethinking the imaginative role that women, and especially women in the settlement house movement, first played in the building of the modern social welfare state. Women are now viewed as pivotal agents of change at the century's turn in two respects. First, because they were still denied the vote and the right to participate in electoral politics, women had no choice but to work outside conventional political and governmental structures. As a result, they built voluntary organizations like the settlement houses, which raised the issues of private well-being that have since become central to this nation's public life. They constructed what sociologist, Theda Skocpol, has identified as "nation-spanning federations" to bring to public attention pressing moral and social questions, and, in so doing, they radically altered the discourse of politics and the manner in which government has since organized itself to meet the needs of citizens. Progressive women helped create our modern, issue-driven, lobby-dependent civic culture. Denied entrance to the smoked-filled rooms of political lore, they constructed alternative arrangements that tamed the intemperance and corruption of conventional politics and made government more directly responsive to human need.[11]

But there is a second, perhaps even more important, dimension to this argument—a consideration of whether these progressive women may have envisioned a better government than the one we wound up actually getting, because it was intended to be a government rooted in morality rather than self-interest. In the writings of prominent theorists like Charlotte Perkins Gilman and Florence Kelley, scholars have now uncovered a compelling alternative to the conventionally understood liberal constellation of an impersonal, patronizing, *paternalist* state that has since been discredited by those on the right—and on the left as well—who fear its excesses. As an alternative to a paternalist state concerned primarily with the distributions of rights among competing individuals and the resolution of conflicts among contending interests, this new scholarship presents a *maternalist* vision where the common good was meant to take precedence, and stereotypically nurturant female capacities were intended to prevail. This maternalist analogue presents the mother/state as an enabler of its children/citizens, less likely to dominate or incapacitate than the state that critics on both left and right have come to fear.[12]

Recent studies pose the question of whether progressive institutions like the settlement houses were especially sensitive to abuses of power and authority, because the women who ran them generally were accustomed themselves to discrimination and to outsider status. Were they also more inclusive of diversity in their larger vision of the body politic? Were they more open to innovation and experimentation and more willing to involve the poor in a creative partnership? And do their pioneering approaches therefore remain instructive today?[13]

The new scholarship also emphasizes the degree to which early settlement house pioneers envisioned and built creative partnerships with government to accomplish social change. Contrary to what so many of us were once taught, progressive reformers never had complete confidence in private philanthropy. Historian Kathryn Kish Sklar reminds us that Florence Kelley, a lawyer, a consumer activist and a resident for many years of the Henry Street Settlement in New York, shunned the term welfare and did not want to be associated just with charity. Her goal was to create a state that would acknowledge the needs of its people, and contribute to their own empowerment. Sklar credits Kelley and her colleagues with having tried to shape an entirely new social compact, one that was meant to provide far more than the frayed safety-net of public regulation and social insurance that became the New Deal's flawed legacy.

Far from sentimental agents of voluntarism, these tough-minded women did their best to engineer federal support for local solutions to social problems. They lobbied for and then themselves staffed the first two agencies in Washington that funded specific programs for women and children through the Children's Bureau (founded in 1912) and the Women's Bureau (1920) of the U.S. Department of Labor, the agency then responsible for social welfare. In an early example of federal revenue sharing, funds were dispensed nationally, but spent locally, often in conjunction with supportive public investment at the municipal level. The same women who descended on Washington returned home and designed imaginative prototypes for municipal services to serve urban families under stress, including social, educational, and cultural programs; public housing, public parks, and playgrounds; and perhaps most important of all, neighborhood family health clinics emphasizing disease prevention. Tragically, federal funding for these clinics survived through the 1920s but was killed when private physicians protested that they would lead to the socialization of medicine, a canard that prevailed and effectively killed meaningful national health insurance initiatives during the New Deal, a critical oversight.[14]

In sum, new interpretations force us to recognize that progressive reformers, many of them women living in the settlements, were bold social theorists and resourceful political operatives, whose exemplary strategies may indeed merit renewed attention today. They created an enduring model for public-private partnerships in addressing social need, by recognizing the necessity of public support for the poor while never losing sight of the virtue of compassionate administration of social policy. Jane Addams founded Hull House in a vintage Victorian mansion that now seems faintly anachronistic, but it is well worth remembering that the facility quickly developed into a comprehensive, multiservice center, whose services spilled over into a campus of buildings that for many years filled twelve square blocks in the heart of Chicago. Conventional images of Addams and her colleagues as madonna-like figures obscure the more forceful personality traits and practical inclinations evident in their successes as able managers, shrewd fundraisers, persuasive lobbyists and dynamic public speakers.

A single anecdote may be especially inspiring to contemporary reformers. It is said that Florence Kelly, upon listening to an admirer pay homage to Addams said this: "Do you know what I would do if that woman calls you a saint again? I'd show her my teeth, and if that didn't convince her, I'd bite her."[15]

## REINVENTIONS FOR THE FUTURE

Inspired by this rethinking of the past, contemporary social welfare theorists are reversing earlier stereotypes and embracing progressive era strategies that address deficiencies in recent policy approaches. A decade ago, a landmark report was prepared for the Koch administration under the direction of a private commission headed by New York lawyer and former federal health and human services official, Richard I. Beattie. It called for the creation of a Family and Children's Services

Agency within the city's Human Resources Administration (HRA), which would decentralize all its services to the community district level, where all nonshelter social services (including income maintenance and food stamps) would be co-located. This bureaucratic rearrangement was not meant as an end in itself, but rather as a step toward case management of social services that would allow for one social worker to coordinate and address as many of a single family's needs as possible. The objective quite simply was to integrate as many programs as possible—including income subsidy, family planning, daycare, after-school care, drug treatment, personal counseling, job training, and the like—making them mutually supportive and more accessible to hard-pressed clients who have trouble negotiating multiple and often distant public bureaucracies. In an integrated, case-managed system, the family served is the unit around which the bureaucracy is constructed, rather than the shuttlecock that the bureaucracy smashes around, the report observed.[16] Yet, no sooner was the recommendation made, than management changes at the HRA, and subsequently at City Hall, prevented its implementation.

One could argue that the spirit of the Beattie Commission report endures today, however, in the work of local settlement houses. With a grant from the Ford Foundation, United Neighborhood Houses, now under the gifted leadership of Executive Director Emily Menlo Marks, has recently undertaken an initiative to reshape member settlements into more comprehensive, integrated and cost-effective institutions that meet the perceived need for decentralized one-stop shopping in social services. The effort is replicating pioneering progressive strategies for dealing with the poor, not as needy "clients," but as deserving "citizens" of local communities, a perspective which many now believe was too casually discarded by New Deal and Great Society advocates of top-down, categorical, social welfare provision.

The UNH Settlement House Initiative began by taking stock of existing resources and by identifying obstacles that restrict more effective management and delivery of programs. It found that its affiliated institutions in New York currently provide direct services to 182,000 people a year, while their larger reach extends to another 300,000. The research has also established that these facilities are integral to the city's neighborhoods, reasonably well managed, and capable of doing far more—and doing it better—than current resources and administrative practices permit.

Now in its fourth year, the UNH Settlement House Initiative has also resulted in noteworthy practical accomplishments that are making the integration of categorical programs more feasible. These include accounting and reporting modifications that have streamlined government reimbursement practices, while also improving the settlements' own staffing and internal management and information systems to accomplish the same ends.

What may seem sane and simple in theory, however, is not always easy to put into practice. Currently under way, for example, at Hudson Guild, University Settlement, and Eastside Settlement are three pilot programs attempting to integrate Head Start and Day Care to form model child development programs that provide year-round, unified, high-quality services to eligible young people and their families, most especially when both parents, or a single mother, is at work. Combining these two public programs is intended to enrich the experiences of children by improving curriculum and staff. It would save time and avoid confusion for the parents of participants, while also providing them linkages to other services such as literacy, employment training, personal counseling, and recreation. And, finally, it would reduce public costs by avoiding duplication and waste. The effort is slowly moving forward, though byzantine bureaucratic and political barriers, including competitive union locals, are complicating implementation. The success of prior program integration in other jurisdictions, such as Westchester County, serves as continued inspiration to the dedicated settlement personnel who are trying to negotiate changes, as does their intense commitment to the long-term goal of providing a strong continuum of services for children, from infancy through adolescence.[17]

Lynn Videka-Sherman, Dean of the School of Social Welfare at Rockefeller College of the New York State University at Albany, distinguishes settlements from other social service agencies in four respects: first, a focus on the well-being of entire neighborhoods, rather than on the specific troubles of individuals or families; second, a historic commitment to positive, normalizing, enriching programs that educate and socialize and provide individuals with a sense of ownership in their communities—not just programs that address specific problems in need of resolution; third, a mutigenerational emphasis, which brings together and sustains relationships among children, parents and the elderly; and, finally, a strong sensitivity to, and respect for, ethnic, cultural, and (in recent years) racial diversity.[18]

As established private, nonprofit institutions, settlements provide sponsorship and a central location in a given neighborhood for the distribution of categorical government programs. Private money, in turn, helps support overhead and core functions that are not traditionally paid for with public funds, such as social clubs, cultural activities, recreation and gardening. The whole tends to add up to something far greater than the sum of its parts. Settlements serve as vehicles for improved coordination of social services that have long been compromised by isolation from one another and from the individuals and families they are intended to serve. They also help guard against the waste and fraud that plague many independent, community-based programs, because they allow for centralized funding and audits. Though accountable to government funders, settlement-run programs also benefit from the supervision of local boards of directors as well, which today tend to recruit a mix of highly committed volunteers from the immediate neighborhood, along with middle-class professionals and more affluent benefactors from elsewhere in the city.

In a recent article in *The Public Interest,* Howard Husock also points out that the typical settlement house climate adds an intangible factor to social service provision. Settlements provide a kind of common living room for their communities, and this atmosphere invariably politicizes and, under the best circumstances, empowers individuals who are part of it. Even troubled clients who participate because of the need for specific, therapeutic programs may not feel stigmatized. Instead, they come out of the experience with greater self-esteem and a more positive social and political outlook than imparted during the more standard interventions, located in isolated settings. Settlements thus contribute forcefully to "community building," a term, reminiscent of the progressives, that is now again in fashion, because it describes the process of strengthening social networks and relations, and of building local leadership skills, that has also been a missing ingredient in contemporary social policy.[19]

So what more can now be done? Private, voluntary efforts, however well-intentioned, can only hope to accomplish so much. What is needed is a long-term, national commitment to the reorganization and integration of social services at a neighborhood level. Officials in the Clinton administration have studied the settlement paradigm as part of their commitment to break down the welfare state as we know it and transfer resources from cash stipends to investments aimed at helping individuals and families sustain themselves. But with efforts bogged down on the problem of creating welfare-to-work opportunities, little progress has been achieved on other fronts.

En route to the Democratic National Convention in New York in 1992, Bill Clinton, then still a presidential candidate, made a much publicized campaign stop at the Henry Street Settlement, where he met a young boy who lingered in his memory as he delivered an impassioned nomination address the following night at Madison Square Garden.

"This election is about putting power back in your hands and putting government back on your side. It's about putting people first," Clinton intoned on the settlement house steps, repeating the key line of his standard stump speech. But the boy, he recalled, responded cynically: "That sounds good, Bill. But you're a politician. Why should I trust you?"

Clinton used the incident as a rhetorical bridge to his central theme that night, his hope that Americans would enter into a New Covenant with their government, a solemn agreement "based not simply on what each of us can take but on what all of us must give to our nation." He promised, if elected President, to work toward a government that "offers more empowerment and less entitlement . . . a government that expands opportunity, not bureaucracy . . . a new choice based on old values."

"One of the reasons we have so many children in so much trouble in so many places in this nation," Clinton continued, "is because they have seen so little opportunity, so little responsibility, and so little loving, caring community that they literally cannot imagine the life we are calling them to lead."

Clinton called on all Americans to look beyond the country's deep divisions to find a sense of common community. "All of us, we need each other," he said. "We don't have a person to waste. And yet, for too long, politicians have told the most of us who are doing all right that what's really wrong in America is the rest of us. Them. Them the minorities. Them the liberals. Them the poor. Them the homeless. Them the people with disabilities. Them the gays. We've gotten to where we've nearly them'd ourselves to death. Them, and them, and them. But this is America. There is no them. There is only us."[20]

This was vintage campaign-speak—a bit hokey, perhaps—and yet the candidate sounded like a man with genuine conviction, a man who really believed what he was saying. After all, he'd just spent an afternoon in a settlement house. Maybe we need to bring him back, too.

# 9

# THE RISE OF THE PRIVATE CITY

## PAUL GOLDBERGER

"*T*he street is a room by agreement," the architect Louis Kahn wrote, and this line, with Kahn's characteristically gentle, poetic tone to it, tells all. The street is the building block of urban design and, by extension, of urban life; the city with vibrant street life is the city that works as a viable urban environment. It is the street, not the individual building, that is the key to making a city work as a piece of design, for the street is, as Kahn put it, the true room of the city—more even than its ceremonial plazas and squares. Indeed, if plazas, to paraphrase Napoleon's famous remark about St. Mark's Square, are the drawing rooms of cities, than streets are the kitchens, the places where the real life goes on.

Or so conventional urban theory would have it. Urbanists are trained to believe that a collection of buildings, however distinguished, does not a city make—witness Houston, say, or Minneapolis—but add a few great streets and you have something far more potent: New Orleans, perhaps, or San Francisco.

Even if there is no reason to believe this theory wrong—and who could question the intuitive sense that there is more urban energy to a city like San Francisco than to one like Phoenix?—it is increasingly inadequate as a way of discussing American cities at the end of the twentieth century. The traditional, dense city for which streets are the measure of success is less and less a design paradigm. It is increasingly being replaced by a model that values automobile access more than pedestrian accommodation, a model that seems designed to offer the ease and convenience of the suburbs. Yet this new model seems determined to demonstrate that it can offer many of the benefits of traditional cities: a variety of shops, restaurants, and public gathering places; facilities for the performing and visual arts, and the general level of excitement and stimulation associated with older, street-oriented cities.

That the cities of this new urbanism are characterized by sprawl more than density seems, oddly, not to matter. It is not street life that attracts people to Charlotte, or to Minneapolis, or Dallas, or Seattle, to name but four cities that have become known as attractive places to live and work even in an age of urban decline. The magnet these and other so-called attractive cities possess might be described as a combination of ease of living and the presence of a gentle sprinkling of those aspects of traditional urbanism that middle-class residents value in small doses: lively shopping, a mix of places to eat and meet others, and cultural institutions. Downtown Dallas, for example, has an "arts district," with an Edward Larrabee Barnes-designed art museum and an I. M. Pei-designed concert hall, as well as a restaurant and entertainment district, the West End, in which older buildings filled with bars and eating places serve as a lure for locals and tourists alike. Seattle's waterfront, its urban parks, and its new downtown art museum—not to mention Pioneer Square, its twenty-year old shopping and entertainment district made up of restored older buildings—serve similar functions.

It is worth noting that both Dallas and Seattle, as well as Charlotte, Minneapolis, and numerous other successful examples of the new urbanism, provide middle-class residents with close-in neighborhoods of detached houses with ample, and private, yards, allowing them to live what is essentially a suburban life within city limits. This may be the single most important aspect of the appeal of these cities to many of their residents: that once they go home at night, they do not feel as if they are in a city. It is not merely the esthetics of a back yard, of course, but also the fact that such cities are able to dangle before their residents a sense of relative freedom from the serious problems of crime and poverty that are so conspicuous in such cities as Detroit, St. Louis, Los Angeles, and New York.

The desire is clearly to have certain benefits of an urban place— energy, variety, visual stimulation, cultural opportunities, the fruits of a consumerist culture—without exposure to the problems that have always come along with urban life: specifically, crime and poverty. It seems inherently clear that achieving a quasiurban environment that is free of these problems results in places that are not only primarily middle class but also primarily white. Indeed, while segregation may not be the goal, it is surely the result of the new urbanism—though, given the ample presence of middle-class blacks and Hispanics in many of the areas that can be called examples of the new urbanism, it must be said that this segregation is generally more class-driven than race-driven. But it is no exaggeration to say that the new urban paradigm can be defined, in part, by the desire to provide some measure of urban experience without encouraging the mixing of different classes of people: making the city safe for the middle class.

This represents a sea change in attitude from the premise on which traditional cities have always been based. It is not that they do not value safety (though they have not always been successful in providing it), but rather that they emerge from the premise that both security and more uplifting values such as visual and intellectual stimulation emerge naturally out of the juxtaposition of different people and different cultures in close physical proximity. Traditional cities view engagement as a virtue. The new urban paradigm is the precise opposite; it sanctions disengagement, denying the premise of the traditional city even as it professes to celebrate the virtues of urbanity.

We can see this in older cities, too, such as Baltimore, which has been particularly successful in remaking its waterfront core, the Inner Harbor, into a complex of shops, restaurants and hotels, with Harborplace, a Rouse-built marketplace of shops and eating places, as the centerpiece. The National Aquarium is adjacent, and just a short walk away is the justly celebrated new baseball field, Oriole Park at Camden Yards. It all exudes prosperity. Yet before the Camden Yards ballpark was built in 1992, there was virtually no connection between any of this development and the rest of the city, and even now, Camden Yards provides the only significant link. The visitor must struggle to reach any other part of Baltimore, even the extraordinary and urbane Mount Vernon Square just a short distance away. The Inner Harbor has become a tourist island, a middle-class, suburban mecca hovering at the edge of a city that it seems to have almost no connection to.

It is possible to visit the Inner Harbor or Camden Yards and have little sense of crime, drugs, or poverty. Nothing would be better, of course, than to have these problems truly absent. But of course they are there, just blocks away, hidden by the Potemkin village of the new urbanism. And it could be argued that they are even made worse by being hidden, easier to deny, as more of society's limited resources are put into visible developments like the Inner Harbor, and fewer into solving social problems that are out of sight, out of mind.

In its social attitude, the new urban paradigm is less truly urban than it is a kind of blurring of traditional differences between the city and suburb. This blurring exists all the more in what may be the purest examples of all of the new urban model, those clusters of shopping malls, hotels, and high-rise office buildings built on the outskirts of older cities, often at the intersection of major freeways. These so-called edge cities (an awkward term; I have always preferred the less high-sounding "out-town") would seem to have every quality of cities except streets. Such places as City Post Oak in Houston, Tyson's Corners outside Washington, Buckhead north of Atlanta, and Las Colinas outside Dallas are gleaming and relatively new, and represent an attempt to take on the more benign characteristics once associated with larger cities without acquiring any other qualities of urban downtowns. The message is obvious: urbanity is attractive, so long as it can be rendered friendly and harmless by excluding poverty and all that is associated with it—crime, drugs, and violence.

These "out-towns" have now grown to the point at which they have taken on many of the public functions once reserved for central cities. They possess not only stores and offices, but also sports stadiums, arenas, and cultural centers. One of the most significant developments to have come to Southern California in recent years was the opening of the immense performing arts center in Costa Mesa, in Orange County, which for many southern Californians who already lived and worked in Orange County removed the last reason they had for going to Los Angeles. The Costa Mesa center, a huge granite complex situated opposite a cluster of shopping malls and hotels, is not a small-scale, local arts center: it competes with Los Angeles's cultural facilities as the southern California locale for major national bookings. And not far away from the Costa Mesa Performing Arts Center is the Newport Harbor Art Museum, an institution whose trustees have taken as their mission the determination to create as high and serious a profile in the visual arts as the Costa Mesa center seeks to create in the performing arts.

The agglomeration of high-profile cultural facilities in prosperous Orange County, quite intentionally rivaling those of Los Angeles, may be extreme, but it is not unique. Arts facilities in suburban Stamford, Connecticut, Westchester County, and Long Island now compete with Manhattan-based organizations for audiences in the New York metropolitan area, not only in the summertime but all year round.

While New York's cultural facilities are hardly suffering— many of them are international in stature and stay busy through the continuous flow of tourists—it is no longer essential that suburban residents travel to Manhattan to experience culture.

Paradoxically, what might be called suburban values have by now come to play a significant role in defining the urban experience. This is true not only in areas outside of cities, but in entire urban regions, often even including portions of older central cities themselves. By suburban values I mean much more than matters of geography, and much more than accommodation to the automobile, though this is surely a part of it: no longer need a suburbanite's night at the symphony naturally be combined with a stroll on a city street or a visit to an urban cafe or restaurant. The orchestra hall in many places is just as likely to be driven to, and driven home from, as it is to be walked to along city streets.

Underlying this are two much more subtle, but ultimately far more profound, aspects of suburban values: the presumption of disengagement and, going hand-in-hand with this, an acceptance, even an elevation, of the notion of private space. Indeed, the truly defining characteristic of our time may be this privatization of the public realm, and it has come to affect our culture's very notions of urbanism.

Suburbs have traditionally valued private space—the single- family, detached house, the yard, even the automobile itself—over public space, which they have possessed in limited enough quantities under the best of circumstances. And most suburbs now have even less truly public space than they once did. Not only are malls taking the place of streets in the commercial life of many small towns, the privatization of the public realm has advanced even more dramatically with the huge increase in the number of gated, guarded suburban communities, places in which residential streets are now technically private places rather than public ones. In literally thousands of such communities, entire neighborhoods become, in effect, one vast piece of private property.

The rise of suburban values means much more than the growth of suburban sprawl, then. It has meant a change in the way public and private spaces work in both suburbs and cities. And it has meant that many cities, even ones that pride themselves on their energy, prosperity, and urbanity have come to take on certain characteristics once associated mainly with the suburbs. Now in both city and suburb, expressions of urbanity, which we might define as the making of public places where people can come together for both commercial and civic purposes, increasingly occur in private, enclosed places: shopping malls, both urban and suburban; "festival marketplaces" that seem to straddle the urban/suburban models; atrium hotel lobbies, which in some cities have become virtual town squares; lobbies of multiplex cinemas, which often contain a dozen or more theaters and thus exist at significant civic scale, and office building gallerias, arcades, and lobbies.

Private places all, yet they serve the function that was once reserved for public places such as the street, the town square, and the park. The magnificent and civilized balance Louis Kahn evoked in his musing on the street—a balance established over time, across the generations, not only between commercial and civic concerns but also between different architects who knew the street belonged to none of them individually but was in and of itself a part of the commonweal—is essentially a thing of the past. It is gone because it emerges from the implicit assumption that the street is a public place. The great streets of the great cities of the world are all arenas in which private enterprise has made what might almost be called a kind of sacrificial gesture, in which architects have worked together to create a sense of place that is larger and more consistent, not to mention considerably more complex, than anything any individual building can possibly attain.

This is not to say that such a balance between public and private concerns is not respected today. But it is rarely imitated. Indeed, genuine street life exists today mainly where it has managed to survive. There are significant numbers of great old streets in American cities, many of which are healthy both as economic entities and as expressions of a lively urban culture (the two often go hand in hand). But there are few, if any, great new ones. There is no late twentieth-century equivalent of Madison Avenue, or Newbury Street, or North Michigan Avenue. Indeed, North Michigan Avenue in Chicago, for all its continued power as a majestic urban boulevard, seems as much an example of the new form of urbanism as the old: it is intersected by several large vertical shopping malls, punctuation marks of the new urbanism amid the old.

Our culture now creates what might be called urbanoid environments with a vengeance. From the South Street Seaport in New York, where a mall and food court sit on the edge of the most vibrant traditional cities in the world; to Grand Avenue in Milwaukee, where an interior mall has brought some modest, but limited, commercial activity to a troubled downtown, to Horton Plaza in San Diego, a kind of pseudo theme park-urban mall, we are awash from coast to coast in places that purport to offer some degree of urban experience in an entertaining, sealed-off, private environment. That they exist and prosper stands as proof that our culture has not discarded the most important urban value of all, the desire for physical proximity to others in a shared place. But even as these urbanoid environments show that we crave the satisfactions being in public places can give us, they make it equally clear that we are inclined to satisfy those cravings in places very different from traditional streets.

The urbanoid environment—the pseudo-street, the pseudo-square, the pseudo-piazza—is at bottom a kind of theme park, and in this sense, a descendant of that Southern California project from the 1950s that surely had more long-term influence on the American urban landscape than Le Corbusier: Disneyland. The architect Charles Moore was perhaps the first to see Disneyland's significance in terms of American attitudes toward public space; in 1965, in an essay entitled "You Have to Pay for the Public Life," he wrote: "Disneyland, it appears, is enormously important and successful just because it recreates all the chances to respond to a public environment, which Los Angeles in particular does not any longer have. It allows play-acting, both to be watched and to be participated in, in a public sphere. In as unlikely a place as could be conceived, just off the Santa Ana Freeway, a little over an hour from the Los Angeles City Hall, in an unchartable sea of suburbia, Disney has created a place, indeed a whole public world, full of sequential occurrences, of big and little drama, of hierarchies of importance and excitement, with opportunities to respond at the speed of rocketing bobsleds or of horse-drawn streetcars. . . . No raw edges spoil the picture at Disneyland; everything is as immaculate as in the musical comedy villages Hollywood has provided for our viewing pleasure for the last three generations. . . . Everything works, in a way it doesn't seem to any more in the world outside."

As we seek to find places in which "everything works," Disneyland, and the private, pseudo-urban environment that it represents, has become the model. We see it in the biggest of the sprawling suburban malls, where the parade of shops, itself a series of changing stage sets in the manner of Disneyland, gives way every few hundred yards to some form of entertainment—often children's rides right out of an amusement park. CityWalk in Universal City, California, a pseudo-city street of shops and entertainment produced by Disney's competition, raises the curious question: Is it a city street masquerading as a theme park, or a theme park masquerading as a city street? We are not quite sure.

There is nearly as remarkable an ambiguity in the upmarket version of CityWalk, 2 Rodeo Drive in Beverly Hills. That is Disneyland's Main Street for grownups; instead of cute little shops selling mouse ears and stuffed animals, there are mock Art Deco and Spanish Colonial buildings, selling Tiffany jewelry and Hermes scarfs, all lined up on a make-believe street over underground parking. If nothing else, it is proof that the theme park has come a long way. Once a protected pretend-city, it has now broken out of its gates to become a kind of mutated urban form. Charles Moore showed us how the theme park "wanted" to be a city—we see now how the world outside its gates wants to be a theme park. Is it the real city playing at being entertaining, or entertainment playing at being a city?

The same question might be asked of a new Disney venture, the planned rehabilitation of the historic New Amsterdam Theater on West 42nd Street in New York, one of the first efforts in the city's long-planned Times Square renewal effort to show signs of life. That the Walt Disney Company, a private corporation whose innovative designs have all but created the new, private urban paradigm, would step in to restore a landmark theater off Times Square when public efforts to push an urban renewal project for Times Square ahead have so far borne so little fruit, might seem to be a metaphor for the moment. In this case a city is not looking to Disney for inspiration, but quite literally turning over a piece of the urban fabric to it.

Such places as CityWalk, 2 Rodeo Drive and virtually every urban mall in any city are sources of entertainment as much as commercial interaction. Indeed, it is no exaggeration to say that a key characteristic of the urban impulse right now is that it has become more closely wedded to the entertainment impulse than ever before. In an age in which electronic media have come to render many kinds of face-to-face contacts unnecessary, people are as likely to go to a public place in search of relief from boredom as anything else. But this is hardly unprecedented in the history of cities, which, after all, have always been in part sources of entertainment. Nineteenth-century Paris, that high point of Western urbanity, was an entertaining public culture; strolling on a boulevard or sitting in a cafe to watch the world go by were both forms of entertainment. There have always been close ties between the urban impulse and the entertainment impulse. The city grew up as a marketplace, but it flourished also as a stimulating, entertaining environment.

What, in the face of competition from out-towns, suburbs, and suburbanized cities in which disengagement is valued above en-gagement, is the traditional, dense, truly urban city to do? If there is anything that older, street-oriented cities can offer, it is a sense of authenticity, a sense that their pleasures, if not as instantly easy or comfortable as those of the new urban paradigm, are at least real.

They are authentic. They are places not made out of whole cloth; they exist in time, they grow and change, like living beings. "In a city, time becomes visible," Lewis Mumford has said, and that is the one thing that the new urban paradigm has not managed to figure out how to replicate. In the mall and the theme park, things are ever new, ever perfect: there is no sense of the ravages of time, but also no sense of its depths.

There is open space in the suburbs, but not of the richness and complexity of Central Park; there is culture in Costa Mesa, but not with the powerful interaction between performance and city that exists at Lincoln Center or Carnegie Hall; there is big public space in suburban malls, but it is not capable of being as continually enriched and revived and redefined as the gestalt of Madison Avenue. Streets are not only rooms, as Kahn said; they are also arteries, carrying people and things and, most important of all, a sense of time. It is in the very nature of a street that it is different from one year to the next, while the most important quality of a mall is that it tries to remain the same.

Cities can offer reality, then: the reality of time as well as the reality of engagement. Whether that will be enough to satisfy a generation brought up to value other things—to value convenience and ease and entertainment over what older cities can offer— remains to be seen. Longevity—the mere act of survival—is clearly not enough for a city to possess, or Buffalo, Detroit and St. Louis would occupy the same role in American urban culture that Seattle, Dallas and San Diego do. Cities must appear vital and possessed of an urgent present, even as they also possess deep and resonant pasts; they must truly make the whole arc of time visible, from embracing and enlivening the past to holding out the promise of a future.

This is a noble ambition, and perhaps this notion in and of itself marks the difference between traditional urbanity and the new urban paradigm. Cities have great reach: They inspire and ennoble, and they surely challenge. The new urban paradigm seems to shrink from challenge, preferring to embrace ease and comfort. It is the familiar and the tame that are acceptable, not the new and different.

But it is clear that, whatever short-term economic benefits may come from the new urban paradigm's fondness for imitating suburbs, the ability of this model to have a real impact on the condition of older cities is limited indeed. Baltimore, once again, is a good case in point: its Inner Harbor project has managed to bring middle-class suburbanites into the city limits, and it has encouraged a considerable amount of benign thinking about the notion of the city. But the Inner Harbor is really an island unto itself, with little connection, either physical or conceptual, with the rest of the city. The prosperous Inner Harbor throws off tax dollars which affect the rest of the city, but it does not change the basic nature of Baltimore. We should be grateful that it has not remade the rest of the city in its suburban image, but its lack of connection also means that it has had little effect on the city's deeper problems. It is numb to the city's traditional urban virtue of engagement.

Cities must play to their strengths, and their greatest strength is authenticity. It is no small irony that Disney, the company that has done so much to devalue authenticity in the new urban paradigm, would be taking on the restoration of the New Amsterdam Theater in New York, a building whose very selling point is its authenticity. The New Amsterdam is real, with a long and distinguished history, and it is in a very real and very troubled place, 42nd Street. Conceptually at least, it is best to think of Disney mainly as a source of financing here, since what is planned for the New Amsterdam is really quite un-Disneyesque. As the New Amsterdam is restored, this will not be the invention of a make- believe past; it will be the reinvigoration of a very real one. This is the kind of remake of an urban icon that more cities need.

Does the spread of the new urban paradigm mean that the glass of urbanism is half-empty or half full? The urban impulse is obviously alive in this country, even if it is being fulfilled in a manner that is more contained, more controlled, and ultimately less free than traditional streets and public open spaces have been. There must be a reason that urbanity is now highly prized in this culture, even if it is so often expressed in a manner that would seem to contradict the values of the traditional city. But what are the consequences of the new urbanism? Does it ultimately matter that so many public places today are not, technically, very public?

With their resources strained, it is all most cities can do to maintain the public places that they have (and many are not even able to do that adequately). In a climate that makes it impolitic to devote significant public funds to the creation of new public places, most cities have welcomed the willingness of the private sector to create what is, in effect, a new public realm. Indeed, more than a few of the products of the new urbanism, such as atrium lobbies and public arcades in office buildings, are mandated by zoning codes designed to encourage the creation of public space within private buildings. To cash-starved urban officials, allowing public places to become a function of private enterprise is a fair price to pay; they see the alternative as having no new public places at all.

Yet as the new urbanism turns over financial responsibility for public places to the private sector, it implicitly cedes control of the public realm as well. No matter how strict a municipality's regulations may be in requiring open access for all, both the design and the user population can fairly be described as likely to be more homogeneous than in "real" public places, especially in the new out-towns. Good news for the urbanophobe, perhaps, who moves cautiously into urban life from a safe suburban refuge, but far less encouraging for those who value the harsher edge of traditional urban environments. Public places that are not truly public almost invariably possess a measured quality that makes them different from older streets, parks, esplanades and squares. They may be cleaner and safer, but they have a tendency to be flatter and duller; the voltage is almost always reduced. Everything is so right that it becomes, by consequence, wrong, for no matter how physically handsome these places may be, they are almost always missing a certain kind of serendipity, the randomness that provides the element of surprise that is so critical to a real urban experience.

This failing is most obvious in such examples of the new urbanism as open outdoor plazas, interior atriums, and office-building lobbies that double as public arcades. Architecture is almost always at the forefront here, but for all the determination of private developers and the city officials regulating their work to maintain a high standard of design, few of these places manage to transcend the limitations of this now-common genre and project any real sense of traditional urbanity. Their role as private places ultimately overshadows their public mission, whatever the architectural achievement they represent. They are, for the most part, upright and dull, bespeaking good taste above all. And if rampant propriety and dullness are less likely to be the case in many of the more purely commercial examples of the new urbanism, such as theme parks, which at least offer a high level of visual stimulation and occasionally even wit, even the most entertaining of such places possesses none of the complexities and inconsistencies of real urban form. They are not made over time, like real streets; they are manufactured by designers, seeking to reproduce and package and make in an instant something that elsewhere developed over generations.

It is the role of all places to consume culture, but it is the privilege of a special few to create culture. Those places that manage to create culture in a more than incidental way tend, almost always, to be great cities: New York and Los Angeles rank above all others in this country in this regard, and it is no accident that they are both complicated, rough, difficult cities, profoundly original in their physical makeup and highly diverse in their population. Los Angeles may have spawned Disneyland, but it is not itself Disneyland, any more than New York is the "festival marketplace" of the South Street Seaport. New York and Los Angeles may be as different in their physical form as they are in their climate, but they share an intensity and a power, not to mention a certain sense of disorder—even, if this is not too extreme a word, anarchy.

Is it their extraordinary complexity that makes both of these cities so attractive to younger artists, musicians, writers, painters, dancers and architects? Or the way in which each borders on chaos? This is not the place in which to answer the question of why particular kinds of environments seem to encourage creativity. But it seems impossible to argue that it is large, difficult, "real" cities that are most hospitable to the creation of culture, as opposed to the consumption of it.

The new urban paradigm seems to celebrate consumption of culture, not creation. The Costa Mesa Performing Arts Center in Orange County may rival Los Angeles in the artistic events it presents, but it has spawned no community of artists and performers around it to challenge that of Los Angeles, any more than the new suburban cultural facilities around New York have made a dent on the role of New York City as a cultural incubator. The "festival marketplace" of the South Street Seaport may be an economic boon to the lower Manhattan neighborhood, but its shops and cafes are filled with consumers of culture, not with the makers and shapers of it.

Cities that have the capability of making culture—New York, Los Angeles, to a certain extent Seattle, San Francisco, perhaps Boston and Miami—have little to fear from the new urbanism. They are incubators, creators of culture, and as such possess what might be called the ultimate form of urban authenticity. They can make what the new urbanism can only imitate. Their economies will ebb and flow, but it is difficult to believe that the new urbanism can replace the essential role these cities, and others like them, play.

But many older cities, those not lucky enough to possess the power of shaping culture, are highly vulnerable to the lure of the new urban paradigm. They can offer little that the middle class truly wants, and thus they seek refuge in trying to save themselves by becoming ever more suburbanized. Atlanta, Charlotte, Dallas, Denver, Phoenix— these cities are already heavily suburban in feeling, and it is hard to believe that they will develop in a different way over the next generation. And whatever happens to the cores of these older cities, it is all the more likely that more and more commercial business will be done in out-towns, those clusters of high-rise buildings that stand as the new urban paradigm's alternative to the old commercial centers.

Intimately tied to consumerism, to entertainment, and to popular culture, the urbanism of today seeks to provide a measured, controlled, organized kind of city experience, which is the precise opposite of the rough-edged, somewhat disorganized reality of older streets and older cities. The new American urbanism is packaged for easy use; it disdains the randomness, the difficulty, and the inconsistency of real cities. It is without hard edges, without a past, and without a respect for the pain and complexity of authentic urban experience. It is suburban in its values, and middle- class to its core. That it exists at all, for all its flaws, is probably a good thing, given how determined this country seemed at the peak of the frenzy of urban renewal in the 1960s to eschew any kind of urban life altogether. Yes, we seek an urbanism still. What we do not have—yet—is a true public realm.

# PART III   PERSPECTIVES FROM THE FIELD

# 10

# THE HEALTH AND WELFARE OF CITIES

## DONNA E. SHALALA

merican cities have been the centers of great innovations in medicine and major breakthroughs in public health. The nation's first hospitals—Bellevue and New York Hospital—were founded in New York City in the eighteenth century, and this country's first health department was established in New York City in 1886, setting the stage for American cities to lead the way in controlling the scourge of disease.[1]

Cities were health leaders because they had to be. City dwellers' close proximity to one another encouraged epidemics and produced new health problems—from the cholera epidemics that swept American cities in the late eighteenth century to the pandemic of AIDS that afflicts cities today. By the beginning of the twentieth century, aggressive urban efforts to improve sanitation, sewerage, water quality, and hygiene had virtually eliminated cholera, typhus, and typhoid fever. Together with antiseptic and antibiotic medicine, these innovations have helped dramatically increase the life expectancy in the United States, from 47 years in 1900 to 75 years in 1990.

Urbanites today have a shorter life expectancy, higher rates of pneumonia and tuberculosis, and higher mortality rates from cancer and coronary disease than the general population.[2] American cities face a plethora of health problems that require new approaches to controlling disease and countering environmental and behavioral factors that lead to premature death and disability. Cities have too much violence and too few immunizations, too many teen pregnancies and too few healthy babies, too much unsafe sex and too few condoms, too much environmental pollution and too few resources to combat it. Achieving real improvement in health and the quality of urban life will require changes in individual behavior, in environmental quality, and in health services.

Such improvements will also require a coordinated strategy involving governments at the federal, state, and local level; doctors, nurses, and other health professionals; community organizations; and communities themselves. The knowledge to reverse these trends is available. But completing the public health revolution begun in earnest in American cities two centuries ago will take public commitment and support.

## PUBLIC HEALTH AND PURE WATER

The tasks of protecting the water supply and disposing of waste drove the agendas of early public health officials. Between 1850 and 1859, scarlet fever killed as many as 272 of every 100,000 Chicagoans. Beginning in the 1850s, Chicago responded by aggressively attacking water pollution by creating sewer systems. Those efforts, inspired by Ellis Sylvester Chesbrough, led the Illinois State Legislature to establish the Chicago Board of Sewerage Commissioners in 1855. In his first report to the board, Chesbrough noted that not one U.S. city had a comprehensive sewer system, a sharp contrast to European cities of the day.[3]

In 1798, Benjamin Latrobe urged the city of Philadelphia to clean up its water supply. His early warnings did not result in any action, however, and throughout the nineteenth century polluted water supplies continued to cause epidemics of typhoid. Philadelphia did not begin filtration of its water supply until the twentieth century, when it was introduced in two of the city's six water regions, in 1902 and 1904, with remarkable results: those two areas were virtually untouched by the typhoid epidemic that swept the rest of Philadelphia in 1906. By 1909, when installation of filtration was complete, Philadelphia experienced no further outbreaks of typhoid, which had killed as many as 1,000 Philadelphians a year.[4]

Throughout the nineteenth century, public health officials also spent much of their energy attacking the high rate of infant mortality. Between

1850 and 1900, an estimated 15–20 percent of children born in the United States died before their first birthday. Contributing factors included a low standard of living and infections spread through the water supply and breast milk.[5]

## SANITATION, IMMUNIZATION, AND COMMUNITY HEALTH

Between 1860 and 1910, the proportion of the American population living in cities rose from 19 to 45 percent, largely because of massive immigration from Europe and internal migration from farms to cities. With this population shift, the initiative in controlling disease also shifted—from individual physicians, family members, and neighbors to governments and voluntary associations. Settlement houses and civic organizations began to provide medical assistance in the squalid slums. State and city governments began to finance and organize the delivery of medical care. The creation of the New York City Metropolitan Board of Health in 1866 was a turning point in this effort and served as a model for other cities.[6]

Public health moved from an emphasis on sanitation to encompass improvements in living conditions; provision of medication, immunization, nutrition, prenatal and infant care; and, most recently, environmental intervention. From 1850 to 1880, most efforts to reduce infant mortality overlapped the work to clean up the water supply and sewerage systems of American cities. From 1880 to the 1920s, health officials concentrated on digestive and nutritional disorders and tried to improve the quality of the milk supply. In 1907, the New York Milk Committee, established to reduce infant mortality, set up infant milk depots in poor neighborhoods and gave free milk to families who needed it.[7]

The supervision of pregnancy by physicians had been haphazard, left mostly to midwives until the creation of the Federal Children's Bureau in 1912, which served to change that pattern. By the 1920s, maternal and child health functions had become a standard part of health departments. In 1935, the enactment of the Social Security program brought with it an increased availability of resources for such programs through the new federal Maternal and Child Health program, which provides grants to states to provide prenatal and primary care to women and postnatal care to infants.

The introduction and subsequent broad application of childhood immunization programs served to reduce the death rate of infants and children. Childhood diseases ranging from diphtheria to whooping cough were brought under control as states and cities passed mandatory immunization laws and the federal government provided financial and technical assistance to assure a sufficient supply of safe vaccine.

From 1900 to 1930, government efforts to deal with the spread of disease expanded tremendously—particularly in cities. In 1900, the three leading causes of death in the United States were influenza and pneumonia, tuberculosis (TB), and gastrointestinal infections. Together, they accounted for nearly one-third of all deaths.[8] Annual mortality rates fluctuated wildly due to epidemics of dysentery, typhoid fever, smallpox, diphtheria, and scarlet fever.

If the second half of the nineteenth century was noteworthy for a revolution in the sanitary conditions of cities, the first half of the twentieth was remarkable for progress on the scientific front. Most notably, after World War II, the widespread use of sulfa drugs, penicillin, and other antibiotics had a dramatic impact on the prevalence of syphilis, gonorrhea, tuberculosis, and other diseases.

## New Challenges, New Solutions

By the middle of the twentieth century, sweeping epidemics seemed to be a thing of the past in the United States. Public health programs at federal, state, and municipal levels provided a relatively clean environment, safe water supplies, and an increasing number of physicians and other professionals to meet the health care needs of the vast majority of Americans.

Beginning in 1953, states and municipalities got a new partner when President Dwight D. Eisenhower established the U.S. Department of Health, Education, and Welfare (HEW) to coordinate federal efforts. Coming nearly a century after the creation of the first citywide health department, HEW was a late arrival. In 1980, with the establishment of a separate Department of Education, HEW became the Department of Health and Human Services (HHS). Policymakers and public health professionals turned their attention to two major contributors to morbidity and mortality in cities: poverty and human behavior.

Attempts at alleviating poverty have included assistance programs aimed at both health care and economic needs. The most critical advance was the Social Security Act of 1935, which provides retired workers with a guaranteed pension, helping to lift millions of senior citizens out of poverty. The Social Security Act also addresses poverty through Aid to Families with Dependent Children (AFDC), Supplemental Security Income (SSI), and the maternal and child health care block grant program to the states.

Thirty years later, Congress added two new programs to the Social Security Act—Medicare and Medicaid—to provide direct health care benefits to the elderly, the poor, and the disabled. Medicaid was particularly important to poor urbanites. A. B. Ford's study of the health status of low-income Americans living in nineteen U.S. cities between 1969 and 1971 revealed that incidences of low birth weight, infant mortality, lack of prenatal care, illegitimate birth, death from tuberculosis, and death from violent causes were all far higher in the inner city than in other neighborhoods.[9]

Medicaid has had a remarkable record of success in improving access to health care services for low-income Americans. Prior to Medicaid's enactment, these Americans saw a physician about 20 percent less often than did those above the poverty line. By 1975, the poor visited doctors 18 percent more often than the nonpoor. The program has had an even more dramatic effect on racial gaps in health care access. In 1964, black Americans saw a doctor 42 percent less often than whites. By 1975, that gap had narrowed to 13 percent.[10]

Another significant contribution of the expanded federal role in health care was the further expansion of the National Institutes of Health (NIH), which had been set up to conduct and fund biomedical research. Advances in science, clinical research, and epidemiology led to a reduction in the 1970s in mortality from cardiovascular diseases. Reductions in the rate of smoking and other behaviors helped spur what Dr. Milton Terris calls the "second public health revolution."[11]

## New Systemic Problems

Medicaid has not been untarnished, however. Due to uneven eligibility rules (by tying Medicaid eligibility to AFDC and SSI, Congress left to the states the establishment of income levels for eligibility), more than half the people living in poverty were not covered by the program in the early 1990s. The tie-in to welfare benefits also produced an un-anticipated disincentive for women on AFDC to join the workforce, since they would, more often than not, lose health coverage for themselves and their children.

During the 1980s, Congress voted to establish federal Medicaid eligibility rules for pregnant women and young children, which helped cover millions of additional people. Still, Medicaid remains an uneven way to provide the poor with health care coverage. Huge gaps remain between the health of African-Americans and Hispanic Americans and that of the white majority population, as well as between the poor and the middle class. For example, in 1990–92, sick children who lived in poverty saw a doctor half as many times per year as children in families with higher incomes.[12]

Medicare also had a dramatic impact on the health of cities. Medicare, which spent more than $800 billion between 1966 and 1990, enrolled 68 million Americans, covered 200 million hospital stays, and paid for 2.6 billion visits to a doctor. Not only has the program improved the health of the elderly and disabled, it has provided a consistent source of funding for urban hospitals and has helped support the major academic health centers located in large cities. For millions of senior citizens, Medicare provided access to health care professionals and the medical technology that has improved and extended their lives. In 1965, the average sixty-five-year-old could expect to live about five more years. By 1987, that average was up to seventeen years.[13]

Still, Medicare, too, has significant gaps, including the absence of a prescription drug benefit and coverage of most long-term care for the elderly and disabled who wind up in nursing homes. Limits on coverage and rising deductibles have put pressure on senior citizens' budgets. An attempt to plug these gaps resulted in the enactment of the Medicare Catastrophic Care Act of 1988, but opposition from wealthy retirees led Congress to repeal much of the act in 1989. The act would have extended Medicare coverage to prescription drugs and home health care while limiting the annual amount of out-of-pocket spending by the elderly and disabled.

Costs were another problem. When President Johnson signed Medicare into law in 1965, the program was projected to cost $3.7 billion by 1970. Instead, it cost $7 billion. In succeeding years, costs continued to escalate, in part because of additional benefits voted by Congress and, in part, because of limits placed on premiums paid directly by the elderly, but primarily because of rising health prices and utilization of services. Presidents and Congress have battled to control costs by limiting payments to hospitals, physicians, and other health care providers. But most of those savings were shifted either to other parts of the program or to private payers, including employers.

## SIGNS OF SLIPPAGE

Despite the best efforts of public health and medical professionals, some hard-won advances of the twentieth century's first seventy-five years began to be reversed between 1980 and 1992. Two prime examples: the resurgence of tuberculosis (TB) and the recent outbreaks of measles. A disease that had killed 20 percent of the adult population in the nineteenth century, TB was slowed in the early twentieth century with the advent of improved sanitation and effectively halted after 1950 by antibiotics. Between 1953 and 1984, the number of TB cases dropped steadily. By 1985, 40 percent of U.S. counties reported that they had no cases of TB; 90 percent had fewer than ten cases.

But TB came roaring back in the 1980s. Its resurgence was caused in part by the AIDS epidemic and its concomitant lowering of immunity, but chiefly due to a failure to follow up on earlier progress. In 1985, the total TB caseload in the United States was 22,201. By 1991, that number had risen to 26,283. In 1989, nearly 2,000 Americans died of a disease that was supposed to be a thing of the past.[14]

One factor in the resurgence of tuberculosis was cutbacks in federal, state, and municipal government funding to combat the disease. In 1981, President Ronald Reagan convinced Congress to eliminate a federal program aimed at eradicating TB. Given that signal, many states and municipalities ended or curtailed their own programs. By the time the number of TB cases began to rise, it was too late to simply reinstate funding and reverse the trends. Much greater and more expensive solutions were needed, eating up valuable and limited resources.

A similar pattern was followed in the battle against measles (rubella). In 1950, 319,124 cases of rubella were reported in the United States. Although the yearly total rose to 441,703 cases in 1960, the broad vaccination of schoolage children cut the number of cases to 47,351 in 1970, 13,506 in 1980, and 2,822 in 1985. It seemed that the United States was about to eradicate measles within its borders. But there was a reservoir of the disease latent in society, and American borders are not sealed shut. As with TB, government immunization programs were cut back. Privately purchased immunization also declined as prices increased. In some cities, only half of the two-year-olds received measles vaccine. The subsequent rise in the number of cases was dramatic. In 1988, the United States had 3,396 cases of rubella; in 1989, there were 18,193; in 1990, 27,786. Not until 1991 did the measles case total drop—to 9,643. During the 1989-91 outbreak, more than 55,000 cases of measles were reported in the United States, and more than 130 people died.[15]

Of course, the most virulent outbreak of disease in American cities has been the AIDS epidemic. Since the first report in 1981 of a mysterious disease among a handful of homosexual men in Los Angeles, the United States has seen nearly 400,000 cases of AIDS and lost 250,000 people to the disease. The vast majority of those cases have occurred in metropolitan areas.[16]

## TOWARD A NEW CENTURY: THE THIRD
## PUBLIC HEALTH REVOLUTION?

In the face of these somewhat dispiriting trends, what can the nation do to improve the health of those who live in major American cities? The problems require a multipronged approach that encompasses both public health policy and socioeconomic policy.

Dr. Philip Lee, who has served under both Presidents Johnson and Clinton as Assistant Secretary for Health, described his vision for improving the health of the American people in the 1994 Shattuck Lecture to the Massachusetts Medical Society. Dr. Lee noted that only 10 percent of excessive mortality in the United States can be related to the inadequacies in the health care system; most of the rest can be linked to behavior. Yet the United States has poured billions into that system while virtually ignoring public health enterprises. For example, in 1994, less than 1 percent of all that was spent on health care in the United States went to public health prevention programs. Between 1981 and 1993, spending on medical treatment increased 210 percent while spending for population-based activities by state and municipal health agencies rose by two-thirds that amount.[17]

Dr. Lee advocates a set of responsibilities for public health agencies:

1.  Surveillance of communicable and chronic diseases

2.  Control of communicable diseases and injuries

3.  Environmental protection

4.  Public education and community mobilization

5.  Quality assurance

6.  Public health laboratory services

7.  Training and education of public health professionals

8.  Leadership, policy development, and administration

The task before us is to build on the successes of the past and achieve the "third public health revolution." Using tested public health approaches, we can continue to extend the life-span and improve the quality of life of Americans. And, following our national tradition, we can export these successes to other nations around the globe.

The work ahead will be difficult. During the 1980s, American cities were decimated by federal and state budget cuts, and the needs of city residents were virtually ignored. Targeted federal programs such as general revenue sharing were eliminated and, simultaneously, local aid from states to municipalities was sharply reduced. At the same time, the federal budget deficit and the national debt rose greatly, leaving the Congress and the executive branch with diminished resources to invest in the health of cities.

What is needed is a targeted approach utilizing an interdisciplinary team health model rather than the more costly traditional medical model. It is no longer enough to simply treat the medical mani-festations of illness. We must attack the core problems of behavior and focus on prevention. Only a coordinated attack will succeed. Federal, state, and municipal governments must increase their contributions to core public health functions and continue to target specific problems of concern to municipalities. The trick, of course, is to garner the political will to do so.

An excellent example of the interdisciplinary approach is the ongoing response to the AIDS epidemic. Clearly, it is a federal responsibility to fund basic biomedical research. Funds targeted at AIDS research have been steadily increased as the epidemic has grown. Through the Centers for Disease Control and Prevention, the federal government has given states and localities funds to track the progress of the epidemic and identify local needs. Federal and state funds have been devoted to AIDS prevention and education at the state and municipal level.

A greater challenge has been to guarantee access and availability of high-quality services. In 1990, Congress enacted the Ryan White Comprehensive AIDS Resources Emergency Act to provide federal funding to states and cities to provide direct services to people with AIDS. At first funding for that program lagged considerably behind the levels authorized by Congress. Beginning in 1993, however, the federal government sharply increased spending so that the program has reached the full authorization levels provided.

Still, the federal government must step up its own efforts in HIV prevention and education. For the first twelve years of the AIDS epidemic, Washington's refusal to confront the seriousness of AIDS and to use the preventive tools at its disposal actually allowed an epidemic to spread when it could have been contained. In 1982, Congressman Henry Waxman of California put it best when he rhetorically asked, "If AIDS affected rich, white, country club members, would the government's response be so slow?"

In recent years, the federal response has become more aggressive and more inclusive in its approach. Prevention campaigns emphasizing sexual abstinence and the correct and consistent use of latex condoms by those who are sexually active have shown early positive results. Community-based planning has also begun to shift the direction of prevention programs toward the needs of particular local populations. And, by working with, instead of against, community organizers, the federal government is achieving an unprecedented level of dialogue and action.

The remaining gaps in children's health also require a greater federal investment. Combined federal spending on childhood immunization totaled $496 million in 1993, when President Clinton took office. In 1994, spending was increased to $693 million. In 1995, it reached $888 million following the enactment of a comprehensive immunization reform program that includes Vaccines for Children, a program to provide free immunization to all children in low-income families, those who are uninsured, and those who do not have coverage for immunizations as part of their family's insurance plan. Additional investments were made in outreach to families, through the development of a network of qualified physicians and other health professionals to vaccinate children and a coordinated delivery system to ensure that vaccines reach providers in time.

In 1995, $121 million was requested for the Centers for Disease Control and Prevention to assist states and municipalities in controlling TB. Legislation expanding Medicaid coverage of TB treatment will provide another $70 million in direct services. And another $51 million is being spent by the National Institutes of Health to conduct research into ways to prevent, treat, and eradicate this disease. The federal government must continue to target problem areas, increase funding for those efforts, and—most important—maintain that commitment long term.

Federal investments in basic biomedical research must be increased so that state and municipal health officials can gain from new advances in knowledge and technology. The federal commitment to NIH totals $11.5 billion in 1995, with more than half of those funds for basic, rather than directed, research. More money is needed for basic research into health promotion and disease prevention. With so many public health problems rooted in behavior, this funding increase would reap large dividends in improved health and reduced health expenditures.

State and municipal health departments urgently need additional resources to shore up their core public health functions. One of the harshest effects of the 1980s cutbacks in federal assistance to states and cities has been a concomitant reduction in funding to health departments. As a result, in some parts of the country, large geographic areas have no health department at all and depend instead on a centralized office that sends officials out to "ride the circuit." In others, there has been heightened competition for scarcer dollars, often pitting one part of the public health system against another (for example, mental health services against environmental protection).

Since the federal government shares in the blame for this situation, it should share in the solution. Washington must reinvest in core public health functions of states and cities. These new funds should not be earmarked for specific purposes or diseases but should go to shore up what is, in many places, a crumbling public health infrastructure.

## LINKING PUBLIC HEALTH IMPROVEMENT TO WELFARE REFORM

Beyond targeted public health investments, of course, the real need remains for investment in cities and in their people—particularly those people who are poor. Certainly the best investment we can make in people is to create jobs, especially jobs with health benefits. Pulling the American economy out of the recession of 1991–93 has helped to create more than three million private sector jobs in the last two years.

For many low-income city dwellers, however, a job often means only minimum wage, which—however welcome it may be—still fails to lift a family out of poverty. To confront this problem and remove disincentives to work, Congress has expanded the Earned Income Tax Credit (EITC), which frees millions of working Americans from an income tax obligation. Along with expanded child care benefits, this makes low entry-level salaries go farther.

Still, too many families remain trapped in a system that rewards inaction and penalizes advancement—but not for a lack of willingness or efforts to leave it. According to sociologist Donna Pavetti, building on the work of Harvard social scientists David Ellwood and Mary Jo Bane, some 70 percent of today's welfare recipients leave within two years, and 90 percent leave within five years. Yet the vast majority return to the welfare rolls, often because the low-paying jobs they typically obtain do not come with essential benefits like child care and health care.

Some studies suggest that 7–15 percent of the current welfare caseload—at least one million adults and children—are on welfare simply to qualify for Medicaid. And a 1994 Urban Institute study found that over a twenty-month period, only 8 percent of those on AFDC who went to work were able to find a job with health insurance. Parents should not have to choose welfare over work just to get health coverage for their children.

Ninety percent of Americans in a recent poll agreed that values of work and responsibility—helping people help themselves—should form the basis of any attempt at welfare reform. Our welfare system was founded on one of America's most basic values—neighbors helping neighbors through hard times. As Franklin Roosevelt said, "Continued dependence on relief induces a spiritual and moral disintegration," which is really at the root of why so many people—on welfare and off—dislike the current system.

I believe that by strengthening supports for working Americans—by expanding the Earned Income Tax Credit, by guaranteeing health care with every job, by putting real muscle into child support enforcement, and by providing child care—we will build a solid platform for millions of women who are struggling to make the transition from welfare to work. Today, more than two-thirds of all women with children are in the workforce. As Mary Jo Bane has noted, her own and others' research is beginning to show that children of women on welfare are better off—both financially and developmentally—when they see their parents going to work every day.

## THE TIE THAT BINDS: HEALTH CARE REFORM

No effort to improve the health of urban Americans can succeed without a fundamental change in the system of financing health care. The United States has the finest medical care available in the world—for those who have access to the system. For them, the supply of superb medical professionals, technology, and facilities is abundant. For those without the means to access the system, it must seem a cruel hoax.

Nearly every examination of the health problems of cities points to a lack of universal insurance coverage for a large number of Americans. Those without insurance visit doctors less often, use hospital emergency rooms more frequently, postpone needed care, suffer more disabling conditions, and die prematurely. The continuing gaps in life expectancy between races can be traced back to this lack of coverage. (The disproportionate representation of blacks among welfare and poor populations is reflected in life expectancy statistics.) Without coverage for prenatal care, an uninsured woman must either delay care—endangering both her child and herself—or search for free or reduced cost treatment. A senior citizen with no insurance for prescription drugs must sometimes choose between paying for medicine or for heat.

Health reform must provide all Americans—in cities, suburbs, or rural areas—with coverage for a comprehensive set of benefits that cannot be taken away. Benefits must include a full set of preventive services, including screenings, immunizations, prenatal and well-baby care, mammograms, Pap smears, cholesterol screening, routine physicals, and other services.

Policies should be made available to all Americans—including those with preexisting medical conditions. They should be portable from job to job or from employment to unemployment. They should be renewable and should not be able to be canceled for any reason other than nonpayment of premiums.

Making coverage available is not enough; it must be affordable. In the past fifty years, however, the cost of health care and health care coverage has risen at nearly two-and-a-half times the rate of general inflation. At the same time, there has been a steady rise in the number of uninsured. From 1980 to 1992, the percentage of Americans living without insurance rose from 12.5 percent to 17.2 percent. That means another 13 million people are without coverage, for a total of 38 million people.[18]

Having nearly 40 million people without health insurance taxes health care facilities, emergency rooms, and public health systems. It also puts a strain on individuals and businesses. Those companies that provide coverage to their workers are paying an estimated $25 billion a year in additional premium costs to cover the expense incurred by hospitals in providing care to uninsured individuals. And rising insurance costs have taken an average of $600 per year from each American worker's earnings.

A comprehensive health reform plan would also make the kind of investments cited above in core public health programs, basic biomedical research, and the training of health care professionals to practice in currently underserved areas. While not a panacea, it is a strong first step.

## CONCLUSION

We have the means to improve the health of Americans. As history has shown, a combination of knowledge, skill, and commitment has so improved the quality of health in our cities that it rivals or exceeds that of most cities around the world. And our innovations have provided a model for other nations to follow.

To sustain that progress we must continue to invest in our knowledge base, hone the skills of our talented professionals, and further improve available technology. Most of all, however, we need to strengthen our commitment to improving the standard of living as well as the quality of life in cities. We have the know-how; what we need is the political will and skilled leadership to move ahead.

# 11

# NEW YORK UNDERGROUND: RESCUING THE MTA

## ROBERT R. KILEY

"Underground" has long been a term rich with meaning. It conveys at once the unseen, the unsavory, the avant-garde. It implies mystery and secrecy, so it sometimes inspires fear. Since antiquity, the underground world—whether Plato's cave or the realm of Hades—has also suggested a reality more fundamental than those perceived in the light of day.

The inception, development, and near-demise of one aspect of the New York underground, its subway system, is a story that reflects our municipal and national life over the same period. It tells a great deal about who we were and what we may become.

That story, however, may be best understood by another story, of an incident that happened above ground in New York City. On December 15, 1973, a dump truck carrying a load of asphalt for use as patching material set out for the West Side Highway. There was nothing unusual about the truck or its mission, except one thing: The truck fell through the pavement of the West Side Highway and onto the street below.

General alarm at the condition of the highway precipitated a response that was both typical and symptomatic. The idea of Westway was born—an ambitious scheme, whatever one's opinion of the project itself. Few, however, were willing to face the full implications of the event: If the West Side Highway, which was built in the 1930s, was rotten to the core, maybe other pieces of public infrastructure—especially those half a century older—were in similar straits.

There was, and still is, something peculiarly American about the Westway attitude. First, when a problem becomes acute, we attack it by replacing its apparent cause with something new, preferably more complicated, and almost certainly larger. Second, we don't stop to consider the greater reality that may be demanding attention. The saga of the subway system may help explain how this came to be.

## NINETEENTH CENTURY GRIDLOCK

For cities like New York, building an underground transportation system was a course of last resort. Travel underground had not been considered practical since Roman times. But desperate conditions called for desperate measures.

By the end of the Civil War, New York had become "America's first industrial metropolis," in the words of Charles Cheape. The Port of New York was moving 75 percent of the nation's imports and exports. Half the city's population of one million lived below 14th Street in an area two miles square. Three-quarters of them lived in tenement slums. The city's population density had surpassed London's in 1850.

While cattle were still grazing on 42nd Street, the city's streets were choked with pedestrian and vehicular traffic. Omnibuses—the large, sometimes elegant, urban stagecoaches that first appeared in the 1820s—rumbled up and down some streets every thirteen seconds. The congestion was compounded in the 1850s by the advent of the horse-drawn railways. By 1860, they carried 45 million passengers in New York; and by 1870, nearly three times that number. Not surprisingly, it took an hour to get to City Hall from the 30th Street railroad terminal.

The city was being packed to its limits. It was often easier to get to New Jersey than to go downtown. In 1867 the *New York Post* called New York "the most inconveniently arranged commercial city in the world . . . [A] considerable part of the working population . . . spends a sixth of their working day on the street cars or omnibuses."

This was America's first great age of invention, and many solutions were suggested. None seemed more comprehensive and far-reaching, however, than the one being tried in London: an underground railroad. In 1864, a bill was introduced in the New York State

Legislature calling for one to be built from the Battery to Central Park. It was defeated, and the *New York Times* accused the legislature of having surrendered to "the omnibus proprietors, railroad corporations and political jobbers."

## THE AGE OF VENALITY

The nineteenth century was not only the age of invention, it was also the age of venality. "The paths to fortune are innumerable and all open," Mark Twain commented wryly in his novel *The Gilded Age*. Private interests blocked progress on the subway for years, with the help of their ally, William Marcy Tweed.

One of the few men with the vision, courage, and power to oppose Tweed and serve the broader needs of the city was Alfred Ely Beach, the wealthy editor of *Scientific American* and co-publisher of the *New York Sun*. Beach was also an inventor who exemplified the clear-sighted practicality we like to regard as the American birthright. As early as 1849, Beach had imagined an underground railway running the length of Broadway.

By the late 1860s, Beach was aware that London's underground steam engines had been proven to cause illness and death. He decided that pneumatic power was the proper choice for subway locomotion in New York, and he wanted to build a prototype. But with Boss Tweed in control, he could not do so openly. So Beach pulled off a bit of legislative legerdemain. He obtained permission from the legislature to construct a pneumatic system to deliver mail in lower Manhattan. Later, he had the bill amended to allow for construction of a tube large enough to carry a passenger rail car.

Remarkable as this was, it pales beside what Beach did next. In complete secrecy, he built a 312-foot tunnel under Broadway, between Warren and Murray streets, installed a fan weighing fifty tons, and put in place a subway car that had seats for twenty-two people. To dispel passengers' fears of being underground, Beach tried to make the experience as enticing as possible. For the waiting room, he built a luxurious salon with frescoes, a piano, and even a fountain filled with goldfish.

Beach opened his subway to the public in 1870. It was an immediate success and helped create support for his proposal to build a line all the way to Central Park. Tweed's faction responded by proposing an elevated train—or "Viaduct Railway." Both proposals passed the legislature, but Beach's was vetoed by the governor, a Tweed crony. By the time Beach's bill finally passed, the country had been hit by the Financial Panic of 1873. No money was available for the subway, and the plan died.

Meanwhile, traffic congestion worsened, and pressure for action intensified. But the comprehensive solution was still avoided; the larger reality ignored. Public pressure was channeled into building more of what already existed: elevated trains. For the last three decades of the nineteenth century, the transit needs of the many and the greedy desires of the few were met by elevated railways. Government action, including creation of the first Rapid Transit Commission in 1875, furthered private interests.

Jay Gould, who received no small credit for starting the Panic of 1873, soon took over management, and then ownership, of the city's elevated systems. "Gould, who began his career in New York as a boy with the invention of the mousetrap, now snapped it shut on the whole town," Benson Bobrick writes in his immensely informative book, *Labyrinths of Iron*. The avenues of New York became tunnels, hidden from the light but exposed to showers of grease, cinders, and noise. "The els helped transform the city into a larger version of its old self," Bobrick notes, "and were soon overcrowded in their own right."

As early as 1886, the Times was saying, "It may be taken as a settled fact that the problem of rapid transit for this city has not been solved by the elevated railroads and that these structures cannot be permitted to remain permanently in the streets." In 1891 a new Rapid Transit Commission was formed. At the time, more than 1.5 million people were living in New York City—over 80 percent of them in slums. In the 1880s, ridership on an unchanging length— 32.5 miles—of elevated lines had more than tripled. The solution was at hand. Or was it?

Merchants and manufacturers joined with the press in calling for a subway system to be built close to the surface, with a four-track roadbed, and to be powered by electricity, as London's Underground was. But the commission required a $3 million security bond and a five-year deadline for completion. Two years passed. Not a single bidder appeared.

By 1894, when the Rapid Transit Commission was reconstituted, the surface and elevated railroads in New York were carrying one billion passenger annually—more than all the rest of the steam railroads in the hemisphere. At last, the New York City subway system came into existence through sheer force of need and the combined genius of Abram Hewitt and William Barclay Parsons.

## BIRTH OF THE SUBWAY

Because the city didn't have the funds to build a subway system outright, financing had always been an obstacle to construction. Abram Hewitt devised what was at the time a highly innovative approach, which today would be called an industrial development revenue bond, and which met its demise in the 1986 tax reform act.

The city would put the entire project out for bid, then lend the winning contractor the bid amount by floating bonds. The contractor would be obligated to pay interest on the bonds, to put a certain amount each year toward the principal, and to provide all the subway's rolling stock, power stations, and so forth, as collateral on the loan. When the lease expired, the city could buy back the entire operation at a price set by arbitration, if the contractor did not wish to renew. New York stood to gain immediate construction of a subway at minimal cost to taxpayers, while the contractor could finance and make a profit from his work using a low-interest municipal loan.

The Rapid Transit Commission's Chief Engineer, William Barclay Parsons, was as creative and persistent as Hewitt. He did not make his recommendations for New York until he had surveyed the major European transit systems. Among other things he noted that little effort had been made to grace London's underground stations with "a pleasing appearance," as Parsons termed it. "Underground railways have always been associated in the public mind with dark, damp, dank, smoke-laden tunnels—veritable approaches to the lower regions," Parsons wrote. He determined that New York's would be otherwise.

The Interborough Rapid Transit company, builder and operator of the city's first subway, budgeted more than $500,000 so that the IRT stations would be properly decorated with polychromatic terra cotta designs and neo-classical mosaics as station markers, all handsome architectural complements to the prodigious engineering feat of the subway itself.

It was not just stations that were built to a standard of excellence. Its four-track system, offering a local and an express in each direction, set an engineering standard that few of the world's transit systems enjoy even today. Arched-roof tunnel work was abandoned in favor of a rectangular beam construction, which allowed excavation nearer the surface and the widespread entrance of daylight.

The original IRT lines ran up Manhattan's East Side from City Hall to 42nd Street, across 42nd to Broadway, and then up Broadway to 145th Street. The distance they covered—just over nine miles— was more than three times the length of America's first subway system, built in Boston for trolley cars in 1897.

The subway's importance to the city was not lost on New Yorkers of the time. The day the IRT opened for business, October 28, 1904, John Philip Sousa played to a crowd of 25,000 assembled at City Hall. The mayor used a silver spade made by Tiffany's with as wooden handle taken from one of the thirteen trees planted in Washington

Heights by Alexander Hamilton. In the harbor, steam whistles, sirens, and fog bells sounded throughout the day. New York truly had something to celebrate. A fast, clean, relatively energy-efficient means of mobility had been given to a city long stuck in the congestion and chaos its turbulent development had crested. And the linear path of that mobility would extend, define, and in fact confer order on the development that quickly followed in its wake.

The IRT may not have been a perfect solution, but it was certainly a comprehensive, rational one, appropriate to the current and anticipated needs of the time. It was the best that nineteenth century technology and vision could offer, and it only confirmed the burgeoning American sense that the country could solve any problem and meet any challenge.

Chief Engineer Parsons wasn't so sanguine, however. "For New York," he said, "there is no such thing as a solution to the Rapid Transit problem. . . . The instant that this line is finished there will arise a demand for other lines." Four years later Parsons' assessment was even gloomier: "We know only that the great cities of ancient times—Babylon, Carthage, Athens, Rome—grew to the point of decay."

The rest of the IRT lines were soon completed, many of them within weeks of the first section's opening. But, as Parsons had predicted, crowding was a problem literally from the first day. By 1907, the City Club of New York published a list of ways to alleviate it and with others clamored for action. The IRT company installed center doors in the subway cars, lengthened the trains, and made shorter station stops.

It will surprise no one that New Yorkers did not long squander their gratitude for the first IRT lines on the Board of Rapid Transit Commissioners. Instead, the commissioners were assailed, James Blaine Walker tells us, "not because they had not done well with the first subway, but because it was such a great success that they had not multiplied it fast enough. [The board] was denounced by the press which clamored for its abolition." And, in 1907, that is exactly what happened. A new state entity, the Public Service Commission (PSC), took charge.

## PRESERVING THE NICKEL FARE

In 1913, the PSC, the IRT, and the Brooklyn Rapid Transit (BRT) company agreed to more subway construction. They promised to double system track mileage within five years. Despite success in meeting a large portion of this goal, antipathy toward the operators only increased. During a strike in 1918, a Brighton Beach train operated by an inexperienced motorman derailed at Malbone Street in Brooklyn, killing more than a hundred people. Within two months, the BRT declared bankruptcy.

Mayor John Hylan, who took office that same year, prolonged his political career by stoking the flames of public dissatisfaction and by campaigning relentlessly for preserving the nickel fare. Even at that price people didn't think they were getting much. As the City Club said, "We do not get a civilized ride for a nickel today. . . . The trains are like cattle cars."

At a time when it was virtually unthinkable for government to build, own, and operate a transportation system, New York City entered the subway business. Construction of what would be called the Independent line—named for its independence of private interests— was begun in 1925, the last year of Hylan's mayoralty. The IND was completed in 1940. It was, said the Times, "Father Knickerbocker's latest and most gigantic effort to improve his sluggish circulation."

In the 1920s, needless to say, the federal government was not involved in construction of most kinds of public infrastructure. In the recession year of 1921, President Harding opened a Conference on Unemployment (which he had convened at the urging of Herbert Hoover) by saying that federal government spending on public works would only increase the trouble.

The president of the American Construction Council, a fellow named Franklin Roosevelt, pressed for the use of construction work to help "eliminate the peaks of inflation, and the resulting equally harmful valleys of extreme depression." Herbert Hoover did not entirely disagree. But no one came to the rescue of New York's rapid transit. The IRT declared bankruptcy in 1932.

The nickel fare, which had been the standard tariff on New York's elevated and underground lines since 1886, remained in effect until 1948. While new subway cars were sometimes purchased during those years, it is safe to say that capital investment to renew basic infrastructure was simply not made.

With completion of the IND in 1940, the city took over operation of the entire subway system. Indeed, one could look at public transportation as a case of failed privatization, of failed franchised monopolies. Public transportation had been heavily subsidized almost from the beginning, but once the government stepped in, the need for subsidies increased. By the 1950s, state and local government took over, but without really being ready. For one thing, the government wasn't prepared to provide more money. At the same time, government takeover signaled that unionization could begin in earnest, which it did as a sort of precursor to municipal unionization. From then on, some have argued, the problems of moving people in New York only worsened, and the potential for catastrophe only increased.

In 1949, the last year of the nickel fare, ridership topped two billion. The fare went up to a dime in 1948, and ridership fell by a quarter billion in 1949. The fare went to 15 cents in 1953, and ridership fell by another 135 million. By 1977, when the fare was 50 cents, ridership dropped below one billion for the first time since 1917.

Contrary to popular myth, though, fare hikes were not entirely, or even primarily, responsible for the post-war drops in ridership. Indeed, they may have masked more serious problems and trends. Thanks to the Herculean, some would say diabolic, efforts of Robert Moses, automobiles in the region were encouraged to proliferate. And the service offered by public transportation of all kinds was in distinct decline.

## HIGH COST OF LOW FARES

The harbingers of disaster were there to be read in 1973, when the dump truck fell through the West Side Highway. For nearly a decade, subway reliability was declining precipitately, at least as measured by the average number of miles a train could travel without breaking down. Liberalized pension laws covering the New York City Transit Authority since the late 1960s had been depleting the ranks of highly skilled and committed personnel. And the system was getting older.

To have kept up with the basic physical needs of the subway plant during the 1960s and 1970s would have required approximately a $1 billion a year in today's money. Yet during the whole of that period, maybe 30 percent of what should have been spent was spent— $300 million in a very good year. And much of that investment was spent on entirely new subway lines.

And why not new subway lines? After all, in this city and nation we had long been accustomed to solving our transportation and many other problems by trying something new. The MTA's earliest capital improvement plan, covering the years 1968 to 1973, eventually listed ten such projects, including the Second Avenue subway, the Queens Boulevard Bypass via the 63rd Street Tunnel, and various other extensions and relocations.

The core projects were then and remain today of great merit. But all of them—as work on the Second Avenue line soon proved—were exorbitantly expensive even to start. The funds to finish them were far from secure. So the decision was made to put separate, distantly spaced holes in the ground—as was done on Second Avenue and at

63rd Street—on the theory that the mere fact of their existence would create an irresistible momentum toward garnering the necessary funds.

Meanwhile, in the 1970s the federal government had begun a national program to (1) invest in new systems—Los Angeles, Atlanta, Washington, D.C., and (2) renovate old systems—Boston, Philadelphia, Chicago. New York lost out initially because it was still building its system—the Third Avenue and Second Avenue subways were being taken seriously in the capital budget—and then because when it hit its fiscal crisis, it shifted every dollar it could into closing the huge budget gap. (A financial trick known locally as Beame Shuffle, after then-Mayor Abraham Beame, diverted capital money into expense budget.) Thus New York's subway system continued to deteriorate as other systems were being fixed.

So the only momentum that really proved irresistible was that of abuse and neglect of the existing system. By 1980, the New York newspapers were reporting on any given day that one-third of the subway fleet was out of service during the morning rush hour. The collapse of public transportation, never foreseen and only grudgingly admitted even as it unfolded, could no longer be ignored.

## Reversing Decades of Neglect

But a new problem was emerging on the American landscape, and the quicker, more dramatic solutions of the past would not apply. Once the downward spiral of disrepair has advanced in any major piece of infrastructure, a huge amount of money and enormously complicated, persistent efforts are required to reverse the trend. This is especially true of a public service like transit, which is capital- and labor-intensive. Richard Ravitch, MTA chairman from 1970 to 1983, became one of the most important people in the system's history when he devised the financial means and then marshalled the political will to deal with New York's transit problem. The MTA's first five-year, $8-billion capital program, which began in 1982, is his legacy. At the time of its creation, there was nothing like it anywhere else.

By late 1983, however, the effect of this huge amount of money was yet to be felt. In fact, things seemed to be getting worse. Serious subway fires were epidemic. Trains were derailing on average every eighteen days. Red-tag orders on the track cut speeds by 75 percent at more than 400 places around the system. Graffiti had covered the entire subway fleet for half a generation. Decades of neglect had robbed the subway system of more than capital plant. They had drained the organization of hope and motivation and the management structure of sufficient size and authority.

When I arrived in 1984, the Transit Authority had 50,000 workers, but only 300 managers accountable to its president. The track department had 5,000 employees, but only eleven accountable managers. Every foot of rail in the system's 700 miles of track should have been inspected at least twice a week. (That's been the railroad standard for years.) But less than a quarter of the system was receiving twice-weekly inspections.

The Coney Island shop—the largest rapid-transit heavy-repair shop in the hemisphere—runs three shifts a day, seven days a week, fifty-two weeks a year. In 1984, some 1,100 people worked there—under one accountable manager. Employees were repairing their own automobiles on the job, sleeping on couches they had moved into the facility. It's no wonder the TA took twice as long as outside vendors to overhaul a subway car—badly.

Was this happening because government in general and the Transit Authority in particular attract only lazy, nefarious people? No, it was happening because the employees had long ago lost the tools they needed to do their jobs. Because regular maintenance had been abandoned for decades. Because there was time only to do emergency repairs. It was happening because accountable supervision had long before disappeared, and accountable supervision is the only way a large organization can set objectives, measure results, and meet goals.

In February 1984, MTA president David Gunn and I initiated a management reform plan that created more than 1,200 real management positions. We proposed removing existing jobs from the strictures of civil service and collective bargaining and making them directly accountable up the chain of command to the president of the TA. With the support of the mayor and the governor, our plan was put into full effect in August 1984.

The Coney Island shop, for example, was assigned twenty-five managers, and started producing first-rate full-scale car overhauls as good as any done by private vendors. This kind of reorganization occurred in every department of the Transit Authority. In the track department, which had only eleven accountable managers, was assigned 177 line managers. Every inch of track in the system is now examined twice a week, week after week, month after month.

## THE SYSTEM TODAY

There is no doubt that the combination of management control and sufficient investment brought results. In 1983, the IRT lines (the oldest and once the grandest) had the worst cars and track, the lowest reliability, and the most graffiti-scarred fleet. Capital investment was put to work first on these lines. By the end of 1987, the IRT's track was in sound condition, and nearly 85 percent of the its cars were new or rebuilt. Speeds were increased, waiting periods between trains shortened, and trip times reduced. In 1987, the IRT fleet ran more than four times better than it had five years before.

In fact, the subway fleet as a whole ran four times as reliably in 1990 as it had in 1982. By December 1990 the entire fleet's average number of miles traveled between breakdowns was at its highest level (33,000) since 1950. By mid-1988, the entire subway fleet was graffiti-free.

New Yorkers responded. Average weekday ridership on the IRT rose 4.2 percent in 1986 and 6.5 percent through the first eleven months of 1987. This helped boost average weekday ridership systemwide by 3.2 percent through the first eleven months of 1987. That was exactly double the pace of 1986. By 1994, ridership was up 8.5 percent over 1984 to 1.08 billion people—the highest level of average weekday ridership since 1974.

During the 1980s, while we struggled to restore reliable, safe service to a system that had been running out of control, our station modernization program was moving at glacial speed. At the rate we were going, it would have taken 104 years and $1.5 billion (in 1986 dollars) to finish. Although patience is a virtue we have long asked of our customers, we thought a century was a bit much.

We devised a multi-faceted approach that should show results much sooner, but not nearly so soon as we and the people of New York would like. The TA's track and cars reached a state of good repair by 1992, but its station lighting and mainline switches, for example, won't get there until around the year 2006. Station rehabilitations, tunnel repairs, and signal cable and equipment won't be completed until after that. And the price tag for all this work? About the same $1.5 billion we spend every year.

## The Work Ahead

The magnitude of the work that lies ahead gives one pause. We must now deal with the consequences of permitting great public works to fall apart. Only in the last few years has the nation begun—just begun—to deal with the calamity its infrastructure policy has been inviting for decades. In 1984, the National Council on Public Works Improvement was created, partly in response to the Mianus River Bridge collapse in 1983. But calamitous episodes are not and should not be the only spur to action.

Ten years ago, the Federal Reserve Bank of Chicago pointed out that in the twenty-year period between 1964 and 1984, investment by government in public infrastructure—roads, bridges, mass transit, water and sewer systems—fell by 82 percent. It fell from a high of 2.4 percent of gross national product in 1966 to 0.3 percent in 1982.

At the same time, the Chicago Fed demonstrated a correlation between public investment of this kind and private-sector economic growth. While a surge of public investment seems at first to depress private investment, sustained expenditures on public works over time stimulate profit and encourage investment in new plant and equipment. Statistical evidence now supports Adam Smith's contention in the Wealth of Nations that the "final duty" of the state, that of erecting and maintaining public works, does indeed facilitate the commerce of society.

It is a duty that the federal government—since Thomas Jefferson's administration built the Cumberland Road—has most willingly performed in the area of highways. To date, for example, the Federal Government has contributed nearly $140 billion for completion of the Interstate Highway System. But its willingness to devote large sums to maintaining the interstate system—let alone the rest of our trillion-dollar stock of public works—is far more doubtful. The Joint Economic Committee of the Congress has said that by the year 2000 it would cost another trillion dollars to fix America's public infrastructure. Others set the price tag at twice that amount.

Yet our debt-financed economy is relentlessly losing the capacity to address such huge needs. Former Secretary of Commerce Peter Peterson has noted that in the 1970s, productivity increased annually only about one-quarter as quickly as it had in the 1950s and 1960s. In the 1980s it fell more. Before the 1970s, we always consumed less than our annual increase in production. Since the early 1980s, we have consumed 325 percent of that increase. And the difference has been made up by borrowing from foreigners. Unless we change our ways, Peterson, and others, see us slipping into parity with Britain as a second- or third-class world economic power. The chief difference is that Britain's decline took seventy-five years. Ours is happening three times as fast.

Clearly, reversing these ominous trends will take patient and persistent action. We have to rectify our attitude and our fiscal priorities on public infrastructure, we have to face this problem in all its dimensions, and we have to deal with it quickly. We can no longer permit bridge inspections by binoculars, as had been done with the Mianus Bridge. We can no longer accept the kind of haphazard maintenance that led to the near-collapse of the subway system. (When the Brooklyn Bridge opened in 1883 it had 200 full-time maintenance workers; in 1994, it has fewer than five.

We can no longer take for granted magnificent public highways, bridges, dams, and monuments. We cannot simply use and ignore them until they fall apart. Most important, we cannot permit the attitudes and assumptions that allowed all this to happen to simply go on unexamined and unchecked.

Was Aristotle right about us human beings when he wrote: "For that which is common to the greatest number has the least care bestowed upon it. Every one thinks chiefly of his own, hardly at all of the common interest; (and only when he is himself concerned as an individual.")

Yet I cannot believe that we are so lacking in imagination and foresight that this must be so. I cannot believe that we must wait for ourselves and our own families to be engulfed by the rising flood before we act. I believe that what we are now doing to resuscitate and restore New York's underground railroad shows what can be accomplished for the good of all people when sufficient resources and will are applied to the essential public works that sustain and enhance life for us all.

# 12

# THE FUTURE OF PUBLIC EDUCATION

## JOSEPH A. FERNANDEZ

N owhere does the national resolve to strengthen education face
a tougher test than in inner cities, perhaps most dauntingly in
New York, but also including Detroit, Chicago, Los Angeles,
and Miami, among others. Of the nation's 15,000 school districts, the
fifty largest enroll about 14 percent of the country's disabled children,
25 percent of its poor children, 38 percent of its children with limited
proficiency in English, and 40 percent of its African-, Latino-, and
Asian-American children.

Every problem that could possibly affect school children is more
pronounced in the great cities, and every solution harder to implement.
The litany is familiar: poverty, drug abuse, family instability, dysfunctional communities, overcrowding, aging buildings and facilities,
teen pregnancy, poor health care, violence, racism and bigotry, AIDS,
malnutrition. Although these problems are limitless, the resources are
severely limited. While the average large-city school system spent
about $5,200 per student in 1990–91, the average suburban school
system spent $6,073. That disparity between urban and suburban
schools amounts to a difference of nearly $22,000 annually for a

class of twenty-five children. This disparity in funding between rich and poor schools is a national disgrace. What makes this situation even worse is that efforts to address these problems must be conducted in an atmosphere of enormous complexity and diversity—political, demographic, economic, cultural, social, and religious. And school officials usually must tackle these complex problems with very little political backing.

In 1990, at the urging of Bob Wagner, I went to New York as chancellor of the city's school system in the hope of shaping public education to meet the changing needs of children and promoting public education as a force for social change. New York's school system is huge: if it were a private entity, the New York City school system would be the twelfth-largest corporation in the country. Its operating budget is over $7 billion, larger than twenty-six state budgets; its capital budget nearly $5 billion; and it employs over 125,000 people. It oversees more than a thousand schools and just under a million students.

The problems I encountered from the start were enormous. Half the students did not read at grade level; 60 percent of the high school students failed at least one subject every semester; more than 25 percent of high schoolers took five years to graduate; 10 percent spoke little or no English.

## SOCIAL PROBLEMS

New York City's predicament is more understandable given that educational problems have always gone hand in hand with social problems. Six out of ten New York City schoolchildren are from one-parent homes. An estimated 80 percent of the city's teenagers are sexually active. Of the country's reported cases of full-blown AIDS among adolescents, about 10 percent live in New York City. During my first year as chancellor, some 3,000 babies who had been born addicted to crack were among our 60,000 kindergartners.

New York (and other large city school systems) grapples with problems that seem relentless—even though solutions to these problems are fairly well known. Even when people know what to do, however, they can't necessarily do it. For example, despite the national consensus on the importance of preparing children to start school, such programs are rare. What's more, young children live in such precarious situations in this country that, for many of them, participation in preschool would be a tremendous struggle—even if it were available. Statistics on babies, infants, and preschool children show them to be frighteningly vulnerable:

▼ Some 15–20 percent of all babies in the country are born exposed to illegal drugs.

▼ Some 7 percent of all babies and 13 percent of African-American babies have low birth weights.

▼ Some 20 percent of all prekindergarten students are not vaccinated against polio.

▼ Only 33 percent of eligible children receive Head Start services.

▼ Some 25 percent of pregnant women receive no prenatal care during the first trimester.

Yet urban schools may be doing better than other American schools in developing solutions in preschool education. Some 58 percent of urban school districts now assess the school readiness of children using a combination of measures of cognitive development, immunizations, health, social development, weight, and age. The bad news, though, is that some 20 percent of urban districts still use only a birth certificate to assess readiness for school.

Few efforts would provide a greater payoff than coordinating social, family, and health activities with those of other public and private agencies and groups throughout the cities. Here, New York is a model for the nation. Intermediate School 218 (IS 218) in Washington Heights is a cooperative venture with the Children's Aid Society. Open fifteen hours a day, six days a week, fifty-two weeks a year, for use by parents and neighbors as well as by its 1,100 students, IS 218 is a community school that functions as the hub of the neighborhood. In addition to providing education to children, IS 218 keeps its doors open so that adults can come for study, medical or dental treatment, drug counseling, or cultural and entertainment events.

## DROPOUTS

One problem that is particularly troublesome for urban schools is the high number of dropouts: 31 percent of students entering big city public high schools in 1986 failed to graduate in 1990. Most of these dropouts are Latino and black, and while the gap in the dropout rate between African-American students and whites is narrowing, the gap between whites and Latino students remains wide. (The Latino dropout rate is in the neighborhood of 10–15 percent annually.)

With more than one million teen pregnancies a year nationally in large urban school systems, pregnancy still leads the list of reasons girls dropout.

Yet school administrators have clearly learned over the years to tailor programs better to the many reasons why youngsters drop out of school. Across the country, city schools must be doing something right, as these figures demonstrate.

▼   The median annual dropout rate in urban high schools fell from 10.6 percent in 1988–89 to 8.8 percent in 1990–91.

▼   The median four-year dropout rate in urban high schools declined from 32.1 percent in 1988–89 to 26.1 percent in 1990–91.

The bad news is that dropout rates in urban school districts are still about twice as high as the national average.

## ACHIEVEMENT

Another troubling area is the low level of achievement of students in our schools. The national figures concerning achievement are now driving much of the current debate on standards and assessments:

▼   The United States ranks roughly twelfth of fourteen on international tests of math and science knowledge.

▼   Some 58 percent of thirteen-year-old American public school students display only moderate reading ability.

▼   Only 18 percent of American eighth graders in public schools meet new national standards in mathematics.

Urban schools are making some progress:

▼   About 67 percent of urban school districts showed increasing achievement test scores in reading and math between 1988–89 and 1990–91 at the elementary grade levels; about half increased their scores in the secondary grades.

▼   The average urban student scored at about the fiftieth percentile in math in 1990–91, although lower in reading.

▼    Urban public school students were completing advanced place-
     ment or international baccalaureate courses in literature, math,
     and science at about twice the national average.

These are promising indicators, but the bad news continues to outstrip
the good. Only one-third of urban students have completed a first-year
course in algebra by the end of their tenth grade. The achievement of
African-American and Latino students is far too low: Only 10 percent
score in the top quartile in math by the tenth grade, though 25 percent
had scored in the top quartile in second grade. While urban systems
enroll 32 percent of the nation's Latino youth, they produce fewer
than 1,000 Latino students each year who score in the top quartile in
math.

The new standards development process may help in this regard,
but urban educators must make more headway with more cooperative
learning models, less tracking, fewer courses in remedial skills, and
more intensive instructional approaches.

## TEACHERS

The United States has some of the most dedicated and talented
teachers in the world, but a large proportion of the nation's teachers
are expected to retire in the next ten years. What's worse, the shortage
of teachers in urban areas is already about 2.5 times higher than the
national average. Urban schools, by and large, reflect national trends
in this area, although there are positive indicators as well. One bright
spot is that urban teachers are likely to be more experienced than
the average teacher.

Today, however, urban school systems are unable to pay teachers
much more than the national average, thereby cutting their ability to
attract individuals willing to work in the most difficult schools. Nor can
they attract enough teachers who mirror the ethnic and racial makeup
of the student population. In fact, the demographics of urban teachers
are almost the exact opposite of urban students. Why? Primarily
because fewer African-Americans, Latinos, and Asians are pursuing
careers in teaching.

The ability to correct these trends will rest largely on the nation's
willingness to spend more on professional development, to improve
working conditions in inner-city schools, and to reach out aggressively
to African-, Latino-, and Asian-American communities to encourage
more individuals to pursue teaching as a career.

## Illiteracy and Crime

With regard to post-secondary opportunities, the nation is paying the price now for years of underinvestment in education and literacy. Some 27 million Americans are judged to be illiterate.

▼   The average youth unemployment rate is about 15–20 percent, yet it is about 30 percent in the inner cities.

▼   About 75 percent of all new jobs between now and the year 2000 will be in the suburbs.

Finally, there are the challenges of safety, drug-abuse, and facilities. These are areas where schools nationally are facing serious problems, but where the public has a difficult time investing resources to correct the problems. The national statistics are troubling:

▼   Each day, an estimated 16,000 crimes occur on or near school property.

▼   Some 100,000 students bring weapons to school each day.

▼   Drug abuse among teens continues to be high.

▼   Some $50–$100 billion in capital is needed across the nation for school facilities.

What should we be doing to save the schools? My hunch is that we as a nation are doing better with public schools than most people realize or than most critics suggest. But even if the critics are entirely wrong—and they're not—there is no reason to think that schools shouldn't be substantially improved. Some good ideas would actually cost surprisingly little money.

First, schools not only need to be more open to educational re-form, but actually need to lead it. They should be leading the parade, not marching in the back of the procession. In fact, much of the reform movement that has now been somewhat co-opted by the states grew out of initiatives and experiments in schools. Yet, education is often viewed as entrenched, immovable, self-protective, and sluggish due to bureaucracy. In too many instances this is the case, but the reformers within education can easily serve as models to the rest. It is, in fact, good to reform, and it is better yet for schools to reform themselves—schools are in the best position to do that. That is what School-Based Management is all about. For example, with their new freedom, Miami schools changed textbooks, created smaller classes, and eliminated redundant jobs to divert the funds to more crucial areas. Some created schools within schools, where teachers would advance along with their students from ninth grade through twelfth; others set up night schools for students who worked. One key is to make sure School-Based Management comes along with a school-based budget and that every idea is tested and measured by student progress. That must always be the bottom line: How will children be better served by these changes?

Second, educators are trained in ideas, and ideas should be their strength. I think that every idea, however extreme at first glance, however outlandish, should be considered. Many radical ideas get stopped before they ever have a chance to be tested. Take, for example, the idea of all-male academies for inner-city black students. This is an emergency measure that should be explored further. Such an academy, offering a disciplined, integrated curriculum aimed at raising self-esteem while providing a disciplined environment geared to young males and free of sexual distraction, could indeed save many youngsters now dropping out of school.

I recommend this strategy even though I am opposed to school segregation. Why? Because otherwise, thousands of hostile, tuned-out young men, now prey to every evil influence inflicted by poverty, will simply be lost to society. You can't make the school mandatory, but that's fine. At least offer it. Many will take it. In fact, many did take it when it was offered in Dade County.

Many urban systems could benefit if such programs were tried. For example, over 90 percent of Detroit's public school students are black; over half of black males entering the system fail to graduate. As "a last desperate measure," according to proponents, Detroit put together a plan for an all-boys model in 1991: three all-male, all-black academies, starting in elementary school. The American Civil Liberties Union joined with the National Organization for Women to sue the school board, charging discrimination against female students. A U.S. district court judge ruled that the academies were "unnecessary and unconstitutional." U.S. Secretary of Education Lamar Alexander delivered the final blow, saying Detroit would have to find ways to help black males without "segregating them in violation of federal law." Although the parents of 1,200 children signed for the 536 available slots, the

Detroit Board of Education backed off from appealing the order and dropped the plan, saying it could not justify a costly court battle over an issue it had "little chance of winning."

Third, try the outlandish ideas, but also do the obvious: take back the schools physically, make them inviting and pleasant, clean them up, landscape the grounds, give students a chance to take pride in their school and campus. And when you've made the schools inviting, invite the community in. Schools need to increase their collaborative arrangements with the community at large. I said earlier that the closer collaboration with other public and community agencies was necessary to deliver comprehensive services to children. It also means keeping facilities open to the community and designing our programs around the schedules and needs of the community—not our own.

Fourth, schools need to stop treating parents as the enemy. Urban education has amazingly few friends. Not only can it not afford to alienate anyone, but it must develop better strategies to reach out to parents—on whatever terms or grounds they find themselves. Parents should be treated not only as the schools number one customer, but as their number one ally. And it is here that we must understand the many different communities that school administrators must interact with, particularly those that have limited proficiency in English. Educators must be inclusive and not exclusive.

Fifth, school leaders need to stop chewing themselves up on political agendas. I am not sure how this can be done, but there are many examples in every city where the fractured and desperate nature of the community is leading educational leadership into gridlock.

Sixth, schools need to do everything they can to stop sorting and tracking kids, while raising standards and expectations for students. Too often tracking results in differentiation only by race, sex, and rather than the abilities or efforts of students. Educators must believe that all children can learn, and practice that belief.

Seventh, we need to return our schools to a human scale. New York, for example, began to put in place a process that has lead to a series of smaller high schools. It is important to reduce the size of urban schools, even if this means only developing schools-within-schools. Children need warmth and individual attention to thrive, and it is too hard to give it to them with schools the size of factories.

There are also things that the states and the federal government could do to help, particularly regarding increasing the resources of urban school systems. While I don't think money cures all, I am a firm believer that money matters in school as it does everywhere else. I saw it every day in my work—from the time I was a high school math teacher in Miami through my time as chancellor of the New York City public schools. Part of that belief rests on the fact that urban schools just don't have the resources of other school systems.

Urban schools form one of the crucibles of American democracy. They are one of the last frontiers of democratic ideal. The nation cannot afford to survey the urban landscape, with its difficult terrain, and conclude that conquering our troubles is a lost cause.

# 13

# LIFEBLOOD OF THE CITY: THE ARTS IN NEW YORK

*NATHAN LEVENTHAL*

T he arts are consumed by and consume New Yorkers. No other city has New York's volume and diversity of art, along with perhaps the best-informed and most sophisticated audiences on the globe.

But the arts do not merely feed New Yorkers' souls. They also feed its economy. A number of recent studies have quantified what we all knew: The arts are big business—$9.8 billion annually, according to the Port Authority of New York and New Jersey, which estimated the total economic impact of the arts on the New York metropolitan region in 1992. Louis Harris and Associates found, in a 1991 survey, that the arts were a key reason for people moving to New York: 56 percent of recent "in-migrants" cited New York's active cultural life as an important attraction.

The New York Urban Center has argued persuasively that, with New York's days as a manufacturing center long gone, the city's real strength is its intellectual capital. The center's report further claims that a lively arts scene is critical to attracting the best and brightest minds. New York corporations have long recognized the importance of a healthy arts sector to their own success. Companies like Philip

Morris, Citibank, Chase Manhattan, NYNEX, Consolidated Edison, and others have given millions to support the arts and have set the standard for companies around the country.

The case of Lincoln Center, which Bob Wagner always referred to as one of the most successful redevelopment projects in city history, is instructive. Before construction began in 1959, the upper west side of Manhattan was an impoverished area. In 1954, the Committee for Slum Clearance, under the chairmanship of Robert Moses and Mayor Robert F. Wagner, designated a seventeen-block area between West 62nd and West 70th Streets as a candidate for revitalization. In 1955, both the Metropolitan Opera Association and the New York Philharmonic-Symphony Society decided, for a variety of reasons, to relocate to this site. The concept of a performing arts center was born.

It would be not be an understatement to say that Lincoln Center transformed the upper west side. By 1984, the impact of the performing arts complex was not just artistic, but economic. That year, on the occasion of the twenty-fifth anniversary of the center's ground-breaking, a study by former Deputy Mayor Karen Gerard measured the center's economic impact. The direct impact of the various organizations that comprised Lincoln Center was enormous, totalling nearly $175 million (in 1984 dollars).

More important, the study documented a significant "multiplier" effect, as wage earners and patrons alike spent dollars throughout the local economy. In particular, tourists spent an estimated $42 million over and above the price of their tickets on food, hotels, transportation, and so forth; these dollars are the economic equivalent of exports, bringing new money into the city that would not otherwise arrive here. In total, Lincoln Center generated more than $500 million annually for the city in 1984, a sum which has only grown since then as performance activity continues to expand.

Gerard also discovered that while the population of Manhattan had declined by about 16 percent between 1959 and 1984, the population of the Lincoln Center area had held firm—and the number of households had actually increased by 14 percent. Real estate values in the area skyrocketed in the wake of Lincoln Center. Assessed property values increased 223 percent (to $1.2 billion), a rate of increase 77 percent higher than the city in general. New or fully renovated properties valued at more than $500 million were an important component of this total.

The Gerard report also calculated a ratio of population to employees, an important measure of economic activity. In the Lincoln Center area, the population-employee ratio was 1.8 to 1, compared to an overall density in the city of 2.5 to 1. This finding means, in effect, that there are 10,000 "extra" employees in the Lincoln Center area, most of whom owe their livelihood to the cultural complex. About 20 percent of all employees in the area worked for corporations and non-profits that were either newly formed or had moved here since Lincoln Center was built, and about 5 percent of employees work for businesses that directly serve visitors to the complex.

In 1984, these factors combined to generate more than $250 million in sales, personal, property, and income taxes, a figure that far outweighed the city's initial and ongoing investments in Lincoln Center. Taking all of these factors into account—direct spending by Lincoln Center-based organizations, patron and visitor expenditures, real estate improvements, related business activity, and taxes generated—the overall economic impact of Lincoln Center was, and continues to be, in excess of $1 billion annually.

Of course, economic arguments barely begin to estimate the impact that Lincoln Center, and all the other performing and visual arts entities, have on the life of the city. It helps make it a magnet for those who are enticed by culture and those who want to be a part of the world of the arts. It adds glamor, excitement, and a spirit of joy and creativity. It makes the city something far more splendid and far more a representative of what is best about America. That that kind of commitment is even possible certainly says something about the city.

# 14

# THE CONTINUITY OF PURPOSE

## STANLEY BREZENOFF AND ROGER COHEN

The American political system has no use for royalty. The nation's founders so detested the idea that they wrote a constitutional prohibition on granting titles of nobility. American political culture, on the other hand, has embraced dynastic politics since the earliest days of the Republic. The Adamses, Harrisons, Tafts, Stevensons, Roosevelts, Longs, Rockefellers, and Kennedys are only the most familiar in a long line of families who, generation after generation, have devoted themselves to public affairs.

In New York City, the first family of public service may well be the Wagners. The careers of three generations of Robert Ferdinand Wagners—a senator, a mayor, and a renaissance man of urban affairs—parallel much of the course of progressive government in New York. Their careers stretch across not quite one hundred momentous years—a period when New York City virtually embodied America's ascendancy to the front-rank of leadership of the modern world—a period that might legitimately be called "the New York Century."

In an institution like the Port Authority of New York and New Jersey, whose history has coincided with and contributed to New York's ascendancy, the Wagner family legacy resonates powerfully. Each generation of the family has affected the agency in a different way. But one element common to each man has been the idea of long-term continuity of purpose.

It was the second member of the Wagner dynasty, New York's three-term mayor, whose association with the Port Authority was the deepest. Known affectionately around World Trade Center offices simply as "the Mayor," he served as the Port Authority's vice chairman for fourteen years until his death in 1991.

From a philosophical perspective, however, it is the youngest, the late Bob Wagner, whose influence is felt most keenly at the Port Authority today. His prominence is remarkable considering that Bob Wagner's bulging portfolio of postings never included a tour of duty at the Port Authority. Yet his core values are a continuing source of inspiration to those of us who work in an agency that—like the dynasty he was part of—strives to maintain and nurture continuity of purpose.

## THE MAYOR'S LEGACY

During his three memorable terms, Mayor Robert F. Wagner was instrumental in launching some of the most important projects in the Port Authority's history: the third tube of the Lincoln Tunnel, the lower deck of the George Washington Bridge, and the Central Terminal at LaGuardia Airport. Two other projects the mayor pushed are significant: conversion of makeshift air terminals in the remote Queens marshes known as Idlewild into a great international airport; and development of the World Trade Center, along with its companion project, the transformation of the bankrupt, rickety Hudson Tubes into the modernized PATH system.

Like most major capital projects, these two required long-range time horizons. A World Trade Center proposal was first discussed after World War II in the administration of Governor Thomas E. Dewey. It was conceptualized by David Rockefeller and other business leaders in the late 1950s; developed by the Port Authority throughout the 1960s; and opened for occupancy in the early 1970s. However, the Trade Center was not profitable until the 1980s.

Although he was out of office well before ground was broken, Mayor Wagner was a prime mover in the Trade Center project. All three generations of Wagners believed in aggressively using the authority form to its fullest potential. Both the World Trade Center and the PATH takeover were on such large scales that only the public sector was inclined to take them on. At the same time, each entailed sufficiently large risks that they were unsuitable for general government.

Bringing these two disparate public works efforts together under the aegis of the single, multipurpose public authority enabled both to proceed (it is probable that neither of them would have advanced without their having been linked), and to generate extraordinary benefits to the city and the region. By constructing the Trade Center on top of the downtown terminus of the Hudson Tubes (the first proposed site had been at the East River end of Wall Street), the two facilities spawned a new generation of growth in Lower Manhattan and linked it to the New Jersey labor force.

It is presumptuous to suggest that Mayor Wagner, sitting at his desk in City Hall back in 1962, considering whether to give his assent to these two major projects, focused on each specific factor that argued for doing them, or for the Port Authority to take responsibility for them. What is clear, however, is that he recognized the urgent need for both public investments and understood their suitability to the mechanism of the public authority.

## THE SENATOR'S LEGACY

If Mayor Wagner made vigorous use of the public authority as a tool to advance his agenda for New York City, he acquired the inclination directly from his father. For twenty-two years, Senator Robert F. Wagner represented New York and the principles of progressive, activist government in the U.S. Senate. His direct involvement with the Port Authority was limited, but significant.

A state legislator when the Port Compact creating the bi-state agency was first proposed, he had left Albany for a Manhattan judgeship by the time the legislation was enacted in 1921. His principles, however, resonate within the agency. He was, after all, a protege of one of the most re-markable men of twentieth-century American politics, Alfred E. Smith.

As governor of New York and Democratic presidential nominee in 1928, Smith was arguably the fountainhead of modern liberalism. He synthesized the reformist agenda of progressive Republicans, such as Theodore Roosevelt and Charles Evans Hughes, with the high-minded idealism of Democrats such as Woodrow Wilson, and then fused both with the Democrats' big-city party structure. Smith was the trailblazer for Franklin Roosevelt's grand coalition that defined American politics in the mid-twentieth century.

So close were Smith and Wagner that when Smith sought reelection as governor in 1926, knowing that his presidential hopes hinged on a decisive victory, he persuaded Wagner to abandon the comfort and security of the judiciary to challenge the incumbent Republican senator. Wagner entered Congress as a freshman senator in 1927, already bearing the glow of prestige that came of the widely held perception that he was Al Smith's voice in Washington.

Smith left other progeny in government—the Port Authority is one of these. Proponents of a unified harbor, including Woodrow Wilson, had been advocating bi-state cooperation in the development and operation of the port. It was Smith, however, who championed the cause and husbanded the politically tortuous creation of the nation's first modern public authority.

Senator Wagner, in turn, drew amply upon the Smith model. Although best today remembered as the author of the National Labor Relations Act and as the New Deal's floor general in the creation of the illfated National Recovery Administration, in the 1930s and 1940s, Wagner was also widely recognized for his commitment to public investment in housing. Through a series of acts, Senator Wagner continuously pushed the federal government's role in housing development and assistance to tenants and homeowners. The United States Housing Authority, whose creation Wagner authored, lives on today in the Office of the Federal Housing Commissioner of the Department of Housing and Urban Development.

Thus, while Senator Wagner's agenda only rarely intersected with the trade and transportation concerns of the Port Authority, it is clear that a shared philosophy was at work—one of continuous public investment over the long term, and use of the authority form as a tool for effecting those investments.

## BOB WAGNER: LINKED TO THE PAST, FOCUSED ON THE FUTURE

Bob Wagner's patrimony gave him a unique understanding of public service. Lacking the political flair of his elders, Bob Wagner was absorbed with both the strategies of public policy (like his grandfather) and the implementation of those policies (like his father). Above all, he shared with them an abiding commitment to the future of New York City. His conception of government service was a constant reminder to his colleagues not to shortchange the future to serve the immediate needs of the present.

Bob Wagner's focus on the future was a recurrent theme in all his assignments, particularly as deputy mayor, chairman of the City Planning Commission, Board of Education president, and chairman of the mayoral Commission on the Year 2000. In these posts, as well as in his earlier tenure as a City Council member and as president of the Health and Hospitals Corporation, he held a fixed core of critical beliefs that informed his actions. He believed in:

▼    the quality and value of public services

▼    the economic competitiveness of New York City and the metro-
     politan region

▼    the bonds of community and New Yorkers' commitment to one
     another

Improving service quality was a prominent management objective of Wagner's when he was at the Health and Hospitals Corporation, the Board of Education and as deputy mayor. In *New York Ascendant: The Report of the Commission on the Year 2000*, he makes clear that service quality bears long-term consequences for the city's future. "Basic services are the public sector's contribution to the life of the city—and the public sector must be held to that contribution," the report declares. "By 2000, no excuse should be made or accepted for shabby or inefficient services."

In measuring city services, Bob Wagner focused less on the range of services provided and more on how effective each was at meeting a policy objective. He was always asking: Which services should the city provide? Which ones must it provide? Above all, what can it provide well? Implicit in these inquiries was a willingness to make politically tough decisions among competing, compelling demands for limited public resources. Wagner's concern went beyond efficiency and effectiveness. He believed public services have to be responsive to the citizens who use and pay for them.

In the eras of Bob's father and grandfather, New York City's dominant standing among the great cities of the world was taken for granted. In recent years, of course, that leadership has been challenged by metropolitan centers in the United States and around the world. Bob Wagner never lost sight of this fundamental economic shift and recognized that New York must strive to stay competitive.

He advocated two major approaches to strengthen New York City's competitiveness: investment in the city's capital plant and investment in the social and human development of New Yorkers. As deputy mayor, Wagner played a crucial role in advancing the long-awaited development of Battery Park City. As Board of Education president, he made facility investment a top priority by pressing for creation of the School Construction Authority. He eloquently and tirelessly championed education, which he saw as the most effective public weapon against chronic poverty and social dependency.

At every stage of his career, Bob Wagner articulated the viewpoint that the city's future depends on its cohesion as a community. He saw the city's neighborhoods and schools as the basic building blocks of civic renewal. As the main gateway for a nation of immigrants, New York has always been ethnically rich. Today, the city's diversity is greater than ever. The dizzying variety of its citizens presents unique opportunities in trade and cultural linkages to the entire world—a significant competitive advantage. The complexity of so many ethnic, religious, linguistic, racial, and national groups living so close together, however, adds a new dimension to the challenge of melding the city into a vigorous community.

Wagner saw certain elements as essential to a strong, harmonious community, such as social justice, broadbased economic opportunity, and tolerance. To these he added a tone of civility in public discourse and respect for divergent points-of-view, philosophies, and lifestyles. Finally, he saw a pressing need to rejuvenate New Yorkers' belief in the possibilities of the future and in their own ability to work together to effect positive change.

## The Vision of New York Ascendant— A Wagner Agenda

The far-ranging themes of Bob Wagner's interests came together in his work with the Commission on the Year 2000. The Commission's report, written in 1986 and 1987, reflects a time of explosive growth in New York, but also conveys a cautionary tone. As a result, the report proved even more valuable when the economy fell into a severe recession in 1989, and it stayed instructive into the slow recovery.

Both optimistic and realistic in its assessment of the city's prospects, this work was identifiably Wagner's. Its optimism was grounded in a sound accounting of the city's tremendous assets and competitive advantages. Its realism stemmed from a sober recognition of the depth of the challenges the city still faces. The report focuses, first, on the city's deteriorating physical condition: stagnating neighborhoods and crumbling infrastructure in areas of decline; massive congestion, worsening environmental quality, and inadequate infrastructure in areas of growth. Second, it emphasizes the stubborn social ills, particularly the problems of chronic poverty, dependency, and discord between the races.

These difficulties could be overcome, Wagner believed, only if the city built on its traditional strengths. "We kept coming back to the city's past," he wrote, "to those characteristics that have defined New

York, given it its special nature, pace and spirit, that have made it, at its best, to use E. B. White's phrase, 'the loftiest of cities.'" Wagner's report portrays four dimensions of what New York—at its best—is and can be:

The World City—gateway for cargo and travelers, leader in international finance and commerce, center of global communications, culture, and entertainment, and destination of immigrants from virtually everywhere on earth.

The City of Neighborhoods—a powerful generator of community cohesion through its institutions, such as families, schools, and businesses.

The City of Opportunity—center of both the unbridled energy and creativity that gives New York its unique character and the incredible diversity and quality of a labor force that has long been a powerful competitive advantage.

The Civil City—a community marked by tolerance and mutual respect, equity and access to public decision makers, and effective, high-quality public services.

Vision—as represented by these four dimensions of New Yorks—was the unique gift of the youngest of the Wagner dynasty. But he neglected neither his grandfather's passion for a programmatic agenda nor his father's emphasis on implementation. To build for the future, he knew what had be to done in the present.

First and foremost, Wagner believed educational quality must improve significantly. He argued passionately that access to education needs to be broadened for all New Yorkers, and school facilities must be made more integral centers of their communities. He said that welfare dependency must be reduced; a goal he believed could be attained by reorienting the objectives of the social service system toward getting recipients into employment.

Wagner advocated aggressive investment in public infrastructure, both to support greater efficiency and to enhance the quality of life for all. He believed that the development of more affordable housing is the key to stabilizing neighborhoods. And he envisioned new possibilities for reorganizing public service delivery by shifting emphasis from the "inputs" of resource allocation to the "outputs" of higher-quality services and greater accountability. To achieve these ends, he encouraged a broad renewal of civic values. This renewal would only be possible through public leadership that stresses our shared stake in the future, advocates the urgent need for greater tolerance and civility in public and private interactions, and demonstrates a commitment to the long term, including the necessity to defer some current consumption in exchange for greater benefits in the future.

In attempting to implement such an ambitious agenda, Wagner emphasized the limits of resource availability, of government's capacity to deliver effectively, and of the need to maintain the city's competitive position. But he saw an equally pressing need to reinvigorate "our sense of daring" through prudent risks. He sought what he described as "a balance between what needs to be remembered and what needs to be done to secure the kind of future the city deserves."

## How the Port Authority Advances the Wagner Agenda

How then does an agency like the Port Authority internalize and apply the lessons of a career so broad in scope as that of Robert Wagner, Jr.? On the most practical level, a number of the specific projects and investments that were given high priority in New York Ascendant have been undertaken by the Port Authority:

▼ Wagner's report identified capital investment in the region's airports as critical to securing the city's economic competitiveness. Since the report was published in 1987, the Port Authority has invested over $2 billion in airport improvements and plans to invest another $1.9 billion through 1998.

▼ Wagner warned that New York cannot afford to let another generation pass without improving ground access to the airports. The Port Authority has begun planning transit connections to each of the three airports, financed with a user fee paid by air passengers.

▼ The report urged more aggressive use of technology to maximize capacity and manage demand on the transit system. In partnership with regional transportation agencies, the Port Authority has begun to integrate such new technologies as fare cards, electronic toll collection, and advanced incident management and communications systems.

▼   The commission insisted that the obstacles that have blocked renewal of New York's spectacular waterfront for decades be cleared away. The Port Authority has teamed up with city and state agencies to begin this effort with the proposed Hudson River Park and the ambitious Queens West mixed-use development in Hunters Point.

▼   The report called for reestablishment of commuter ferries around New York Harbor. Under Port Authority sponsorship, ferry service resumed between Lower Manhattan and New Jersey in 1989. Its success has brought many proposed new ferry routes and services that promise to alter commuting patterns significantly in the 1990s.

But more than the projects or proposals he put forward, Bob Wagner's influence is felt most pointedly in the principles he stood for. He repeatedly cautioned officials not to reduce their commitment to sustained, high levels of capital investment and maintenance, even when hard economic times or pressing immediate concerns made that a difficult commitment to fulfill. Since 1984, the Port Authority's rate of annual capital investment has grown more than three-fold.

He repeatedly emphasized that service quality matters. Enhanced service quality has been a central management objective of the Port Authority Business Plan. He admonished all government to respect resource limits. Fiscal discipline is mandatory at the Port Authority, as a self-financed organization that receives no tax revenues.

He believed that public investment must move beyond physical improvements, such as infrastructure, and include investment in the capabilities of citizens. Issues such as social equity and quality of life must increasingly inform our investment decisions.

Bob Wagner was often exasperated by the infrequent, sometimes inept, attempts at cooperation among various agencies of government. With resources scarce and needs great, those in government owe it to the public to work together more often and more effectively across jurisdictional, functional, and institutional boundaries to develop effective responses to challenges of growing complexity. The region's transportation agencies recognize that transportation is one area that presents some of the best opportunities—both in planning and operations—to improve co-operation. After all, travelers don't care who runs the trains, as long as they arrive safely and on time.

Finally, Bob Wagner understood how profoundly the future of New York City is bound to that of the metropolitan region. He realized that while the city is the heart of the region, the health of the whole is vital. "We view the city in the context of our region with which we are inextricably linked," notes *New York Ascendant*. "New York is a world city in part because it is the economic engine for one of the world's most important economic regions."

Ours is indeed a global region, whose economic strength is tied to international commerce, travel, and tourism—a region of extraordinary opportunity. Through its capital program and the economic impact of its facilities, the Port Authority has long sought to expand opportunity in the region and ensure it is shared equitably among its citizens. And by advancing the idea of regional citizenship, we have sought to foster a civil region, one whose people and communities are committed to the long-term future and to each other.

# 15

## BELOVED CITY

### WILLIAM J. DEAN

*B*ob Wagner and Walt Whitman loved their city. It is impossible to imagine either living anywhere else. "Remember," Whitman wrote of *Leaves of Grass*, "the book arose out of my life in Brooklyn and New York . . . absorbing a million people. . . ."

Like Whitman, Bob enjoyed walking everywhere and experiencing the city in its many manifestations. Whitman chronicled the city from his vantage points "afoot," along the city's streets and avenues. Each day he looked upon the East River and the New York and Brooklyn skylines from the pilot's deck of the Fulton Street Ferry as he travelled to and from his home in Brooklyn. He knew the city from having worked for ten of the city's newspapers. He knew it as a sensitive observer of life about him. As Justin Kaplan writes in *Walt Whitman, A Life*, "America's first urban poet began as a student of the city's rhythms and sounds."

Bob knew his city through his service as an active participant in its public affairs. Some of Bob's most personal views of the city find expression in the wonderful poetry of Whitman.

Both were enthralled with the city's beauty. In Whitman's words, "The glories strung like beads on my smallest sights and hearings, on the walk in the street and the passage over the river." After viewing the city's busy harbor, bustling with ships, Whitman wrote: "Wasn't it brave! And didn't we laugh (not outwardly—that would have been vulgar; but in the inward soul's bedchamber) with very excess of delight and gladness? O, it is a beautiful world we live in, after all!"

Both men knew well the vibrancy of the city: "The blab of the pave. . . the tires of carts and stuff of bootsoles and talk of the promenaders." And its madness: "Proud and passionate city—mettlesome, mad, extravagant city."

Both knew the dark side of city life, its terrible poverty and crime. Whitman, writing in praise of Charles Dickens, said: "Mr. Dickens never maligns the poor. He puts the searing iron to wickedness, whether among poor or rich; and yet when he describes the guilty, poor and oppressed man, we are always in some way reminded how much need there is that certain systems of law and habit which lead to this poverty and consequent crime should be remedied. . . . "

Whitman's love of democracy especially appealed to Bob. Whitman preferred calling his city "Mannahatta." "New York" sounded too English, too redolent of a colonial past. "Mannahatta! How fit a name for America's great democratic island city! The word itself, how beautiful! how aboriginal! how it seems to rise with tall spires, glistening in sunshine, with such New World atmosphere, vista and action!"

Both men shared a love of history. As a young man in 1833, Whitman saw President Andrew Jackson ride up Fulton Street in an open carriage. In February 1861, he saw President-elect Lincoln enter the Astor House, where he was spending the night on his way to Washington. Whitman learned of the bombardment of Fort Sumter while walking down Broadway to the Fulton Ferry after attending a performance of Verdi's "A Masked Ball" at the Academy of Music. Hearing of Lincoln's death, he crossed over from Brooklyn to Manhattan by boat and walked up Broadway. As he saw the city go into deep mourning, he wrote in his notebook: "Black clouds driving overhead. Lincoln's death—black, black, black—as you look toward the sky—long broad black like great serpents."

Both viewed the city as a timeless pageant. Whitman writes in his magnificent poem, "Crossing Brooklyn Ferry":

*It avails not, time nor place—distance avails not,*

*I am with you, men and women of a generation, or ever so many generations hence,*

*Just as you feel when you look on the river and sky, so I felt,*

*Just as any of you is one of a living crowd, I was one of a crowd,*

*Just as you are refresh'd by the gladness of the river and the bright flow, I was refresh'd,*

*Just as you stand and lean on the rail, yet hurry with the swift current, I stood yet was hurried,*

*Just as you look on the numberless masts of ships and the thick-stemm'd pipes of steamboats, I look'd.*

Like Walt Whitman, Bob Wagner will forever be part of the pageant that is New York City.

# 16

## EPILOGUE

### JULIA VITULLO-MARTIN

C ities work, but not in the understandable, systematic ways that social scientists prefer. They work on their own terms— in unpredictable, erratic, and energetic ways. One simply has to face the truth up front: cities are wild, dirty, noisy, dangerous, often ugly places. New York is not Scarsdale, Chicago is not Wilmette, Los Angeles is not Beverly Hills. At their best, cities are exciting, fabulous, compelling, hip agglomerations of people. They are the channels of upward mobility, the incubators of new businesses, and the cultivators of the arts. They triumph over the drive for orderliness proposed by bureaucrats and planners. Their very impossibility—what Rem Koolhaas calls "their culture of congestion," for example—is what makes them wonderful.[1]

American cities are governmentally dependent: creatures of their states (a legal fiction, since many cities preceded their states) and economic vassals of the federal government. Cities do not control the nation's economy; they do not patrol the nation's borders; they cannot even restrict who enters their own jurisdictions. Yet cities must bear the costs of national economic shortcomings. They must endure a plague of guns, admitted by interstate commerce, and drugs, admitted by unguarded borders. They must pay for services to immigrants, even illegal aliens.

Cities are responsible for the health, housing, and education of poor people. Indeed, they bear the brunt of providing the safety net of services for the unproductive poor, including teenage mothers and ailing senior citizens, priced out of wealthier jurisdictions. And yet federal tax policy extracts tremendous amounts of revenue from urban tax bases while offering tax relief and incentives to businesses relocating beyond central cities, further exacerbating the problems. In general, American cities have been left to deal with what are national structural problems—handled in every other advanced economy by the national government.

Such burdens on cities are not fair. Those problems that transcend urban borders are the responsibility of all citizens and therefore Washington must help solve them—and pay for the solutions. Eli Ginzberg points out that of the ten large American cities that lost double-digit percentages of population during the 1980s, seven were major midwestern manufacturing centers seriously hurt by simultaneous causes, including technological obsolescence and an overvalued dollar that depressed markets at home and abroad.[2]

Of course, some city problems are self-imposed. Many city governments are poorly organized for delivering basic services. The federal government is not the primary reason why, for example, Detroit is dangerous, Boston's streets are pot-holed, or Los Angeles ripped up its light rail lines after World War II, and so has only rudimentary public transportation. The federal government did not force New York City to become a "social democracy," in Lou Winnick's phrase, a democracy acting as its own government to "tax the rich to help the poor."[3] Nor is Washington responsible for the stranglehold of civil service on so many city governments. Federal policy forces are strong, but cities often set their own fates.

The question thus becomes, What can cities do? The first thing is to determine what role Washington is likely to play in the future—and whether or not it can be pushed to play a stronger role than it would if a concerted effort to force action were not made. The next is to take an unflinching look at the history of liberalism and its effects on urban policy as well as the shifts in thinking over the past decades that have added the concept of victimization to the equation, and the repercussions of that shift. Drawing upon all the material presented by the authors of the essays throughout this analysis, clues to how cities can survive—and arguments that will help convince Americans that they should—emerge. After all, convincing Americans that they want and need cities is the first step in obtaining the support cities need to flourish.

## CITIES AND WASHINGTON: CAUGHT IN THE FEDERAL TRAP

When Donna Shalala was assistant secretary of the Division of Policy, Development and Research at the Department of Housing and Urban Development (HUD) in the late 1970s, President Carter told her what he meant by a national policy, "I want you to design an urban policy that includes New York and . . . Plains," he said. Shalala later recalled, "Neither I nor any of the urban experts with whom I was working had any idea of what to make of this directive from our commander-in-chief."[4]

The demand to accommodate such different circumstances set off a departmental debate focused not on policy but on process, not on understanding goals and means but on devising workable formulas. Community Development Block Grants, Revenue Sharing, Comprehensive Employment & Training acts became mired in disputed formulas. Even the new programs that were initiated, such as Urban Development Action Grants, provoked little serious debate about ideas; the debate was about which jurisdictions would get the bulk of the funds. Today, with cities even weaker politically, their ability to drive federal debates about policy has deteriorated even further.

To a certain extent, federal funds have always been distributed according to political influence with little regard for merit. It was no accident that the first public housing projects went to Lyndon Johnson's and Sam Rayburn's Austin, Texas, to Robert F. Wagner's New York City, Huey Long's New Orleans, and to John McCormack's Boston. New Deal funds went to the power districts. As it happened, many of those elected officials represented urban areas and urban states, for the time was one of the ascendancy of cities.

In the 1950s, cities began losing population and relative voting strength. By the 1970s, when urban voting dominance was gone, Congress further divorced need from programmatic awards. The Community Development Block Grant program, which had replaced the traditional urban categorical programs like urban renewal, probably became the most outrageous—vividly symbolized by Scottsdale, Arizona, which used federal dollars allocated to fund housing for the poor to pay for a swimming pool for the affluent instead.

Yet in a fundamental political sense, President Carter was right: Getting any urban program through Congress meant designing programs that would benefit sections of the country that had no large, impoverished cities. In facing up to the suburbanization of American politics, mayors will have to change their strategies. Rather than pursuing the traditional urban strategy of more federal funding for welfare, for example, mayors may be shrewder to seek financing for regional infrastructure (where they can find allies), freeing up local dollars to fund unpopular social policies. Such a strategy would fit into the long-standing federal practice of helping the disadvantaged, whether people or places, by including them in a category that encompasses the advantaged—and politically influential—as well.

This practice thins funds for the most disadvantaged Americans, but does get them something.

Attempts to address these problems today are facing a great deal of popular resistance, in part because a serious change in political views has occurred. According to the Roper Center, in 1964 some 73 percent of Americans agreed that the government had a responsibility to eliminate poverty; today only 34 percent of Americans agree. Yet while the absolute number of Americans living below the poverty level is about the same today (36.8 million) as in 1964 (36 million), the racial base has shifted. In 1964, 15 percent of whites and 50 percent of minorities lived in poverty versus 12 percent of whites and 32 percent of minorities today.

Examining these changes in attitudes against these numbers raises a number of interesting questions about the future of cities. Who is responsible for dealing with urban poverty? What about the deteriorating urban infrastructure? Does a potential political coalition between cities and suburbs exist?

Phil Thompson argues in this volume that Congress is not the right venue for dealing with urban poverty, in part because political consensus is elusive, and in part because the consequences of poverty are best handled at the state and local levels, where political differences can be brokered more easily. He also notes realistically that no meaningful transfer of resources from Washington to states and localities is likely to occur.

Programs crucial to the physical operation of cities—capital funds for public transit, for example—have been cut disproportionately in Washington. Perhaps more than any other program, public transit reflects the disturbing conflicts within American federalism. Large Northern and Midwestern cities built transit systems in the first half of this century; in the second half, these systems declined precipitously. Much of the decline was due to the lack of basic maintenance. Robert Kiley calculates that to have kept up with the basic physical needs of New York City's subway plant during the 1960s and 1970s, the city would have had to spend about $1 billion annually in today's money. Instead, it spent at best 30 percent of what was needed—$300 million in a very good year, and much of that on new subway lines. For the most part, the federal government saw maintenance as a local responsibility and helped out only reluctantly and erratically. Washington may have been right theoretically, but the result was disastrous for many cities.

In the 1970s, notes Kiley, the federal government began a national program to (1) invest in new systems—Los Angeles, Atlanta,

Washington, D.C., and (2) renovate old systems—Boston, Philadelphia, Chicago. New York lost out initially because it was still building its system—the Third Avenue and Second Avenue subways were being taken seriously in the capital budget—and then because when it hit its fiscal crisis, it shifted every dollar it could into closing the huge budget gap. Thus New York's subway system continued to deteriorate as other systems were being fixed.

Then the New Federalism came along—two Republican administrations during which Congress first shifted national priorities and then removed many constraints on how states spent federal money. The relationship between highway funds and public transit funds went from a two-to-one ratio in 1980 ($2 for highways to every $1 for transit) to a five-to-one ratio in 1990, according to Louis Gambaccini, general manager of the Philadelphia region's Southeast Pennsylvania Transportation Authority.[5]

Overall, Congress decreased the sum total of grants to state and local governments by more than 11 percent over the decade on the theory that lower jurisdictions would make programs more efficient and cost-effective. Instead, most states raised taxes.[6]

Despite Republican campaign attacks on onerous federal regulations and unfunded mandates (by which the federal government requires states and localities to provide services that it refuses to pay for), Republican control of the U.S. Senate and House in the early 1990s produced no easing of the federal stranglehold on cities. By 1995, Washington had substantially reduced its aid to cities, but had abolished almost no unfunded mandates and had eased very few regulations. The American sense of fair play alone demands that even if Republican elected officials refuse to support cities, they should at least cut them loose from federal restrictions to make their way as best they can with their own resources and their own strategies.

## THE LIBERAL BASE OF URBAN POLICY: KEEP WHAT WORKS, ELIMINATE WHAT DOES NOT

Redistributive policies—as well as urban policies that tend to take from the wealthy to give to the poor—are not very popular with voters. During the New Deal such policies were controversial but successful as a response to a desperate economic situation. They also garnered support during the economically strong 1960s, but their popularity ended with the advent of the recession in the early 1970s.

Ester Fuchs argues that the "end of the liberal experiment" has arrived. The signs are clear in the conservative uprisings in New York,

Los Angeles, San Francisco, Philadelphia, and Indianapolis. Even cities that still have Democratic mayors—Baltimore, Chicago, Pittsburgh, Detroit, Boston—are showing a new conservatism in social policy. Large numbers of voters, disgruntled over traditional social programs, have used the voting booth to indicate their unhappiness with redistributive social policies, which they believe are not working.

Liberalism flourishes in a reasonably well-run city. The essence of twentieth-century liberalism is centered on ideals of compassion, fairness, equality, generosity, and, in its earlier incarnation, justice for the working person. The decline of liberalism as a moral and political force has coincided with the decline of liberalism's respect for workers, as espoused by Senator Robert F. Wagner. (Wagner's investigation of the Triangle Shirtwaist Factory fire in 1911 had been a profound turning point for him, and for his friend and coinvestigator Al Smith. The horrifying deaths of the Triangle workers never left Wagner, according to his biographer.)[7]

In many cities, the declining interest in the fate of workers coincided with the increasing contempt liberals were willing to show for white ethnics, especially as white ethnics clashed with black civil rights protestors in Chicago, Detroit, Boston, Philadelphia, and New York. This point has been made repeatedly over the years by journalist Jim Sleeper, who wrote about "the embitterment beyond words, of white ethnics [who found themselves] suddenly marginal to civic cultures they struggled hard to make their own."[8]

This bitterness is fundamental to the decline of liberalism. The New Deal was the source of the programs considered at the heart of liberalism today—the Wagner Labor Act, subsidized housing, social security as a safety net. Yet the true obsession of the New Deal was with jobs. The Works Progress Administration was a jobs bill; public housing was passed as a jobs bill, actually a union jobs bill; Civilian Conservation Corps was a jobs bill.

New Deal liberalism was predicated on the assumption that (1) Americans believe that upward mobility should be available to all who are willing to work hard to better themselves; and (2) jobs are crucial to dignity and happiness. Jobs are the main road out. The New Deal's objectives, wrote Senator Wagner, were "first to see that the hungry are fed, but second and more important, to see that men are reemployed, and third, to prevent a recurrence of so prolonged a depression as the one we are now experiencing."[9] But the goals held an internal conflict.

Public housing is a case in point. It was the ultimate liberal program, and one that began pretty well. Yet, as my own essay argues, one of the weak elements from the start was that it was not so much a housing program as a jobs program. Nonetheless New York, through most of Mayor Wagner's administration (1954–65), built pretty good housing projects, in part because the New York City Housing Authority (NYCHA) defied Washington on design standards. This sounds paradoxical, but the federal government sets "minimum design standards" above which quality must not rise. New York built to far higher standards than almost anywhere else, and included such prohibited "amenities" as security systems.[10] (This is one reason New York's projects stayed safe and sound far longer than high-rise family projects in most cities.)

Federal "minimum design standards" were designed to keep costs down. But, in part because public housing was a fully unionized program, construction costs were astronomical, often as high as or higher than in privately built housing constructed to much higher design standards. In other words, public housing embodied the deep contradictions embedded in liberal programs: benefit the poor by building decent housing; benefit the working class by employing union labor. But what happens when the system benefits one far more than the other, or one at the expense of the other? What happens when the union protects labor without regard to the quality of its effort and product?

At some point liberal concern for workers moved from the protection of the weak and exploited to protection of entrenched, destructive interests. In practice, liberalism in New York has included an unshakable commitment to job tenure at all sorts of levels, such as civil service jobs that reach to very high levels of management, or union jobs that prevent flexibility through the ranks—both common enough throughout the country.

Unfortunately, liberalism in New York also embraced extreme practices like the Board of Education's "building tenure" for school principals. Indeed, Bob Wagner estimated the proportion of incompetent principals—who could not be removed because of the tenure system—to be as high as 25 percent. In 1991, Chancellor Joseph Fernandez challenged this practice, arguing that it rewarded incompetence with invulnerability.[11] The principals' union fought bitterly, even though nearly everyone recognized that grossly incompetent principals were being protected.

If a well-intentioned, liberally designed system is not helping —is even hurting—its intended beneficiaries, what is to be done? Do liberals continue to defend the system because any criticism will be used by conservatives to undo the entire liberal structure? Is it better to sacrifice a few disadvantaged people in the name of liberalism rather than endanger the entire movement? Has liberalism failed or have its programs simply aged?

Phil Thompson confronts these issues directly, asking why did black politics founder and liberals lose their faith? What are the prospects for a renewed black politics, and a renewed black/liberal alliance? Should this even be a goal? Thompson cites former Atlanta mayor and civil rights leader Andrew Young, who argues that the ineffectiveness of black electoral politics in helping poor urban blacks had two causes: the lack of open criticism, or elitism, within the ranks of black mayors and the middle-class bias of the civil rights movement and its subsequent legislative program.

Similarly, aging New Deal and Great Society programs prompt two sets of questions: First, is this the way the program would be constructed if we were starting over today? Second, which programs or program elements should be salvaged or jettisoned? Almost no one would propose setting up public housing as it now is. So why not make the changes agreed upon by nearly every thoughtful local housing official? Similarly, why not reconsider the fundamental structure and delivery of public education, as both Diane Ravitch and Joseph Fernandez urge?

Perhaps Erik Erikson's theory about personality development—that each stage of life from infancy forward is associated with a specific psychological struggle that contributes to personality integration—is applicable as well to the maturing of social policy. Each stage has a psychological and intellectual struggle which, if successfully resolved, allows a program to move forward. Most social policy programs begin with a tension between the beneficiaries to be served (poor people, for example) and beneficiaries to be employed or rewarded (civil service workers or labor unions). Thus public housing's ostensible reason-for-being was to provide decent shelter to those who could not afford it. But public housing's passage through Congress required support from labor, and the provision of jobs became dominant. Washington's prevailing wage requirements, by which all workers building or rehabilitating any government-subsidized housing must be paid union scale, adds exponentially to the cost of low-income housing while substantially decreasing the supply.

Ironically, the provision of jobs for public housing residents themselves was not part of the mix until the late 1980s. Until then, for example, the San Antonio Housing Authority (SAHA) had hired only sixty-eight residents over two decades. Its 1989 annual report noted, "Prior to 1979, employment of public housing residents was not a high priority of management, and any opportunity for advancement for those few who were hired was limited." During the 1980s, SAHA hired 301 residents, trying to resolve a destructive dichotomy that had been there from the start.

## VICTIMIZATION: WHOSE RIGHTS ARE PARAMOUNT?

Over the past twenty years, a new concept has been added to the old liberal ideas of compassion and equality: victimization. Victimization is in turn often tied to rights—for older liberals, the right to medical care and the right to housing, for example; for newer liberals, the right to live on the streets or in public parks. Perhaps more than any other idea, the idea of victimization separates liberals from their older loyalties to working people, white and black, for whom the right to a job and a corresponding obligation to society is often paramount.

Liberals understand the alienation of Catholic white ethnics—and may even welcome it—but they are often distressed by what seems to be equal anger from prominent African-Americans. Former Chicago Housing Authority (CHA) chairman Vincent Lane reflected the views of many black people when he said, "If the Ku Klux Klan had set out to destroy black people, they couldn't have done a better, more systematic job of it than this combination we have of welfare and public housing. We need more working people in public housing. We need the right role models to compete with the gangs and drug dealers."[12]

In Lane's view, what has kept working people out and drug dealers in has been a deadly combination of misguided federal policies and aggressive suits by the American Civil Liberties Union (ACLU) and other advocates—all in the name of helping poor people. The real result, he argues, has been to destroy poor neighborhoods. In earlier times, the essence of liberalism was to ensure that everyone was given a fair opportunity to make a productive and good life. But at some point the concept of a productive life as part of the equation was lost. As far back as 1977, Peter C. Goldmark, Jr., then director of the New York State Budget Office, told the New York Times, "Welfare is hated by those who administer it, mistrusted by those who pay for it, and held in contempt by those who receive it."[13]

Ellen Chesler argues that truly decentralizing social services to the neighborhood level—as was so effectively done by the settlement house founders—would result in far better programs to help troubled families. Even though the public welfare bureaucracy was meant to render settlement houses obsolete, quite the opposite has happened, says Chesler: 300 comprehensive social service facilities thrive in 80 cities, compared to 413 institutions in 32 states in 1913, when the reputation and influence of settlement houses was preeminent. Settlement houses work on the premise that with good will and hard work social harmony can be achieved, even among people of substantially different class, ethnicity, race, and religion. Yet since the 1960s, most liberal thinkers, argues Chesler, have advanced a rights-based agenda that sets individuals and groups in opposition to one another.

The obsession of the past few decades with individual rights has, ironically, moved the liberal agenda away from its traditional concern for a just society. The concept of the whole has fallen before the dominance of the individual. For hundreds of urban neighborhoods throughout the country, this distortion is unacceptable. Whether they use the old Saul Alinsky confrontational strategy or the milder and newer Local Initiatives Support Corporation model, neighborhood organizations are reasserting their integrity. Such groups are far more likely than government bureaucrats to figure out how to balance the needs of the truly troubled and weak with the struggles of poor neighborhoods to right themselves.

However much middle-class urban dwellers fear and loath crime— and every survey shows they do—most urban crime is committed by poor people against poor people. Many poor neighborhoods are so overwhelmed by crime that every detail of life is affected. When sociologist James E. Rosenbaum of Northwestern University studied families that had moved to the suburbs from Chicago's public housing projects, he found that many newly working mothers said they had not worked while living in public housing because they feared for the physical safety of their children in their absence. They had arranged their lives so that they and their children were inside by dusk—4:00 p.m. in the Chicago winter—when the shooting routinely began outside.[14]

The FBI's Uniform Crime Report has shown a decline in violent index crimes (murder, non-negligent manslaughter, forcible rape, robbery, and aggravated assault) for several major cities since 1990. New York City, for example, has seen a 12 percent decline. Yet New Yorkers do not seem impressed. While 60 percent of urban Americans rate their cities as good places to live, only 34 percent of New Yorkers do.[15] Vera Institute of Justice director Christopher Stone argues that crime figures tend to aggregate too much, that bundling crime categories together obscures the real increase in specific violence like urban gunfire. The problem, he writes, is that no one lives in the city as a whole. People live and work in neighborhoods. Data examined at a neighborhood level show that the gradual decline in violent crime citywide is the product of an increase in violent crime in traditionally safe neighborhoods combined with a decline in high crime neighbor-hoods. Most of these now threatened, traditionally safe neighborhoods are racially integrated or black neighborhoods. Stone also argues that it will be difficult, perhaps impossible, to combat drug-related crime decisively without a strong economy offering jobs as an economic alternative.

Taking a somewhat different view, economist Dick Netzer argues that one must divide those who can benefit from the economy from those who must take other steps first. He notes that the 1980s saw considerable absorption into New York City's labor market of young minority people who would have been trapped in poverty had the economy not grown. This demonstrates that when jobs are available, large numbers of people will move from welfare rolls to employment rolls. At the same time, however, he says that huge numbers of people were left behind in poverty, and for them the answer is not the economy but a revolution in education to prepare them for the job market.

This view holds both good and bad news for the Clinton ad-ministration's welfare reform program, which requires that most recip-ients move from welfare to work. If the jobs are there, many people will take them. But a large group of unemployed people will need sub-stantial support and training before they will be employable even if they are among those who want to work.

As a member, along with Netzer, of Mayor Edward Koch's Commission on the Year 2000, chaired by Bob Wagner, Donna Shalala argued in the mid-1980s that a welfare system divorced from em-ployment could not continue. Her ideas were then shocking to many as she argued that, like it or not, working mothers had become the norm for American families trying to reach or stay in the middle class; that these families could not be expected to support a system of per-manently nonworking mothers on welfare; and that lifetimes of un-employment were degrading to human beings. Ten years later these ideas became accepted into President Clinton's Work and Responsi-bility Act, which proposes to overhaul the country's welfare program while, in Shalala's words, "restoring dignity and a fighting chance at economic self-sufficiency to millions of women and their children." Shalala is optimistic that welfare reform will work.

Many, however, believe that there can be little optimism for impoverished urban neighborhoods without a scenario for greatly improved—revolutionized—schools. Education is the key to work and some 45 percent of the country's urban Latinos and 35 percent of urban blacks drop out of high school. The problem facing front-line educators, according to Diane Ravitch, is that the school system is premised on the idea that—except for the Chancellor—no one can make a decision without getting the approval of someone else. The system is girdled with rules, regulations, obstacle courses, and checkpoints, to assure that no one does the wrong thing, which promotes the hierarchical, bureaucracy that is strangling the schools. She argues that it needn't be this way, since in every private and parochial school, the adults in charge make many decisions about staff, students, schedules, repairs, and purchases of goods and services without the oversight of a phalanx of supervisors. She proposes a system of public charter schools (PCS). One PCS already exists, though not by Ravitch's name. The Wildcat Academy, a public high school whose charter was negotiated by founder Amalia Betanzos with Chancellor Fernandez in 1991, opened in 1992. Says Betanzos, "We take kids that really don't fit well into the system—one-third are on parole and another third are suspended from other public schools. We choose our own teachers; we handle our own maintenance contracts; we do our own security. Last year we graduated thirty-one kids, of whom twenty-one went onto college; four went into the armed services; six took jobs."[16]

Ravitch argues for a revolution to free up individual schools and a parallel financial revolution to give means-tested scholarships to poor students, with priority going to students in schools that have been identified by public authorities as "educationally bankrupt." These children, as much as 5 percent of the total enrollment, says Ravitch, should be eligible for scholarships that may be used in any school—public, private, or religious.

Joseph Fernandez, former schools chancellor in both Miami and New York City, recommends two courses of action to solve the education problem: first, take back the schools physically, make them inviting and pleasant, clean them up, landscape the grounds, give students a chance to take pride in their school and campus; and, second, listen seriously to the outlandish, trying even radical ideas that in the past have been stopped before they even have a chance to be tested—such as the all-male academies for inner-city black students. Like Vince Lane, Fernandez is willing to try deeply controversial strategies—including those he instinctively dislikes—if they have a chance of succeeding where others have failed. Of course, both Fernandez and Lane are out of office, replaced by quieter men chosen to institute some innovations while abandoning others.

HUD insists that it will carry on Lane's innovations but with a far more efficient administrative structure.

## FACING THE FUTURE: MAKING CITIES LIVABLE AGAIN

Even as cities contend with the continuing problems created by the extremes of rich and poor, they must deal with a new set of problems: the much-heralded communications revolution is here and it has, as long predicted, freed jobs and businesses to locate anywhere. No one has to be in cities anymore, particularly after making initial contacts. It is still helpful to come to the big city young, fight your way toward the top, make contacts, establish your credentials—before leaving for your favorite playground. Aspen, Santa Fe, Key West are now outposts of New York, Chicago, Dallas, and Los Angeles, populated by professionals in finance, advertising, publishing, entertainment, indeed, most every field short of old-time manufacturing.

When E. B. White wrote his famous *Here Is New York* essay in 1949, Boston was thriving, Chicago was clean, San Francisco was lovely. The White essay was almost a source of pride for some New Yorkers who said we have this fabulous city, and we're not concerned about petit bourgeois matters like a little dirt and noise. New York was filthy, dangerous, ugly, and still the greatest city in America. Today it is still filthy, dangerous, and ugly, so why can't it stay great? Why can't Los Angeles? Or Miami? Or Boston? Is decline inevitable?

The communications revolution is making extreme dispersion possible and seemingly relentless. The outward flow from city to suburb and countryside won't be reversed, but it can be stanched, if cities take full advantage of the resources they have. There are also a few trends working in the favor of cities. Economist Michael Porter notes that just as a handful of nations tend to dominate any one industry, so vital competitors tend to bunch tightly in a narrow geographic area within a nation because they nourish one another; thus the garment industry congregated in New York and Los Angeles; the electronics industry congregated outside Boston and San Jose.[17] In the future, some cities, including these four, will continue to attract competitors.

Almost no one will have to live in cities in the twenty-first century—only those who want to will do so. The crucial question becomes, What do people, particularly upwardly mobile people, want in a city? A New York foundation, the Commonwealth Fund, commissioned a series of surveys by Louis Harris and analysis by the Manhattan Institute to find out why people move to or from New York City.[18]

In a stratified sample of 6,800 households, the surveys found that people move to New York for the jobs—what is, from the government's point of view, the hard part. They leave, angry and disillusioned, over the quality of life—issues that are, from the city's government's point of view, fairly easy to handle. While 34 percent of out-migrants say they moved because of job changes, 55 percent did so to live in a better house or neighborhood; 54 percent were looking for a safer place; 59 percent sought "a better lifestyle," particularly for their families. In addition, 39 percent were trying to reduce their costs of living, and 26 percent specifically mentioned taxes.

The surveys also show that (1) if the jobs were not in New York to begin with, people would not come—and New York would die; and (2) quality of life matters to most people. They want the government to combat and punish crime, pick up the garbage, keep the streets clean, run good schools, control traffic, repair the sidewalks, and in general maintain public order. Yet, as Ester Fuchs notes, local governments are caught in an impossible bind: their permanent fiscal crisis means they put their efforts into cutting their work forces and saving money rather than improving the quality of their services.

Paul Goldberger, looking at what he calls the new urban paradigm—Charlotte, Minneapolis, Dallas, Seattle—believes that what attracts people to cities is a combination of ease of living and the presence of a gentle sprinkling of those aspects of traditional urbanism that middle-class residents value in small doses: lively shopping, a mix of places to eat and meet others, and cultural institutions. And all of this is joined with low crime, or at least low crime in those areas inhabited by the new urbanists. That is what Goldberger says provides middle-class residents with the combination of close-in neighborhoods of detached houses with ample, and private, yards and the amenities of cities—they are essentially choosing a suburban life within city limits. Such cities are able to dangle before their residents a sense of relative freedom from the serious problems of crime and poverty that are so conspicuous in Detroit, St. Louis, Los Angeles, and Miami.

Yet older cities, particularly those led by the new group of what Phil Thompson calls "post-Civil Rights" African-American mayors, are not letting go without a fight. In his 1994 inaugural speech, Detroit's Mayor Dennis Archer charged his largely black audience: "Sweep the sidewalk in front of your house. Clean the rubbish from the storm sewer on your street. Pick up the broken glass in your alley. Demand that I get the trash picked up—on time. Insist that I make the buses run—on time." Then he paused, leaned into the microphone, and said, "And get a grip on your life, and the lives of your children!" He received a tumultuous standing ovation. He was calling on his constituents to help make possible the quality of life that would make the difference between these half-way cities and his own far smaller.

Archer's Detroit may encapsulate the new urban problems as well as any place: once the country's dominant industrial manufacturing center, Detroit is today a wounded giant trying to make its way into the new world of information and communications. In the old manufacturing economy, a great deal of crime was tolerated and no one much cared what the city looked like. Beauty was not part of the economic equation—and crime was—for Birmingham, England, or Gary, Indiana. Today the urban manufacturing economy is minuscule. Writes Peter Drucker, "By the year 2000 there will be no developed country where traditional workers making and moving goods account for more than one sixth or one eighth of the work force."[19] Looks and serenity are very much part of the economic equation of the information economy: the city's face is its fortune, notes Peter Salins.

Competitive factors—taxes, quality of life, safety, schools— will count more than ever as people coolly calculate their options and ask themselves: Do I have to live in the city? Unfortunately, at the moment ever increasing numbers can answer "no."

## SOLVING THE PROBLEMS

Every city government spends enormous sums of money—but not necessarily on what matters to those who can leave. To some extent, a city can continue liberal spending policies toward the poor and the needy if it also provides good basic services to everyone. In practice, many cities are heading in the opposite direction. Their expenditures on social services and Medicaid have been going up, while expenditures on basic services have often been going down.

New York City, the ultimate American city, faces unique problems because of its size. As a result, it is in a distressed category all its own: It has, for example, nearly one-fifth of the country's entire Aid to Families with Dependent Children (AFDC) caseload. It spends 36 percent of its budget on low-income assistance and one-half of one percent on its parks system, a system that is the most magnificent in the country. The city is living on past capital. Previous generations created and supported these parks; this generation is letting far too many of them sink into decay. The major parks are being saved by organized private groups that have carved out some piece of territory for themselves.

But that is not a criticism—it is a lesson for others. Central Park, for example, again reigns as the greatest of public parks because it was saved—and is saved anew every day—by its relentless and warlike supporters' refusal to bow to the demands of transportation, efficiency, budgetary constraints, homeless advocates, school groups, or any of the many good causes that argue that their interests come before the park.

Every great city has been created and repeatedly saved by its citizens—New York, Chicago, Paris, Berlin, London. Each has more than once been close to destruction, but was pulled back from the abyss by those who cared. What's new on the horizon is that the residents of smaller cities are doing the same. Detroit, for example, which fell faster and further than any American city in history, is fighting its way back. While its economic resurgence has been fueled by the Big Three auto industry, many of its hundreds of new economic enterprises have been started by African-American entrepreneurs determined to invest in their home town. Thus, city dwellers are getting good at what writer Tony Hiss calls "replenishing the places around us."[20]

Detroit's decline, along with the decline of so many American cities, occurred despite large amounts of what had looked like government investment over the past few decades. Much of this investment was unproductive, some of it even destructive. The scale of liberal, government-based solutions has too often been wrong—too big, too aloof, too centralized, too intricate. Nearly every essay in this book argues that we must do an about face and head in the other direction: small, neighborly, decentralized, simple. The world is downshifting from large scale to small scale, a shift that only big government—despite self-serving promises to the contrary—refuses to accept.

At the heart of the liberal love for large scale was a misunderstanding of the nature of large cities. A large city is not one entity but rather a confederation of hundreds of neighborhoods. New York City, whose heritage is one of living collectively, is really just a confederation of countless small towns, each of which cares about its own autonomy and integrity.

Thus, when a huge project of any kind is thrust into one of New York's small towns, its residents are likely to protest—and to turn deaf ears to the entreaties of officials urging them to put the good of the whole before their parochial interests. Liberal public policy itself had long since abandoned any real concept of the good of the whole, and ferocious neighborhood organizers know it.

Many of the problems commanding current national attention—the state of the public schools, the difficult transition from an industrial economy to the hi-tech global economy, the rise of homelessness in a wealthy society—come to a head most starkly and compellingly in cities. Yet while today's urban crisis has its harrowing aspects, this is not the crisis described in the 1960s and early 1970s. Apocalypse is not the danger; the danger is an ongoing gradual decline.

Slow decline is a very difficult force to fight, harder in its way than the great crises like the Great Depression or World War II, when political coalitions more readily overcame differences for the good of society. Bob Wagner came from a family of coalition builders who represented the best in American liberal traditions. As a young man his grandfather, Senator Wagner, had written that Tammany Hall served "the aspirations and needs of the urban industrial masses." It was an assumption of New Deal liberals that all human beings aspire and should aspire to higher things—to better lives, better education, better housing. Yet liberals rarely speak of aspirations anymore. The word seems to have left our vocabulary.

Louis Kahn once said that when children walk through a city they should get a sense of what they want to be when they grow up. That is what liberalism, particularly New York liberalism as embodied in the Wagners, meant. Aspiration and betterment, not embitterment, for all.

# NOTES

## CHAPTER 2

1. Paul Brophy, "Emerging Approaches to Community Development," in *Interwoven Destinies* (New York: W. W. Norton & Company, 1993), p. 215.

2. David Rusk, *Cities Without Suburbs* (Washington, D.C.: Woodrow Wilson Center Press, 1993).

3. For an analysis of post-war development policy, see John Mollenkopf, *The Contested City* (Princeton, N.J.: Princeton University Press, 1983). For an analysis of white suburbanization, discriminatory housing practices in the suburbs, and its impact in the central city, see J. T. Darden, et al., *Detroit: Race and Uneven Development* (Philadelphia: Temple University Press, 1987) and Gary Orfield and Carol Ashkinaze, *The Closing Door: Conservative Policy and Black Opportunity* (Chicago: The University of Chicago Press, 1991). For an overview of deteriorating city revenues and their impact on services, see Demetrios Caraley, "Washington Abandons the Cities," *Political Science Quarterly* 107 (Spring 1992): 1–30, and also Carol O'Cleireacain, "Cities' Role in the Metropolitan Economy and the Federal Structure," in *Interwoven Destinies*, pp. 167–86.

4. Latinos accounted for the largest increases in city populations in the 1970s and 1980s. See John D. Kasarda, "Cities As Places Where People Live and Work: Urban Change and Neighborhood Crisis," in *Interwoven Destinies*, p. 84.

5. Data on cities taken from Kasarda in *Interwoven Destinies*. There were significant variations in poverty growth rates in different regions of the country in the 1970s and 1980s. Using the number of blacks living in census tracts with poverty rates 40 percent and above as an indicator, Paul Jargowsky found slightly lower poverty rates in the Eastern cities, significantly higher rates in Midwestern cities, and slightly higher rates in the West. See Paul A. Jargowsky, "Ghetto Poverty Among Blacks in the 1980s," *Journal of Policy Analysis and Management* 13, no. 2 (1993): 288–310.

6. Eli Ginzberg, "The Changing Urban Scene: 1960–1990 and Beyond," *Interwoven Destinies*, p. 38.

7. E. R. Ricketts and R. Mincy, "Growth of the Underclass 1970–1980," *Journal of Human Resources* 25, no. 1 (1990): 137–45. Also see Jargowsky for a discussion of trends in the 1980s.

8. Kasarda in *Interwoven Destinies*, p. 96.

9. Roland Anglin and Briavel Holcomb, "Poverty in Urban America: Policy Options," *Journal of Urban Affairs* 14, nos. 3, 4 (1992): 447–68.

10. Phillip Thompson and Charles Brecher, "Poverty and Public Related Spending in New York City," background paper prepared for the New York Citizens Budget Commission, 1994.

11. William Julius Wilson, *The Declining Significance of Race*, 2nd ed. (Chicago: The University of Chicago Press, 1980).

12. Norman Fainstein, "The Underclass/Mismatch Hypothesis as an Explanation for Black Economic Deprivation," *Politics & Society* 15, no. 4 (1986–87): 403–51. See also Bart Landry, *The New Black Middle Class* (Berkeley: University of California Press, 1987).

13. This was despite the loss of large numbers of whites, whose departure no doubt lowered the city's poverty level when using 50 percent of median family income as the poverty threshold.

14. Michael B. Katz, *The Undeserving Poor: From the War on Poverty to the War on Welfare* (New York: Pantheon Books, 1989).

15. Christopher Jencks, *Rethinking Social Policy* (New York: Harper Perennial, 1992), pp. 129–30.

16. Douglass S. Massey and Nancy A. Denton, *American Apartheid: Segregation and the Making of the Underclass* (Cambridge, Mass: Harvard University Press, 1994).

17. Ibid.

18. William Julius Wilson, *The Truly Disadvantaged: The Inner City, the Underclass, and Public Policy* (Chicago: The University of Chicago Press, 1987).

19. John Kasarda, "Urban Change and Minority Opportunities," in *The New Urban Reality* (Washington, D.C.: The Brookings Institution, 1985).

20. Wage inequality has been rising for the past two decades, with the proportion of minorities earning poverty wages increasing by more than 10 percent in the 1980s. See Gary Burtless and Lawrence Mishel, "Recent Wage Trends: The Implications for Low-wage Workers," background memorandum prepared for the Social Science Research Council Policy Conference on Persistent Urban Poverty, November 9–10, 1993, Washington, D.C.

21. Margery A. Turner, Michael Fix, and Raymond J. Struyk, *Opportunities Denied, Opportunities Diminished: Discrimination in Hiring* (Washington, D.C.: The Urban Institute, 1991). Also, see Joleen Kirschenman and Kathryn M. Neckerman, "'We'd love to hire them, but . . .': The Meaning of Race for Employers" in *The Urban Underclass*, Christopher Jencks and Paul Peterson, eds. (Washington, D.C.: The Brookings Institution). Both articles cited in Michael Dawson, *Behind the Mule: Race and Class in African-American Politics* (Princeton, N.J.: Princeton University Press, 1994), pp. 18–44.

22. Katherine Newman, "Culture and Structure in 'The Truly Disadvantaged,'" *City and Society* (Spring 1992): 3–25.

23. Robert J. Sampson, "Concentrated Poverty and Crime: A Synopsis of Prior Community-level Research," background memorandum prepared for the Social Science Research Council Policy Conference on Persistent Urban Poverty, Washington, 1994.

24. Barry Bluestone, Mary Stevenson, and Chris Tilly, "An Assessment of the Impact of 'Deindustrialization' and the Spatial Mismatch on the Labor Market Outcomes of Young White, Black, and Latino Men and Women Who Have Limited Schooling," John W. McCormack Institute of Public Affairs, August, 1992.

25. Estimate computed by author from data presented in Norman Krumholz, "The Kerner Commission Twenty Years Later," in *The Metropolis in White and Black* (New Brunswick: Center for Urban Policy Research, 1992), p. 24.

26. George Galster, "A Cumulative Causation Model of the Underclass: Implications for Urban Economic Development Policy," in *The Metropolis in Black and White*, pp. 206–207.

27. On the latter point, see Margaret Weir, "Poverty and Defensive Localism," *Dissent* (Summer 1994): 337–42. For a concise argument against neighborhood development as a federal policy, see Paul Peterson, "Introduction: Technology, Race, and Urban Policy," in *The New Urban Reality* (Washington, D.C.: The Brookings Institution, 1985), pp. 24–29.

28. Georgia Persons, "Black Mayoralties and the New Black Politics: From Insurgency to Racial Reconciliation," in *Dilemmas of Black Politics* (New York: Harper-Collins Publishers, 1993), pp. 38–65.

29. For a detailing of the historic criticisms of community participation, and a spirited rejoinder, see Jeffrey M. Berry, Kent E. Portney, and Ken Thomson, *The Rebirth of Urban Democracy* (Washington, D.C.: The Brookings Institution, 1993).

30. The black poor appear to be the first to stop voting after initial black electoral victories. See Katherine Tare, *From Protest to Politics: The New Black Voters in American Elections* (Cambridge, Mass.: Harvard University Press, 1993).

31. Public school teachers in New York City, for example, are able to transfer out of low-income neighborhoods on a seniority basis. As a result, schools populated by poor blacks and Latinos have disproportionate numbers of novices and less well-trained teachers. See "Inequity of Opportunity: The Distribution of Novice Teachers Among New York City's 32 Community School Districts," report by the Community Service Society's Department of Public Policy/Education Unit, 1983.

32. Alice M. Rivlin advocates transferring many federal responsibilities to the states. This may get around the problem of anti-urban Senate bias, although this was not her intention. It raises new sets of problems regarding city-suburban and city-rural tensions. See Alice M. Rivlin, *Reviving the American Dream* (Washington, D.C.: The Brookings Institution, 1992).

33. It is wrong to assume that black mayors necessarily have general black progress at the top of their political and policy agenda. Increasingly, black mayors have won office in majority white cities such as Seattle on a completely deracialized basis. Nonetheless, in majority black cities such as Washington, D.C., Newark, and Atlanta, it is impossible to separate the progress of the city from the progress of the black community.

34. Richard Sauerzopf and Todd Swanstrom, "The Urban Electorate in Presidential Elections, 1920–1992: Challenging the Conventional Wisdom," paper prepared for delivery at the Urban Affairs Association Annual Convention, Indianapolis, Indiana, 1993.

35. Andrew Young, foreword to *The Closing Door*. For extensive treatment of the social welfare import of the civil rights movement, see Donna Cooper Hamilton and Charles V. Hamilton, "The Dual Agenda of African-American Organizations Since the New Deal: Social Welfare Policies and Civil Rights," *Political Science Quarterly* 107 (Fall 1992): 435–52.

36. Lani Guinier, "The Triumph of Tokenism: The Voting Rights Act and the Theory of Black Electoral Success," *Michigan Law Review* 89 (1992): 1091–1101.

37. Department of City Planning, *Comments on Proposed Site and Neighborhood Standards* (New York: City of New York, 1992).

38. Susan Saegert and J. Phillip Thompson, "Social Network of Public Housing Residents: Social Deficit or Social Capital?" working paper prepared for the Rockefeller Brothers Fund, 1994.

39. The comparable figure in Washington, D.C., is 42 percent. Data are taken from David J. Rothman, review of Jerome Miller, *Search and Destroy: The Plight of African-American Males in the Criminal Justice System*, in *The New York Review of Books* (February 1994).

40. Robert F. Wagner and Julia Vitullo-Martin, "New Hope for Old Projects: Vincent Lane and the Revival of Public Housing," *City Journal* 4, no. 2 (1994): 21–30.

41. *Black Political Agenda* 2, no. 3 (1994): 5.

42. Data taken from Donald O. Leake and Brenda L. Leake, "Islands of Hope: Milwaukee's African-American Immersion Schools," *Journal of Negro Education* 61, no. 1 (1992): 24.

43. Civil rights organizations have considerable experience in organizing, advocacy, lobbying, communications, and other skills needed in poor communities. They have the organizational capacity to impact on poor communities. The black middle class has a variety of incentives to support increasing the stability, organization, and politicization of poor black (and other) communities. Middle-class blacks frequently live near poor blacks, and would gain from neighborhood improvements. Middle-class blacks are economically threatened, and many of the programs established to benefit them have been justified in the name of fighting black poverty. Without the support of the black poor and working classes, the black middle class is politically imperiled. For evidence of civil rights organizations' weak recruitment of poor blacks, see Tare, *From Protest to Politics*, p. 93.

44. "Political scientists, in particular, have neglected the one area that could lead to the empowerment and involvement of poor individuals in struggles and strategies to improve their status, namely, politics (as distinguished from policy formation)." Quote from Cathy Cohen and Michael Dawson, "Neighborhood Poverty and African-American Politics," *American Political Science Review* 87, no. 2 (June 1993): 286.

## CHAPTER 3

1. Robert Murray Haig, *The Regional Plan of New York and its Environs* (New York: Regional Plan Association, 1929); Raymond Vernon, *The Changing Economic Function of the Central City* (New York: Committee for Economic Development, 1959) and *Metropolis 1985* (Cambridge, Mass.: Harvard University Press, 1960); Edgar M. Hoover and Raymond Vernon, *Anatomy of a Metropolis* (Cambridge, Mass.: Harvard University Press, 1959); Jane Jacobs, *The Death and Life of Great American Cities* (New York: Random House, 1961), *The Economy of Cities* (New York: Random House, 1969), and *Cities and the Wealth of Nations* (New York: Random House, 1984).

2. Mitchell Moss, "The Information City and the Global Economy," in John Brotchie, Michael Batty, Peter Hall, and Peter Newton, eds., *New Technologies and Spatial Systems: Cities of the 21st Century* (New York: Longman-Cheshire, 1991).

3. *Economist*, May 21, 1994, p. 15.

## CHAPTER 4

1. U.S. Advisory Commission on Intergovernmental Relations (ACIR), *A Commission Report: City Financial Emergencies, the Intergovernmental Dimension* (Washington, D.C.: ACIR, 1973), p. 12.

2. Charles R. Morris, *The Cost of Good Intentions: New York City and the Liberal Experiment* (New York: W. W. Norton, 1980).

3. *Dartmouth College v. Woodward*, 4 Wheat. 518 (1819).

4. *City of Clinton v. Cedar Rapids and Missouri River Railroad Co.*, 24 Iowa 455, 475 (1868).

5. Ester R. Fuchs, *Mayors and Money: Fiscal Policy in New York and Chicago* (Chicago: University of Chicago Press, 1992).

6. This conclusion is supported in Roland Liebert, "Municipal Functions, Structure, and Expenditures," *Social Science Quarterly* 5–6 (September 1974): 210–24; Thomas R. Dye and John A. Garcia, "Structure, Function and Policy in American Cities?" *Urban Affairs Quarterly* 14 (September 1978): 103–22; Terry N. Clark and Lorna Ferguson, *City Money* (New York: Columbia University Press, 1983); Helen F. Ladd and John Yinger, *America's Ailing Cities: Fiscal Health and the Design of Urban Policy* (Baltimore: Johns Hopkins University Press, 1989); Ester R. Fuchs, *Mayors and Money*; The New York State Financial Control Board, *Staff Report: Other Ways of Doing Business: Fiscal Comparisons of Major U.S. Cities* (March 1994).

7. Fuchs, *Mayors and Money*, pp. 255–59.

8. U.S. Conference of Mayors, *Impact of Unfunded Federal Mandates on U.S. Cities: A 314-City Survey* (Washington, D.C.: October 1993).

9. "Federal Mandates: It Is Time to Relieve the Funding Crunch," *Dallas Morning News*, May 22, 1994, p. 2J.

10. Mayor Edward G. Rendell, *The New Urban Agenda* (City of Philadelphia, April 1994), p. 14.

11. New York City Washington Office, *New York City 1994 Federal Program* (New York City, 1994), p. 73.

12. Local governments include cities, counties, school districts, townships and public authorities. ACIR, *Significant Features of Fiscal Federalism*, vol. II (Washington, D.C.: ACIR, 1993), table 18.

13. National Conference of State Legislatures, *State Fiscal Outlook for 1992* (Denver, Colo.:January 1992).

14. ACIR, *Significant Features of Fiscal Federalism*.

15. Mark I. Gelland, *A Nation of Cities: The Federal Government and Urban America, 1933–1965* (New York: Oxford University Press, 1975), p. 45.

16. John H. Mollenkopf, *The Contested City* (Princeton, N.J.: Princeton University Press, 1983).

17. ACIR, *Significant Features of Fiscal Federalism*.

18. Ibid.

19. *The New York Times*, November 8, 1984, p. A19.

20. U.S. General Accounting Office, *Federal-State-Local Relations: Trends of the Past Decade and Emerging Issues*, report to Congressional Committees for March 1990.

21. U.S. General Accounting Office, *Federal-State-Local Relations*.

22. U.S. Conference of Mayors (USCM), *The Federal Budget and the Cities* (Washington, D.C.: USCM, 1990), p. ix.

23. Office of Senator Daniel Patrick Moynihan, United States Senate and Taubman Center for State and Local Government, John F. Kennedy School of Government, Harvard University, *The Federal Budget and the States, Fiscal Year 1993* (July 28, 1994).

24. Iris J. Lav and James R. St. George, "Holding the Bag: The Effect on State and Local Governments of the Emerging Fiscal Agenda in the 104th Congress," *Center on Budget and Policy Priorities* (January 31, 1995), pp. 7, 15.

25. Philip M. Dearborn, "The State-Local Fiscal Outlook From a Federal Perspective," *Intergovernmental Perspective* 20, no. 2 (Spring 1994): 20–23. See also Demetrios Caraley, "Washington Abandons the Cities," *Political Science Quarterly* 107 (Spring 1992): 1–30.

26. This description of Philadelphia's fiscal crisis is based on "Philadelphia: Back from the Brink," *Economist*, April 17, 1993; Charles Matheson, "Maybe Philadelphia is Governable After All," *Governing* (April 1993); and Edward G. Rendell, "America's Cities: Can We Save Them?" *City Journal* 4, no. 1 (Winter 1994).

27. Nell Henderson, "D.C.'s Budget Woes Intensify for 1994: Overestimate of U.S. Aid May Cost More Jobs," *Washington Post*, June 13, 1993, p. B1; Rudolph A. Pyatt, Jr., "It's Time for D.C. to Make the Really Tough Financial Calls," *Washington Post*, June 21, 1994, F3.

28. Thomas W. Waldron, "Mayor Barry Upbeat Despite City's Financial Woes, Personal Legal Problems," *Detroit News*, July 2, 1995.

29. Brad Altman, "Los Angeles City Council Passes Fiscal 1995 Budget; Police Get Shifted Funds," *Bond Buyer*, May 23, 1994, p. 1.

30. Karen Pierog, "No Downgrade for Detroit, S&P Saya, Affirming City's BBB Rating for GO Debt," *Bond Buyer*, May 27, 1994, p. 1.

31. "No More Excuses on Budgeting," *Atlanta Journal and Constitution*, August 15, 1994, p. A6; Lyle V. Harris, "Monday's Inauguration of the New Mayor Honeymoon? Despite the Airport Corruption Trial and a Surprise Budget Gap, Campbell Promises a Fast Start and Invites Instant Evaluation," *Atlanta Journal and Constitution*, January 2, 1994, p. C1.

32. Chris Black, "Budget Report Chides Menino," *The Boston Globe*, March 30, 1994, p. 21.

33. Paul E. Peterson, *City Limits* (Chicago: University of Chicago Press, 1981).

## CHAPTER 6

1. Based on preliminary data for the first six months of 1995, reported by the New York City Police Department, July 13, 1995.

2. Federal Bureau of Investigation, *Uniform Crime Reports: 1994 Preliminary Annual Release*, May 21, 1995. This report provides preliminary data for 201 cities of at least 100,000 population.

3. Rural areas showed a 6 percent increase in violent crime recorded by the police between 1993 and 1994. FBI, *Uniform Crime Reports: 1994 Preliminary Annual Release*.

4. U.S. Department of Justice, Bureau of Justice Statistics, *Selected Highlights on Firearms and Crimes of Violence: Selected Findings from National Statistical Series* (Washington, D.C.: U.S. Department of Justice, 1994).

5. U.S. Department of Justice, Bureau of Justice Statistics, (Washington, D.C.: U.S. Department of Justice, forthcoming, 1995).

6. Carol J. DeFrances and Steven K. Smith, U.S. Department of Justice, Bureau of Justice Statistics, *Crime and Neighborhoods* (Washington, D.C.: U.S. Department of Justice, 1994).

7. Port Authority of New York and New Jersey, *Demographic Trends in the NY-NJ Metropolitan Region: Income Distribution and Poverty* (New York: Port Authority of New York and New Jersey, 1994).

8. Since 1992, when South Africa reduced its prison population, the United States has been trading places back and forth with Russia as the nation with the world's highest rate of incarcerating its own people.

9. The report of the National Research Council in Albert J. Reiss, Jr., and Jeffrey A. Roth, eds., *Understanding and Preventing Violence* (Washington, D.C.: National Academy Press, 1993), p. 292.

10. Ibid., p. 293.

11. The report of the National Research Council (pp. 317–18) provides the example of the Violence Prevention Curriculum for Adolescents, a ten-session curriculum developed in Massachusetts by Deborah Prothrow-Stith, which has sold several thousand copies even though an evaluation of the program funded by the National Institute of Justice found only weak evidence of its effectiveness in reducing violent behavior or victimization.

12. For a good example of the explanations offered for the drop in violence in early 1995, see the editorial, "Bringing the Murder Rate Down," *New York Times*, July 17, 1995, p. A12.

13. National Research Council in *Understanding and Preventing Violence*, pp. 315–17.

14. Elizabeth P. Descagnes and Peter W. Greenwood, "Maricopa County's Drug Court: An Innovative Program for First Time Drug Offenders on Probation," *Justice System Journal* 17 (1994): 99–115.

15. *Violent Schools—Safe Schools: The Safe School Study Report to the Congress* (Washington, D.C.: National Institute of Education, 1978).

## CHAPTER 7

1. Interview, September 12, 1993.

2. U.S. Department of Commerce, Bureau of the Census, *1990 Census of Population and Housing* (Washington, D.C.: Government Printing Office, 1990); Michael A. Stegman, *Housing and Vacancy Report New York City, 1991* (City of New York Department of Housing Preservation and Development, June 1993), p. 200.

3. Devereux Bowly, Jr., *The Poorhouse: Subsidized Housing in Chicago, 1895–1976* (Carbondale, Ill.: Southern Illinois University Press, 1978), p. 129.

4. M. W. Newman, "Chicago's $70 million ghetto," *Chicago Daily News*, April 10, 1965.

5. Interview, April 1, 1994.

6. Catherine Bauer, *Architectural Forum*, July 1957, p. 221.

7. Letter to Larry S. Fanning, executive editor, *Chicago Daily News*, April 26, 1965, p.7.

8. Devereux Bowly, Jr., *The Poorhouse*, p. 123.

9. Interview, May 20, 1994.

10. Interview, May 23, 1994.

11. *The Final Report of the National Commission on Severely Distressed Public Housing* (Washington, D.C.: General Printing Office, April 1992), p. 48.

12. Ibid.

13. William Julius Wilson, *The Truly Disadvantaged: The Inner City, the Underclass, and Public Policy* (Chicago: The University of Chicago Press, 1987), p. 143.

14. Robert B. Reich, *The Work of Nations* (New York: Alfred A. Knopf, 1991), p. 282.

15. Interview, April 4, 1994.

16. James E. Rosenbaum, et. al., "Can the Kerner Commission's Housing Strategy Improvement Employment, Education, and Social Integration for Low Income Blacks?" *North Carolina Law Review* 71, no. 5 (June 1993): 1540.

17. Interview, August 23, 1994.

18. Interview, April 5, 1994.

19. Rosenbaum, "Can the Kerner Commission's Housing Strategy Improve Employment, Education, and Social Integration for Low Income Blacks?" pp. 1540–1553, and interview, August 31, 1994.

20. Interviews, August 24, 1994.

21. Interview, April 25, 1994.

22. Evelyn Nieves, "Delays Paralyze Newark's Efforts to Build Housing for the Poor," *New York Times*, February 3, 1992, pp. A1, B1.

23. Interview, July 17, 1995.

24. Jane Jacobs, *The Death and Life of Great American Cities* (New York Random House, 1961), p. 400. She wrote: "It is not enough to raise [maximum income] limits; the tie of residency to income price tags must be abandoned altogether. So long as it remains, not only will all the most successful or lucky inexorably be drained away, but all the others must psychologically identify themselves with their homes either as transients or as 'failures'."

25. Joel Kaplan, "Lane's Vision for Cabrini Made HUD Blink," *Chicago Tribune*, June 9, 1995, sect. 1, p. 20.

26. Interview, July 17, 1995.

27. Samuel G. Freedman, *Upon This Rock: The Miracles of a Black Church* (New York: Harper Collins Publishers, 1993), p. 413.

28. Interview, August 26, 1994.

## CHAPTER 8

1. Fund for the City of New York, *Groundwork: Building Support for Excellence, A Select Interim Report on the DeWitt Wallace–Reader's Digest Management Initiative for New York City Organizations that Serve Youth* (December 1994), pp. 50–55.

2. *UNH Settlement House Initiative: 108 Years and Looking Forward*, a report prepared for the Ford Foundation (United Neighborhood Houses of New York, Inc., February 1995), p. 1. My thanks to Emily Menlo Marks, the executive director of UNH, for providing me a copy of this report, along with many other valuable materials.

3. United Neighborhood Houses of New York, "Budget Cuts, Cripples and Challenges Settlement House Youth Programs," *UNH News* (Spring 1995).

4. Fund for the City of New York, *Groundwork: Building Support for Excellence*, p. 9.

5. Ibid.

6. For this conventional portrait, see Richard Hofstadter, *Age of Reform* (New York: Alfred A. Knopf, 1955); Allen F. Davis, *Spearheads for Reform: The Social Settlements and the Progressive Movement, 1890–1914* (New Brunswick, N.J.: Rutgers University Press, 1965); and Allen F. Davis, *American Heroine: the Life and Legend of Jane Addams* (New York: Oxford University Press, 1973).

7. Howard Husock, "Bringing Back the Settlement House," *The Public Interest* (Fall 1992), p. 54, reprinted in *Public Welfare* 51, no. 4 (Fall 1993).

8. David J. Rothman, "The State as Parent: Social Policy in the Progressive Era," in Willard Gaylin, Ira Glasser, Steven Marcus, and David J, Rothman, eds., *Doing Good: the Limits of Benevolence* (New York: Pantheon, 1978), pp. 69–76. Also see Alan F. Brinkley, *The End of Reform: New Deal Liberalism in Recession and War* (New York: Alfred A. Knopf, 1995).

9. Ira Glasser, "Prisoners of Benevolence: Power versus Liberty in the Welfare State," in Gaylin, et al, eds., *Doing Good*, p. 123.

10. Letter from Jean Bethke Elshtain to Michelle Miller of the Twentieth Century Fund, February 1, 1993, with preliminary proposal for a book on Jane Addams and American public life.

11. See, for example, Theda Skocpol, *Protecting Soldiers and Mothers: The Political Origins of Social Policy in the United States* (Cambridge: Harvard University Press, 1992), pp. 311–540; Robyn Muncy, *Creating a Female Dominion in American Reform: 1890–1935* (New York: Oxford University Press, 1991), passim; Kathryn Kish Sklar, *Florence Kelley and the Nation's Work* (New Haven: Yale University Press, 1995), passim; and Paula Baker, "The Domestication of Politics: Women and American Political Society," in Linda Gordon, ed., *Women, the State, and Welfare* (Madison: University of Wisconsin Press, 1990), pp. 55–91.

12. Seth Koven and Sonya Michel, eds., *Mothers of A New World: Maternalist Politics and the Origins of Welfare States* (New York & London: Routledge, 1993), introduction.

13. Linda Gordon, "The New Feminist Scholarship on the Welfare State," pp. 9–35, and "Family Violence, Feminism and Social Control," pp. 178–98, in Gordon, ed., *Women, the State, and Welfare*; Linda Gordon, *Pitied But Not Entitled: Single Mothers and the History of Welfare* (New York: Free Press, 1994), passim. For a less sympathetic view that emphasizes racism in the settlements, also see Elisabeth Lasch-Quinn, *Black Neighbors: Race and the Limits of Reform in the American Settlement House Movement, 1890–1945* (Chapel Hill: University of North Carolina Press, 1993), passim.

14. Kathryn Kish Sklar, "The Historical Foundations of Women's Power in the Creation of the American Welfare State, 1830–1930," in Koven and Michel, eds., *Mothers of a New World*, pp. 43–93. Also see Clare Coss, ed., *Lillian D. Wald: Progressive Activist* (New York: Feminist Press, 1989), passim; Theda Skocpol, *Protecting Soldiers and Mothers*, pp. 480–524; and Sheila M. Rothman, *Woman's Proper Place* (New York: Basic Books, 1978), pp. 142–53.

15. Allen F. Davis, *American Heroine*, p. 105.

16. The Commission on Human Services Reorganization, Richard I. Beattie, Chairman, *Outline for Action: New Directions for HRA, Final Report to Mayor Edward I. Koch of New York, January 1985*, pp. iv–v. My thanks to Dick Beattie for a copy of this report and for his recollections of its outcome by phone, June 29, 1995. Thanks also to Patricia Glazer, a member of the commission, for her comments.

17. *UNH Settlement House Initiative*, pp. 3–12.

18. Lynn Vedeka-Sherman, "New Style Settlement Houses," *Rockefeller Institute Bulletin* (1992), pp. 41–44.

19. Husock, "Bringing back the Settlement House," pp. 56–59; *UNH Settlement House Initiative*, pp 12–14. Prudence Brown and The Chapin Hall Center for Children at the University of Chicago, "Settlement Houses Today: Their Community Building Role," report prepared for United Neighborhood Houses of New York, 1995.

20. Governor Bill Clinton, "A Vision For America: A New Covenant," speech to the Democratic National Convention, New York, July 16, 1992.

## CHAPTER 10

1. Amasa B. Ford, M.D., *Urban Health in America* (New York: Oxford University Press, 1976), pp. 11–15.

2. Bonnie Bullough and George Rosen, *Preventive Medicine in the United States: 1900–1990* (Philadelphia: Science History Publications, 1992), pp. 7–9.

3. Louis P. Cain, "Raising and Watering a City: Ellis Sylvester Chesbrough and Chicago's First Sanitation System," *Technology and Culture* (Chicago: The University of Chicago Press, 1972), pp. 293–94.

4. Gretchen A. Condran, Henry Williams, and Rose A. Cheney, "The Decline in Mortality in Philadelphia from 1870 to 1930: The Role of Municipal Services," *The Pennsylvania Magazine of History and Biography*, April 1984, pp. 153–77.

5. Richard A. Meckel, *Save the Babies: American Public Health Reform and the Prevention of Infant Mortality, 1850–1929* (Baltimore: The Johns Hopkins University Press, 1990), pp. 1–2.

6. Bullough, *Preventive Medicine*

7. Meckel, *Save the Babies*, p. 2.

8. Ford, *Urban Health in America*, pp. 51–63.

9. Ibid.

10. Robert J. Myers, "How Bad were the Original Actuarial Estimates for Medicare's Hospital Insurance Program?" *The Actuary*, February 1994, pp. 6–7.

11. Milton Terris, "Joseph W. Mountin Lecture," delivered at the U.S. Centers for Disease Control, Atlanta, Oct. 26, 1982.

12. U.S. Department of Health and Human Services, *Health United States, 1993* (Washington, D.C.: Government Printing Office, 1993), p. 36.

13. Janet Firshein and Richard Sorian, "Medicare at 25," *Medicine and Health Perspectives*, July 31, 1990, pp. 1–6.

14. Christina Kent, "Tuberculosis: The White Plague Rises," *Medicine and Health Perspectives*, September 7, 1992, pp. 1–4.

15. U.S. Centers for Disease Control and Prevention, *Morbidity and Mortality Weekly Report* (Atlanta: Public Health Service) 1992.

16. U.S. Centers for Disease Control and Prevention, *Quarterly Surveillance Report*, 2d quarter, 1994.

17. Philip R. Lee, M.D., Shattuck Lecture, Massachusetts Medical Society, Boston, delivered May 21, 1994.

18. U.S. Department of Health & Human Services, Agency for Health Care Policy and Research, "National Medical Expenditure Survey: Annual Expenses and Sources of Payment for Health Care Services," pp. 8–9.

## EPILOGUE

1. Rem Koolhaas, *Delirious New York* (New York: The Monacelli Press, 1994), p. 10.

2. Eli Ginzberg, "The Changing Urban Scene: 1960–1990 and Beyond," in Henry G. Cisneros, ed., *Interwoven Destinies: Cities and the Nation* (New York: W. W. Norton, 1993), pp. 32–47.

3. Quoted in Jerome Charyn, *Metropolis: New York as Myth, Marketplace, and Magical Island* (New York: G. P. Putnam and Sons, 1986), p. 86.

4. Donna E. Shalala and Julia Vitullo-Martin, "Rethinking the Urban Crisis: Proposals for a National Urban Agenda," *The Journal of the American Planning Association*, Winter 1989.

5. Louis Gambaccini, general manager of the Southeast Pennsylvania Transportation Authority, as quoted in Robert F. Wagner, Jr., and Julia Vitullo-Martin, "Can Clinton Save Our Cities? What the Federal Government Can Do," *Journal of the American Planning Association*, Summer 1993.

6. Charles C. Mann, "The Prose (and Poetry) of Mario M. Cuomo," *Atlantic Monthly*, December 1990, p. 108

7. J. Joseph Huthmacher, *Senator Robert F. Wagner and the Rise of Urban Liberalism* (New York: Atheneum, 1968).

8. Jim Sleeper, "In Search of New York," *Dissent*, Fall 1987, p. 416

9. Letter from Senator Robert F. Wagner to Joseph Berran, August 24, 1932.

10. Richard Plunz, *A History of Housing in New York City* (New York: Columbia University Press, 1990).

11. Joseph Fernandez (with John Underwood), *Tales Out of School: Joseph Fernandez's Crusade to Rescue American Education* (Boston: Little Brown & Co., 1993).

12. Interview conducted Sept. 12, 1993, as quoted in Robert F. Wagner Jr. and Julia Vitullo-Martin, "New Hope for Old Projects," *City Journal*, Spring 1994.

13. *New York Times*, May 24, 1977.

14. James E. Rosenbaum, et. al., "Can the Kerner Commission's Housing Strategy Improve Employment, Education, and Social Integration for Low-Income Blacks?" *North Carolina Law Review* 71, no. 5 (June 1993).

15. Louis Harris and Associates, Inc., *Survey of New York City Residents: Improving the Quality of Life in New York City* (New York: Commonwealth Fund, September 17, 1993).

16. Interview, September 11, 1995.

17. Michael E. Porter, *The Comparative Advantage of Nations* (New York: The Free Press, 1985).

18. Louis Harris and Associates, Inc., *Why People Move To and Away from New York City*, A survey conducted for The Manhattan Institute and The Commonwealth Fund (New York: Louis Harris & Associates, 1993).

19. Peter F. Drucker, *Post-Capitalist Society* (New York: HarperCollins, 1993), p. 5.

20. Tony Hiss, *The Experience of Place* (New York: Alfred A. Knopf, 1990), p. 223.

# INDEX

# ABOUT THE AUTHORS

**Stanley Brezenoff** served as executive director of the Port Authority of New York and New Jersey from 1990 to 1995. Previously, he served as first deputy mayor of the City of New York in the administration of Mayor Edward Koch and had been president of the New York City Health and Hospitals Corporation. He had worked with Bob Wagner for many years, regarding him as a friend, advisor, and counselor. Wagner was chairman of the board when Brezenoff was commissioner of the Human Resources Administration, and he had been chairman of the City Planning Commission when Brezenoff was commissioner of the Department of Employment. He is currently the chief executive officer of the Maimonides Medical Center in Brooklyn.

**Ellen Chesler**, currently a fellow of the Twentieth Century Fund, is author of *Woman of Valor: Margaret Sanger and the Birth Control Movement in America*, which was awarded the Martha Albrand citation for a distinguished first work of nonfiction from the American Center of PEN, the international writers' organization. She is at work on a monograph about the evolution of American public policies affecting women and on a biography of the feminist, Betty Friedan. From 1978 to 1983, she served as chief of staff to New York City Council president Carol Bellamy, where she learned a great deal about urban policy and politics from Bob Wagner, Jr. She is a graduate of Vassar College and holds a Ph.D. in history from Columbia University.

**Roger Cohen** is the chief of staff of the Office of Economic and Policy Analysis at the Port Authority of New York and New Jersey. A former journalist with the *Bergen Record*, Cohen has written extensively on the history of the Port Authority.

**William J. Dean** is executive director of Volunteers of Legal Service (VOLS). VOLS develops programs to help meet the civil legal needs of poor people in New York City, and then recruits volunteer lawyers to provide the necessary legal services. He served as a member of the Commission on the Year 2000 and worked with Bob Wagner, Jr., on civic matters over the years. He is a graduate of Harvard College and Columbia Law School.

**Joseph A. Fernandez**, former New York City schools chancellor under Mayor David Dinkins, is currently president and CEO of School Improvement Services, Inc., with headquarters in Winter Park, Florida. This organization, an affiliate of the Teacher Education Institute, is a full-service educational consulting firm with an extensive and rapidly growing client base. Among the firm's clients are Sylvan Learning Systems, Monsanto Company, and IBM South Africa. Some of the most notable educators in the nation are associates of School Improvement Services, which has a vast network throughout the education community.

**Ester R. Fuchs** is director of the Barnard-Columbia Center for Urban Policy, an associate professor of political science and chair of the Urban Affairs Program at Barnard College, and a member of the graduate faculties of political science and the School of International and Public Affairs at Columbia University. She received her Ph.D. from the University of Chicago and taught at the University of Notre Dame. She is the author of *Mayors and Money: Fiscal Policy in New York and Chicago* (University of Chicago Press, 1992) and is currently editing a volume of essays entitled *New York City: The End of the Liberal Experiment?* She has been a consultant to several political campaigns, written political commentary, and appeared as a political analyst on radio and television. She shared Bob Wagner's love of New York City, his penchant for informed political discussion, and a belief in a central and vibrant role for cities in America's future.

**Paul Goldberger** is the chief cultural correspondent of the *New York Times* and the newspaper's longtime architecture critic. The author of *The City Observed: New York, The Skyscraper,* and *On the Rise: Architecture and Design in a Post-Modern Age,* among other books, he won a Pulitzer Prize in 1984 for his architecture criticism in the *Times.* He has also received the Roger Starr Journalism Award from the Citizens Housing and Planning Council, the President's Medal of the Municipal Art Society, and the Medal of Honor of the Landmarks Preservation Foundation of New York. He has also taught at the Yale

School of Architecture, and lectures widely on architecture and urbanism. When he was chairman of City Planning, Bob Wagner valued Goldberger's searching analysis of city projects.

**Peter C. Goldmark, Jr.**, was elected the eleventh president of the Rockefeller Foundation in June 1988. Prior to this appointment, he was senior vice president in charge of five Eastern newspapers for the Times Mirror Company. Before joining the Times Mirror Company in 1985, he served for eight years as executive director of the Port Authority of New York and New Jersey. From 1975 to 1977, he was the director of the budget for the State of New York and for four years prior to that served as Secretary of Human Services for the Commonwealth of Massachusetts. He also served in the budget office of New York City for four years, and was assistant budget director for program planning and analysis before becoming executive assistant to Mayor Lindsay in 1971. When Hugh Carey was governor, Bob Wagner, Jr., was instrumental in Goldmark's appointment as New York State budget director; they worked together on regional economic issues when Goldmark was head of the Port Authority and Wagner was deputy mayor for public policy in the Koch administration; and, most recently, they served together on the Commission on the Year 2000.

**Robert R. Kiley** is the president of the New York City Partnership, an organization of some 200 corporate and nonprofit chief executives. Between 1991 and 1994, he was president of the Fischbach Corporation. From 1983 through 1990, he was chairman and chief executive officer of the Metropolitan Transportation Authority (MTA), which oversees the New York City Transit Authority, the Long Island Railroad, the Metro-North Commuter Railroad, the Triborough Bridge and Tunnel Authority, and the Metropolitan Suburban Bus Authority. He spearheaded the rebuilding of New York's transportation system and restructured its management. As an MTA board member, Bob Wagner had helped recruit Kiley to the chairmanship and proved critical to making the job manageable. They became close friends.

**Nathan Leventhal** has served as president of Lincoln Center for the Performing Arts since March 1984. As president, he oversees the largest performing arts complex in the world. Prior to that, he was New York City deputy mayor for operations under Mayor Ed Koch, serving together with the late Robert F. Wagner, Jr., who was deputy mayor for policy at the time. He also served as New York City housing commissioner, again working closely with Bob Wagner, who was chairman of the City Planning Commission.

**Dick Netzer** has done research and written on urban economics and local public finance for more than forty years. He has been a professor of economics and public administration at New York University since 1961, has served as chair of the New York University Economics Department, dean of its Graduate School of Public Administration, and founding director of its Urban Research Center. He has been a consultant to public agencies and private organizations throughout the United States and in developing countries, and a member of numerous governmental boards and commissions, especially in New York, including membership on the Board of Directors of the Municipal Assistance Corporation for the City of New York since 1975. He began working with Bob Wagner when Bob entered New York City government in the 1970s, and recruited Bob to New York University as an enthusiastic teacher and adviser to the Urban Research Center.

**Diane Ravitch** is senior research scholar and John M. Olin Professor of Educational Policy at New York University and nonresident senior fellow at the Brookings Institution. From 1991 to 1993, she was assistant secretary of education for research in the United States Department of Education. She is the author of numerous books, including *The Great School Wars: New York City, 1805–1973* and *The Troubled Crusade: American Education, 1945–1980*. She holds a B.A. from Wellesley College and a Ph.D. in history from Columbia University. She was a friend of Bob Wagner's for many years.

**Donna E. Shalala** is secretary of health and human services. She joined President Clinton's cabinet after a distinguished career as a scholar and administrator. She served as chancellor of the University of Wisconsin-Madison from 1987 to 1993 and as president of Hunter College from 1980 to 1987. She was assistant secretary of policy development and research at the U.S. Department of Housing and Urban Development during the Carter administration. An expert on state and local government and finance, she was an original member of the board of the Municipal Assistance Corporation in 1975. She received her Ph.D. from Syracuse University and held tenured professorships in political science at City University of New York, Columbia, and the University of Wisconsin. She met Bob Wagner, Jr., in the late 1960s and was one of his closest friends.

**Christopher Stone** is director of the Vera Institute. He joined the Institute in 1986 as director of its London office, where he led Vera's work with the Crown Prosecution Service and Probation Service in England and Wales. He returned to New York in 1988 and was principally responsible for the creation of Vera's Neighborhood Defender Service of Harlem, and the establishment of New York City's Center for Alternative Sentencing and Employment Services, Inc. Before joining Vera, he practiced law as a public defender in Washington, D.C. He is a graduate of Harvard College, the Institute of Criminology at Cambridge University, and Yale Law School. Through his work and professional interest in New York City, he became Bob Wagner's colleague.

**J. Phillip Thompson**, currently a fellow of the Russell Sage Foundation, is assistant professor of political science at Barnard College and assistant professor of public and nonprofit management at Columbia Business School. He is a former deputy general manager of the New York City Housing Authority and former director of the Mayor's Office of Housing Coordination in New York City, during which time he worked with Bob Wagner on a number of issues. He received a B.A. in sociology from Harvard University in 1977, a master of urban planning degree from Hunter College in 1986, and a Ph.D. in political science from the City University of New York in 1990.

**Julia Vitullo-Martin**, currently the director of the Citizens Jury Project at the Vera Institute of Justice, is a writer and editor specializing in public policy, law, business, and finance. She has written for many publications including *Fortune*, *New York*, the *New York Times*, the *New York Review of Books*, and *City Journal*. She is the coeditor (with J. Robert Moskin) of the *Oxford Book of Executive Quotations*. She holds a Ph.D. in political science from the University of Chicago, and has taught at the University of California, the New School for Social Research, and Hunter College. She met Bob Wagner in 1973 and worked with him on several projects in housing and planning, including the Commission on the Year 2000, for which she was managing editor.